The Places of History

The Places of History

Regionalism Revisited in Latin America

EDITED BY DORIS SOMMER

Duke University Press   Durham and London 1999

© 1999 by Duke University Press
All rights reserved
Printed in the United States of America on acid-free paper ∞
Typeset in New Baskerville by Running Feet Books
Library of Congress Cataloging-in-Publication Data
appear on the last printed page of this book.

With the exception of "Translation and Revenge: Castilian
and the Origins of Nationalism in the Philippines," by
Vicente L. Rafael, these essays appeared in "The Places of
History: Regionalism Revisited in Latin America," a special
issue of *Modern Language Quarterly* 57, no. 2 (June 1996).

Contents

The Places of History: Regionalism Revisited in Latin America

DORIS SOMMER

Latin American literatures are being read in many ways, here in the United States and now at the end of the millennium. The variety is often apparent within interpretive essays as well as among them. The chapters that follow take advantage of skills developed in more strident moments and by more single-minded approaches (including Marxist readings of class relations and the peripheral corollaries of dependency theory, deconstructed messages that predictably falter through the medium of language, feminist and gay denunciations of patriarchal codes). But the engagements collected in these essays first published in *Modern Language Quarterly* are generally heterodox, experimental. That is to say, they are essays in reading.

The long list of short pieces was an intentional feature of this collection and was meant to represent a broad range of contemporary criticism within a limited space. The eclectic combination of practices in that range, and inside the essays, would have been a predictable, even a desirable, observation about the sampling. Less predictable, perhaps, was the painstaking attention to history. Readers may sense the attention to the specificities of time and place as a renewed response to the pressures of dramatic "globalization," in culture as well as in economics and politics. Particularities of literary context and strategy emerge as if they were the goal of each chapter.

Pride of place may again be working, as it did in the nineteenth century, to safeguard a sense of personal and collective autonomy, even if the political promise of autonomy may not be immediately apparent. Perhaps the general focus on micrologies, on untranslatable (not movable) particularity, can be called a new *costumbrismo*. Nineteenth-century patriotism cultivated specifically local tastes and historical ties. In response to a globalizing modernity, regionalism, or *costumbrismo*, fostered international competition as a motivation for local productivity, which needed interclass alliances. On one reading, the alliances were brokered by an ascending middle class that offered local color (of popular classes, a euphemism for the masses, or the poor) to a modernizing elite that could identify with "the people" in some productive measure.[1] With this stress on finessing internal differences for the benefit of economic and racial elites who take on a popular style but remain indifferent and often hostile to colorful locals, no wonder that John Beverley worries here about subaltern *testimonios* turning into grist for a *costumbrista* mill. But another dimension of *costumbrismo* was to underline, even to construct, cultural differences between one's own nation and other nations. Differences made sense of economic and military competition. While producers and consumers developed a universalized taste for modern goods, they also defined themselves as culturally particular. However the particularity of values and customs was construed, it was meant to support an ardent patriotism. The elite wrapped itself in lyrical ponchos (as Josefina Ludmer showed for Argentina) or stepped to tropical rhythms (as in Gilberto Freire's idyllic anthropology of Brazil, *The Masters and the Slaves* [1946]), not only to speak *for* one's people but also to speak *to* powerful outside competitors for markets and territories.

Eventually, the culturally consolidating formulas of *costumbrismo* fell prey to the intensity of globalization that pried local elites away from their internal alliances. At the same time, terms like *nationalism* and *local culture* ironically came to describe the internal groups that refused to be homogenized, not the centralized projects that hoped to control them in earlier modernization campaigns. The decision-making autonomy or negotiating position that nation-states hoped to secure by alleging their cultural specificity is being performed by culturally or linguistically identified groups inside unwieldy and porous nations. Ileana Rodríguez, for example, has been noticing a renewed attention to ungovernability. An authoritative vantage point has long

1. Susan Kirkpatrick, "The Ideology of Costumbrismo," *Ideologies and Literature* 2, no. 7 (1978): 28–44, develops this perspective on internal alliance.

been unstable and anxiety provoking. In late-seventeenth-century Guatemala, the Spanish authorities couldn't even get the colony's spelling right. The terrain and the people never quite fit the authorized paradigms, either exceeding them or falling short. One response to Spain's fragile fiction of domination was the Empire's tenacious and aggressive defense of its putative rights. It's because the models of control didn't work that they were put to work so ruthlessly. But the land and the people have been tenacious, too, and Guatemala retains an intractable measure of pre-Hispanic continuity that comes to the fore again, not in the nervousness of an Empire with no clothes but in the postmodern ironies of master narratives that have no master.[2]

Speculations like these, about the concerns and directions in the field of Latin American literary studies, will follow from reading this far-ranging collection of historically detailed essays. They range from Incan architecture to Chicano and Nuyorican habitats, from turn-of-the-century Argentine criminology to Caribbean homophobia, from the rhetorics of independence and dictatorship to Mexicans' ambivalence about opera and Brazil's move beyond monarchy, and from the precarious survival of Spanish language in Latin America to its paradoxical legacy of enlightenment in the Philippines, to mention a few themes. Together, the pieces describe a cultural richness, and a respect for embedded detail, that should become a guide for future work in the field.

History as a focus should be no surprise here and now, in a place and time that veers or reels away from teleological tales and that leaves universal reading formulas behind. Today, issues can remain unresolved without losing political meaning, and approaches to literature become symbiotic as they borrow techniques from neighboring discourses, anthropology, criminology, music, economics. But it is history that occupies a privileged place here, probably because history focuses the same kinds of specificities that have, again, come to the fore in creative literary studies. Literariness, like historicity, is what fits badly into paradigms. Creative specificity doesn't "subvert" those predictable designs, despite the claims of so much hasty criticism, since paradigms

---

2. Illeana Rodríguez, "Reconfiguración de los paisajes tropicales: De las narrativas de Guerra en narrativas ciudadanas," paper presented at LASA, Guadalajara, 1997.

continue to survive their literary entanglements. Instead, literature, like history, can tease those repeatable designs into more flexibility, more tolerance for the ironies of contradiction, than some disciplines may allow. With no single approach to exhaust reading, nor any satisfying metanarrative to fit details into tidy systems, postmodern probing is evidently grounding itself in history as it lifts or loosens one or another methodological mooring.

Heterodox languages, multiple audiences, local culture that both hinders and enhances modernization, the constitutive asymmetries of culture and society—these are the fissures that repeat in one reading after another. One name for the pattern, a name repeatedly invoked in the essays here, is "transculturation." Fernando Ortiz coined it in *Cuban Counterpoint: Tobacco and Sugar* (1940) to distinguish the unresolvable, often violent tension among cultures in conflict from the neat resolutions of difference suggested by such ideal concepts for *costumbrismo* such as syncretism, hybridity, or *mestizaje*.[3] That ultimately seamless ideal has been the banner for consolidation in many countries during the revolutionary struggles against Spain and Portugal and through populist programs for economic and cultural independence, mostly from the United States. One paradigmatic expression of syncretic nationalism was *La raza cósmica* (1925), by José Vasconcelos, which made Mexico the site of humanity's mission to amalgamate all races into a biologically and culturally improved "cosmic" stock. Today, readers are more likely to respond to *La raza cómica* in a parody by Puerto Rican critic Rubén Ríos Avila, who suggests that such missions are madness.[4] Productive differences are more likely to be acknowledged than to be overridden now; they are coded as distinct cultural (including gendered) languages, untranslatable into either competing cultures or transnational codes of class analysis. Perhaps the impression is peculiar to a perspective from North America, where race and ethnicity color political struggles at every level. Yet color-coded politics is com-

3. The reference is to Fernando Ortiz, *Contrapunteo cubano del tabaco y azúcar* (1940). Since then, the metaphor of counterpoint has been standard in discussions of cultural conflict and conflictual creativity in Latin America. See the translation by Harriet de Onís, with an introduction by Fernando Coronil, *Cuban Counterpoint: Tobacco and Sugar*, (Durham, N.C.: Duke University Press, 1995).
4. Ríos Avila, "La raza cómica: Identidad y cuerpo en Pedreira y Palés," *La Torre*, nos. 27–8 (1993): 559–76.

mon to the Americas here and there, countries that share a history of conquering indigenous peoples, of forced immigration of Africans and welcoming arms open to Northern Europeans. This history haunts the hemisphere, North and South. For some reason or reasons, race is an underdeveloped concern in Latin American studies, compared to North American scholarship, perhaps because the discourses of *mestizaje* and *costumbrismo* succeeded somewhat in spreading local color through official national discourse and mitigating the chiaroscuro effect of political antagonisms. Or, long years of pseudoscientific, "positivist," racism continue to contaminate racial terms of identification and solidarity.

Cultural differences, on the other hand, have long provided languages of opposition and political positioning, which is why transculturation is so powerful a concept. Ortiz's neologism for the restless, stressful, sometimes violent change as cultural codes collide in the Americas offers a flexible model for a range of postmodern observations about the incommensurability of "reality" with any one code. Mary Louise Pratt has directed our attention to transculturation in "the contact zone." Roberto Schwarz has suggested it in the "misplaced ideas" of European Enlightenment imported into slave economies. Here he develops the conflict through Machado de Assis's cynical portrait of an aristocratic flirtation with the rights of man and the heart of a woman. Walter D. Mignolo's work has complicated and refined the history of cultural struggles for hegemony by focusing on the Spanish agents as competitors among themselves, since they were variously aligned with regard to indigenous languages.

In Mignolo's contribution, the fissures that constitute New World languages are shown to develop into creative and contestatory games of "languaging," those transgressive borrowings across cultural borders. José Antonio Mazzotti shows an important subtlety of the game played by the first mestizo chronicler, El Inca Garcilaso de la Vega, who managed to position himself favorably for an Andean audience; they and not primarily the Spaniards (who took themselves to be the Inca's ideal readers) would have appreciated his interpretations of local signs of legitimate power. Doubled points of view and the unstable loyalties they produce are themes in Mary M. Gaylord's reading of "transience" in Golden Age literature, which moved between Spain and the Americas, prose and poetry, and between conventional defenses of "real" histories to performances of fiction.

The collective and almost traditional attention to the real, however fissured and performative reality turns out to be, may be an ironic feature of postmodern criticism of Latin America. Backing away from modernist skepticisms and from Marxist devaluations of (ideological) lived experience, it comes full circle to nineteenth- and early-twentieth-century valorizations of local contexts. But the irony is familiar to readers of and in the Latin American peripheries of modern movements, whether or not it becomes a recognizable feature of the center. In the frustrating strain to catch up to the center, Latin America's differences always show up. Those differences from northern Atlantic models of modernity become signs of identity, often coded as obstacles to development. But sometimes they are celebrated as safeguards against the homogenizing anonymity that overrides local distinctiveness in the rush of modernizing movements. Carlos J. Alonso's essay identifies modernity itself as conflictual, transculturated, even thwarted in Spanish America; Arcadio Díaz-Quiñones reads the Puerto Rican struggle for autonomy as performing inside an unstable mix of tradition and revolution; Susana Rotker underlines the literary and political heterodoxy of Simón Rodríguez, Bolívar's mentor; Francine Masiello raises a question about modernity's alleged separation of the public from the private sphere, since gossip continually slips between them to contaminate both. Nancy Vogeley reviews the paradoxical reception of an Italian opera about a Moorish hero in postrevolutionary Mexico, where the elite had just executed a mestizo hero; John Beverley notes the discursive overload between competing agendas in a testimonial genre that had seemed so transparent; and Debra A. Castillo further complicates the assumptions by considering *testimonios* written by professional con artists, Mexican prostitutes who sell their lives to greedy readers.

A culturally fissured and porous nation-state is a precondition for democracy, a contractual system of citizens that Jean-François Lyotard takes care to distinguish from the nation, which is defined by birth.[5] Unfortunately, the fissures are also interpreted as rents in the native

5. Lyotard, "The Other's Rights," in *On Human Rights: The Oxford Amnesty Lectures 1993*, ed. Stephen Shute and Susan Hurley (New York: HarperCollins, 1993), 136–47.

fabric, by those who would defend national compactness by eliminating personal and collective differences. Good-byes to coherent ideals of nationness and family are hard to say, and the difficult work of mourning remains to be done in the wake of projects for cultural engineering in nineteenth-century American states. A country like Argentina managed to produce a work of public mourning for its irretrievable gaucho past in *Martín Fierro* (1872). But the release from the past was deployed as a banner for a new consolidation, a training manual in collective nostalgia for natives and for the potentially overwhelming waves of immigrants at the turn of the century. Since then, more American migrations, internal and external, continue to strain the coherence of national states. At the weakened and defensive centers, the sinister face of nativism and cultural nationalism glares through. In this country it has the face of militiamen, monolingualism, and tightened border controls with expanded budgets. In Argentina's recent history, Diana Taylor shows that monocultural patriotism was the state's official libretto in an obsessively repetitive spectacle of eliminating internal differences. The political etymology of discriminating words such as *legitimate, criminal, crazy* has a history in nineteenth-century medico-legal practices that Josefina Ludmer tracks in her contribution. The monoculture of vigilant masculinity marked Chile's recent dictatorship, too, as Mary Louise Pratt recalls in her attention to women's voices that would not be still and to the perverse combination of dread and desire that dictatorship can produce.

A democratizing promise in enlightened nineteenth-century romance, shortsighted as it may seem now, was at least a relief from the heroic monocultures that preceded and followed. Romance was an invitation to dialogue and to alliance, however controlled. Antonio Benítez-Rojo reaches back to put Mexico's Lizardi in that tradition as he developed the preindependence, enlightened, context for romantic resolutions. Vicente L. Rafael extends the map of enlightened Hispanism outward, to the Philippines, where Lizardi's hero ventured through apparently standard colonial circuits, and where turn-of-the-century promises of autonomy echo the frustrations of Cuba and Puerto Rico. José E. Limón pulls the formula forward in time and outward in territory in his essay on a Texan romance written long after the Anglo-American conquest and local armed resistance, long enough for its authors to imagine how dread is conquered by desire (between men and women and between men) and how one sleeps with the enemy. Perhaps José Martí could imagine erotic resolutions of conflicts between men while he listened to Walt Whitman and wrote about him. Sylvia Molloy's essay underscores Martí's amorous response to the seduction of male bonding and shows how short-lived the possibility would be in Latin America's petrification of Whitman, the patriarch. Martí's troubled response to his own availability for seduction by poetry, and by energetic men, is developed by Julio Ramos, who reads Martí in the literary and historical gap between *fin de siglo* sensitivity and the heroic masculinity of unfinished Caribbean independence movements.

José Martí finally left poetry and propaganda to go to the battlefield, where he charged ahead of his troops on a white horse and staged a heroic death for himself. A century later is an auspicious time to rethink cultural and political projects in Our Americas. While this collection was being prepared, 1995 commemorated at least three centennials. In addition to the martyrdom of Martí, there was the third centennial of the death of Sor Juana Inés de la Cruz, a nun too brilliant and too bold to fit inside Mexico or within her seventeenth century. The year also honored Jorge Isaacs, that universal but unhomogenized figure for the unstable and polymorphous nineteenth century. He was a fissured, Mosaic star, a Colombian Jew, and the century's only Latin American novelist to thrill readers far beyond his own country. But Isaacs's Hebraic habits made him almost unassimilable at home.[6]

The most celebrated centennial was probably that of Martí, author of many works, including the Cuban War of Independence and the influential essay "Our America" (1891). What *our* means in his praise of indigenous and African strains in New World Hispanism is a problem for postmoderns, for two reasons. First, the possessive pronoun neutralizes internal differences and claims ownership in monocultural ways that now seem unproductive. Martí's nineteenth-century nationalism needed to focus on victory by squinting at Cuba, compressing its complexity into a thin but homogeneous *Cubanidad*. The other, more promising problem is that the discriminating pronoun *our* is so shifty, so

---

6. *María* (1867), the classic novel by Isaacs, is the most widely read, pirated, and imitated novel of nineteenth-century Latin America. Required reading in Colombian high schools, it is also on standard syllabi in many other countries.

available for competing positionalities and equivocal meanings. In a New World where commercial, cultural, and political border crossings define so many lives, boundary words like *here* and *there, mine* and *yours, now* and *then* are hardly stable signposts. They are, as always, shifters. Merely to translate the possessive claim to "Nuestra América" as "Our America" is to hear it deformed by the treachery of displacement. It is to move from a defensive position right into the enemy's camp.[7]

Strategists will know that mobility is not only a cause for worry; it is also an opportunity to gain ground. Perhaps Nuestra América has a future history here, up North. Translation, of course, literally means switching ground, a movement in which Puerto Ricans have become expert. They are a nation that maneuvers along the fault line of "autonomy" and grammatical shifters, in the space between here and there, now and then, Our America and theirs. It is a case of an entire population that stays on the move, or potentially so, so much so that Luis Rafael Sánchez makes a hysterical joke about Puerto Rican national identity being grounded in the *guagua aérea* (air bus) shuttling across the Atlantic puddle.[8] Literally a nation of *Luftmenschen*, half is provisionally on the Caribbean island, and half on and around that other Mad Hatter island, which has become the homeland that Tato Laviera calls *AmeRíca*,[9] a practically providential metaphor: AmeRíca transforms what for English or Spanish is just a word into a mot juste in Spanglish. It proclaims doubly marked mainland Ricans as the most representative citizens we have. In the same spirit, Juan Flores's essay, and Latino studies in general, pulls at the seam between belonging and nostalgia to recognize that cultural history is made here, wherever that happens to be.

This energy is evident in all the chapters that follow. They depart

7. Waldo Frank titled his book about the entire hemisphere *Our America* (New York: Boni and Liveright, 1919). Translated in references as *Nuestra América*, it was, for example, an inspiration and model for José Carlos Mariátegui, the major theorist of a particularized, Peruvian Marxism; see *El alma matinal y otras estaciones del hombre de hoy* (Lima: Amauta, 1972), 192, 197. Mariátegui's piece is from 1929. Another disciple of Frank is Walter Benn Michaels, whose new book on "nativism, modernism, and pluralism" bears the title *Our America* (Durham, N.C.: Duke University Press, 1995).
8. Sánchez, "La guagua aérea" [The air bus], trans. Diana Vélez, *Village Voice*, 24 January 1984.
9. Laviera, *AmeRícan* (Houston: Arte Público, 1985).

from ideal projections of syncretic cultures, coherent class orienta-
tions, and patterns of skepticism. The energy opens a space for attending to the historical specificities that fit patterns badly. And the specific
points help anchor our cultural discourses as we witness the endless
movements of transculturation in Our Americas.

The Corpus Delicti

JOSEFINA LUDMER

I would like to use the juridical notion of the corpus delicti, the "body of the crime," in its literal sense of evidence, proof of the truth, and at the same time the literary notion of the corpus, or body of crime, in the sense of a whole group of fictional works linked by their representation of crimes.

The corpus is constituted by a series of narrative texts that traverse the twentieth century, especially in Argentina. The category of corpus questions groupings by authors and the petrified notion of text. The corpus delicti, as a whole body of evidence constituted by reading, has its own form, history, and context. It is a mass of fictions, with different systems of boundaries.

The notion of crime that constitutes the corpus is political, juridical, and cultural at the same time. It serves as the articulator and also as an instrument for defining by exclusion. Crime is one of the most frequently used instruments for defining and founding a culture, that is, for separating it from nonculture and marking what the culture excludes: the murder of the father by the primal horde of sons in Freud, for example, or the feminine "crime" in Genesis. And I want to emphasize that to found a culture upon the crime of the minor, of the second generation, or to found it upon the "crime" of the second sex, would imply not only excluding the anticulture but also postulating a guilty subjectivity. And also a pact. On the face of it, then, this is how fictions of cultural identity seem to deal with crime.

Translated from the Spanish by Donally Suzanne Kennedy and Georgina Dopico-Black.

Crime is also defined by the state and its laws and constitutes the field of state illegality, which is what the state excludes within its interior. Therefore crime is at once a cultural and a juridical category, and it can constitute a literary corpus because it serves to define not only the foundation of a culture (and to articulate it with nonculture) but also the basis of its politics (and to articulate politics with illegality).

In other words, the corpus delicti (body of evidence) can be constituted when it is thought of as a fictional unit from the perspective of the state and *at the same time* from the perspective of crime within the culture.

From the perspective of the state means from the perspective of reason linked with truth and legitimacy. Reasons of state are differential and bureaucratic: they rank things hierarchically, divide and classify them; the hierarchical scale coincides with hierarchies of reason. The differences are to be found, within fictions, between what is true and false, legal and illegal.

The other perspective that constitutes the corpus is that of crime within culture, in a world ranked hierarchically and classified like the state but from another vantage point: from the "crimes" of each of the linguistic, economic, racial, national, sexual, social, and familial parts of the fictions. From the culture's perspective means, therefore, from the perspective of the cultural system of beliefs (ideologies, residuals, archaic remains) in the "crimes" of the diverse regimens or genres of difference in the fictions.

To synthesize: The corpus delicti demonstrates that the modern state defines crime according to a different system than culture does. The apparatus of the state and the cultural apparatus of beliefs and discourses about difference that constitute the subjects of that state are correlated. But their correlation is tense and contradictory. Cultural beliefs (the "genres" of difference and their discourses) are not synchronous with the division of the state; rather, they drag along earlier and sometimes archaic stages or temporalities. The fiction of the corpus puts on stage two dramas or passions: the drama of the cultural world of beliefs in difference and the political drama of the state at each historical juncture.

Delimitation of the Corpus Delicti

The corpus, articulated politically and culturally by crime, can be delimited by four possible variables that could, I believe, define literary-crime texts: first, by the type of subjectivities inscribed or represented in the literary discourse (that of the criminal, victim, witness, or investigator); second, by the dominant type of representation of power (familial, economic, social, sexual, racial, or political) that crime fictions exhibit; third, by the type of justice or penalty that they apply to their crimes (state or nonstate justice); and fourth, by the relationship of that justice with "the truth" or with the specific type of truth postulated by the texts.

Our corpus of crime is constituted upon the guilty subjectivity of the criminal, the representation of power as belonging to the state, the lack of state justice for crime, and the relation of justice to truth as farce. Some of the texts are *El casamiento de Laucha* (1906), by Roberto Payró; *Los siete locos* (1929) and *Los lanzallamas* (1931), by Roberto Arlt; *Las ratas* (1943), by José Bianco; "Emma Zunz" (1946), by Jorge L. Borges; *El túnel* (1951), by Ernesto Sábato; *La casa del ángel* (1955), by Beatriz Guido; *Operación masacre* (1956), by Rodolfo Walsh; and *Boquitas pintadas* (1969), by Manuel Puig. And also some non-Argentine texts, like "Borrador de un informe" (1960), by Augusto Roa Bastos, and *Crónica de una muerte anunciada* (1981), by Gabriel García Márquez.

The corpus delicti recounts at the same time crimes of passion and political crimes, because the corpus always contains, aside from the representation of the criminal character—the one who speaks and confesses his crimes—some representation of the state as criminal. The corpus delicti creates the fiction of the criminal's subjectivity in a criminal state. This fiction differentiates (and separates) the corpus from the tradition of social realism (as a whole culture and not just a literary culture), whose representations of power are economic, social, and political-statist and where guilt for the crime is not subjectivized: in the fictions of social realism the subjectivities of the working-class victims, and not those of the criminal bosses, do the speaking. The center of our corpus, by contrast, is occupied by the criminals' guilty subjectivities. The criminals' discourse also separates it from detective stories (another literary culture that it borders), where the subjectivity is that of the investigator, with his calculations or adventures, and where justice is always done, because truth and justice are fused. Finally, the relation between truth and the farce of truth, which constitutes justice in the fiction of this corpus, differentiates it from both ("higher" or more "literary") cultures, where crime maintains a different relationship with truth, because its fictions are inserted in the space between the genres of detective and fantastic fiction.

As is apparent, crime fiction can be used for all types of divisions and articulations: it can divide into zones the entirety of what could be called a literary culture and thereby define its outlines and layers. Beginning with the representation of the crime, the borders are more or less sharply drawn. In our case, in Argentina, the corpus delimited as such refers to a type of middlebrow culture that is secondary from a historical point of view (that of the children or grandchildren of immigrants), which is produced and read by the advanced sector of the political opposition, rationalist and secular: the progressive modernizing culture, always demanding a transformation of the state in the direction of justice and truth. One of the historical functions of that culture, in its political, cultural, and literary discourses, is the denunciation of the state as criminal.

The corpus delicti is constituted by the most widely read texts of twentieth-century Argentine literature, those that have appeared in the most editions; almost all have been made into movies. There is something of the national literary canon, and not just one strand of culture, in these stories. The corpus of the crime, insofar as it is the corpus of a literary culture, could be read, therefore, as one of the fables of identity that run through and found Argentine culture. These fictions of cultural identity would tell of an exclusion, a guilty conscience, and a pact. The criminal is the one charged with excluding and with making the pact.

Narration of the Corpus Delicti: Fictions of
Exclusion and Dreams of Justice

The crime is recounted, in the corpus, from the secondary status and the guilty conscience of the criminal. This person, who is the central character, the one who speaks and says I, is marked, in this group of fictions, by two kinds of symbolic difference: one of order (hierarchical or numerical) and one of name. He tells us that he enters a space where another stood before him, and he therefore appears right away as a second, the one who comes after the main one: his realm is that of secondariness, whether social, economic, political, military, familial, or sexual. The criminal of the corpus has a nominal deficiency with regard to the other names in the fiction. If the rest of the characters have names, the criminal only has a nickname. If they have two names, he only has one. He may lack a name altogether. His crimes are those of symbolic difference, of number or name. In these fictions the criminal represents or embodies beliefs in the crimes of those who are constituted as "illegitimate" (crimes "against name or honor") and also the crimes of those constituted as "secondary" (minors, subordinates), which are subjected to an authority capable of punishing or annihilating.

In the fictions of the corpus the criminal is associated with what could be called a "first man," who has what he himself lacks, a mark of power in his own name, another name added to his. Generally speaking, he is a representative of the state and can appear in the corpus as a politician, judge, commissioner, priest, or military leader. (He is the astrologer in Arlt, who has the added name that Erdosain lacks and also a third name given to him by Erdosain himself, Lenin; the bishop or the priest in García Márquez; the parish priest Papagna and the commissioner Barraba in Payró, who have the added names that Laucha lacks.)

The first man commits crimes of the state (religious, political, military, or juridical crimes) in the form of farces of truth, which accompany and complement the robberies or murders committed by the central characters. Inasmuch as the reasons of state are rationality linked with truth and legitimacy, the farce of truth is the mode in which the criminal state governs and administers justice: with speech, acts, and ceremonies identical to legitimate ones but devoid of value. They are acts designed to make you believe, like simulations or falsifications (and the corpus can also be read as a reflection upon falsification), because they are spoken or executed in the fictions in the same way as the real ones are, but in another time or place, differently, or by another subject or protagonist, distinct from the legitimate one. Or they might easily accompany an opposite, a different, speech or act.

The sphere of crimes or truth deployed by the corpus supposes differences in beliefs between the actors and the acted upon. It can appear as a farcical marriage, as farces of speeches or political projects, as a farcical blessing by a bishop, as a farcical autopsy, as a juridical farce or a farcical military report. Inasmuch as justice is identified with the truth, the corpus embodies a generalized criminality.

The fiction establishes from the start the closeness, alliance, or symbiosis between the criminal and the representative of the state: they are united by category of illegitimacy and by their shared semantic field of deception or fraud. The alliance between the secondary criminal and the illegitimate representative of the state links and reinforces these two symbolic categories. The relationship may or may not be made explicit in the texts, but the main character of the corpus delicti, his first person, whether he knows it or not, functions as an agent of the state. The illegality of the state and the secondariness of the delinquent constitute the perpetrators of the crimes of the corpus.

To commit his crime, the criminal enters a space where another stood before him. That space is the highest, from the economic, political, or social point of view, represented within the fiction: the place of economic, political, or social power. It is situated someplace other than the capital, the locus of the state, and generally towers over in the fictions. If the corpus is serialized, the house of crime may represent the "real" counterstate at each historical moment, that is to say, the conjunction of those forces of the political opposition that have a shot at power. The crime may occur in the grocery store of the Italian widow in Pago Chico, at the beginning of the century, under the law expelling foreigners (anarchists); in the house of the angel in Belgrano, a conservative haunt during the radical government; at Temperley's country estate, a meeting place of revolutionaries, anarchists, and the military, all conspirators against the Irigoyen government in the coup d'état of 1930. The crime may also occur on the ranch of the oligarchy under Peronism or in a march or popular rally during the military dictatorships. In other words, each house of crime inscribes and includes contemporary political reality in the fictional texts of the corpus. The space of the victim is, each time, a danger or political threat to the "real" state at that historical moment. Each space, that of the state and that of the counterstate, has its discourses and its representations in these fictions. The criminal alternates between the two, and that movement is the very movement of the story of the corpus or of its fiction.

The house of crime is not only the place of power but also that of the "crimes" of difference. It is precisely there, where the criminal interacts with his victim, that the corpus delicti resides. The victim of the fiction of the corpus has a supplement or surplus, another mark of visible or audible difference: another language or another gaze. The supplement can be fused with the representation of the victim in these fictions, like the one-eyed woman in Arlt, the foreigner who speaks Italian in Payró, the Jew who speaks Yiddish in Borges, the blind prostitute in Roa Bastos; or it can be separate from but allied with the victim, like the blind husband in Sábato. Therefore the victim of the corpus (who may or may not be a woman) evokes within the criminal those beliefs and discourses relative to the "crimes" of gender or crimes of the body, like prostitution, loss of virginity, abortion, or adultery.

And the other voice or gaze, that of the victim, evokes within the criminal beliefs relative to the stigmatizing "crimes": the evil eye (the evil of seeing or being seen) and malediction (from *maledictus*, "evil speaking"). These are the most archaic beliefs, beliefs in "evil," associated with gender difference. The point of articulation or collusion among these beliefs is the point where the crime is committed in the fiction of the corpus. The criminal commits the crime in order to empty that space and cut off its progeny. The victim is never a mother.

The corpus of crime as story and cultural fable thus produces a fiction of exclusion, of elimination of difference by means of power, since differences based on gender, nationality, social class, ethnic group, political affiliation, and race, in the space entered by the criminal, mobilize in him the panoply of beliefs and discourses about "crimes of difference," which will help him commit his own crime. Annihilation implies a violent change, the end of a kind of association, the erasure of that space, death without offspring, and a change of place for the criminal. The criminal's entrance, as an agent of the state, into the space of the counterstate culminates in a metaphor of holocaust. The cultural construction of difference and its relation with crime thus appears as an accessory of the criminal national state. The corpus subjectifies and inserts in the narrative this relationship ending in crime.

In the corpus delicti the criminal tells this story, as a confession, to a chronicler, who writes it down. It forms a part of the state's farces of truth and at the same time tells the truth in confession. Or rather, the criminals of the corpus execute two politics at once: the criminal politics of the state (the "fictions of exclusion") and, in the confession, the politics of truth against the criminal state (the "dreams of justice"). They are double agents, characteristic of political textuality. This type of representation of the criminal as stand-in, double agent, and guilty subjectivity and the type of representation of the state as criminal with regard to the truth, occurs only in the corpus of the crime and establishes a zone of Argentine and Latin American culture.

The chronicler of the corpus is clearly opposed to the investigator and even to the savant who appears in the crime fictions of other cultural zones. He represents the instance of truth and hence a possible just state in opposition to the criminal state. Chronicle and confession are the basic narrative discourses of the corpus. And between the two of them, they sustain the narrative pact of truth and justice that serves as a pact of identity in these fictions.

In other words, the pact between discourses of truth, between the truthful confession of the criminal and the written chronicle of the chronicler, constitutes both the narrative system of the corpus and one of the pacts of the fable of progressive modernizing culture in Argentina. The proof of this is that they refer to something real; the fiction of identity established by these discourses has in fact determined professions and "destinies," like all fables of identity. Chronicle and confession occupy the juridical, scientific, medical, journalistic, psychoanalytic, and literary spaces that the representatives of this culture occupy and have occupied.

But the narrative pact of the corpus delicti is founded not only on the truth of these discourses but also on the justice of the chronicler's discourse. In the corpus the criminal does not receive punishment (or "justice") by the state for his crime. The textual, temporal, and spatial "justice-truth" of the chronicler appears, then, after the confession and tells us that the criminal has passed away, committed suicide, or fled the country. (The justice of the chronicler is that of the boundaries or the borders of space and time.) In this supplement of time, the chronicler can also narrate the recompense owed to the criminal.

But something more can happen to justice in the corpus, something that escapes the chronicler, escapes the truth and the justice of the fiction, and ventures once again into political reality—something like a future "justice" or "truth," outside the texts but inside the corpus. The corpus delicti overflows in all directions: beliefs, destinies, professions, states past and future. If the criminals have not died, if they have not been exiled in the fictions (if the chronicler has not meted out justice following the crime), they reappear in the "real" political future, flanking the ruler or as accessories of the state. Outside the text, in reality, the military men not punished by Roa Bastos expelled him from Paraguay; the murderous military assassinated Walsh, and, outside the text, Arlt's astrologer and prostitute attended Perón. (We can read in here the anticipatory function of literature in a world shaped by the relation between the power of state and beliefs.) The corpus delicti thus contains the future histories of the state and the history of the successive contemporary counterstates.

Let me conclude with one of the specific contexts of the corpus. Beliefs in difference and their "crimes," the resulting fictions of exclusion, and the confessions and chronicles that they produce, are linked today, in Argentina, to laws on prostitution, farm labor, Peronists, and foreigners, just as beliefs in honor and name, and their crimes, are linked to laws about private and corporate justice: the law regarding residency or expulsion of undesirable aliens (1902), which almost coincides with Payró's text; another decreeing the closure of brothels (1935–36); the farm labor statute (1945); the laws prohibiting Peronism and imposing martial law (1955); the laws prohibiting dueling (1921) and the exacting of private justice for offenses against honor. Each one of these laws has its exact, precise equivalent in the representation of difference and beliefs in the corpus delicti, which each time excludes or includes someone "different." The history of the corpus is articulated directly also with the history of electoral laws and coups in Argentina, and it accompanies changes in the national state, its transformations, falls, and democratizations, which are, each time, accompanied by laws about difference or about different justices.

The corpus of the most widely read, edited, and filmed texts in Argentina, which recounts one of the fables of progressive, modernizing culture, constitutes a special kind of canon in Argentine literature, if *canon* is understood as a pragmatic instrument and not as an abstraction—as a living canon, one that produces literature, the result of a real war. Each of these texts confronted an official literary institution and won the battle. It suffices to think of Arlt's texts, now canonized. They won one of the wars of the corpus, that of the minor or secondary against the major. They proposed another kind of literature, and thus of reading, neither purely "literary" nor totally "social," neither Catholic nor committed. They tried to erase the opposition between pure literature and social literature and succeeded, because it is impossible to read these works within the boundaries of this opposition. They entered right into the war concerning autonomous literature, the confrontation between pure literature and social literature (or the confrontation over the power of literature), in order to question it and thereby to question literary institutions. The history of the corpus of crime also tells of the struggle for literary power, and not only for state power, of this strand of Latin American culture.

Overwriting Pinochet:
Undoing the Culture of Fear in Chile

MARY LOUISE PRATT

About eight months after the coup of 11 September 1973, General Augusto Pinochet gave a speech to what seems to have been the founding gathering of a new state entity, the National Secretariat for Women, established by the new junta and headed by Lucia Hiriart—de Pinochet, the general's wife.[1] To a highly selective audience, Pinochet proposed to "lay out the thought of the authorities with respect to the role corresponding to women in the plans of the government over which I preside, and the new state that it proposes to install in the future."[2]

It takes little more than Pinochet's opening sentence to grasp the raw authoritarianism that characterized the military regime, especially in its early, triumphal, and extremely violent period. People have roles that "correspond" to them; "thought" is in the hands of the authorities, who do not include women; citizenship consists, as Pinochet loved to say, in either ordering or obeying, and only those who do one or the other well are useful to the state. "In Chile," the speech continues, women have always been "active and effective collaborators in the lives of men"—so Pinochet codes the role that women played in bringing him to power.[3] The women of Chile, he explains (subsuming them all

1. The coup overthrew the socialist coalition Unidad Popular [Popular unity], headed by President Salvador Allende Gossens. Allende died during the coup.
2. Pinochet Ugarte, *Mensaje a la mujer chilena: Texto del discurso*, Santiago: Editorial nacional Gabriela Mistral, [1976]). My translations. On the Pinochet regime's views on gender see also *Valores patrios y valores familiares* (Santiago: Secretaría Nacional de la Mujer, 1982).
3. In the campaign against the Unidad Popular government, right-wing parties and the military sought to mobilize middle- and upper-class women, whose opposition

under the category of those who, at different times and for a host of reasons, came to oppose the Unidad Popular government; homogenization is a central authoritarian tactic), "sought the shelter of a strict authority that would reestablish order and public morality in our country" (7). The authority of the authorities, then, includes command over interpretation as well. Women's desires are *defined*; their actions are assigned a meaning and even an epistemology: "In her feminine instinct" the Chilean woman "saw clearly that what was being defined in those dramatic days was not simply a game of political parties; it was the life or death of the nation" (7). Pinochet speaks of her "clairvoyance" (*clarividencia*: the term not by accident recalls Isabel Allende) in seeing past party politics—which the regime has abolished.

Obviously, I am not quoting this rhetoric for its subtlety. The women are told that, following the traditions of "the West" (*el occidente*), their "mission as women and mothers" has been and remains to defend and transmit spiritual values, serve as a moderating element (against the warlike impulses of men, it seems), educate and instill consciousness and conscience, and serve as repositories of national traditions (8). While acknowledging women's *right* to a profession, the general calls for greater recognition of their contribution in the work that "corresponds" to them, which is of course child rearing. Equality of rights and opportunity are undisputed, he says, but woman's "authentic participation" must "be exercised in relation to her characteristics" (11).

The constant explicit interpellation of women was a hallmark of the Pinochet regime. One of the tragic ironies in Chile, as elsewhere, is that the dictatorship took advantage of the near vacuum in political discourse and party structures as regards women, not because the regime particularly cared about them, but because it saw patriarchal values as the key to the one thing it could not dictate for itself: legitimacy. As Jean Franco has observed, one of the regime's tactics was to mobilize gender ideologies held across society and across the political

---

would appear apolitical. Particularly effective were marches of women banging empty pots to protest shortages caused by a CIA-supported truckers' strike. Even more specifically, a network of highly placed military wives was organized to call for military restoration of order. The coup could then be presented as a response to the demands of a politically disinterested sector.

spectrum.[4] The political parties, from right to left, had never put women into the picture; Pinochet rarely left them out—of the picture, that is. We are not talking about real power. But perhaps in a way we are, for in his seventeen years in power Pinochet presided over a social and political mobilization of women that was unprecedented in Chile, and probably in Latin America, and that had everything to do with his eventual demise. At the same time, the patriarchal ideologies he engaged deeply influenced the way women were seen and saw themselves, unconsciously as well as consciously.

The paternalism and authoritarianism heard in the general's pronouncements were by no means reserved for women, however. They characterized his rhetoric across the board. Scholars have repeatedly commented on the homogenizing, monoglossic, prescriptive, and *abstract* rhetorics of the southern-cone dictatorships.[5] They sought not to replace public discourse with an imposed silence but to simulate it with a relentless drone apparently interpellating all citizens yet actively deterritorializing anyone they chose. Like the martial music played on the radio during a coup, the drone did not just dispel but forbade the idea of culture or the social as the site of conflict, heterogeneity, and negotiation of difference. As Priscilla Archibald has observed, the

4. Franco, "Gender, Death, and Resistance: Facing the Ethical Vacuum," in *Fear at the Edge: State Terror and Resistance in Latin America*, ed. Juan E. Corradi, Patricia Weiss Fagen, and Manuel Antonio Garretón (Berkeley: University of California Press, 1992) 104–20.
5. A vast and rich literature exists on the question of culture, authoritarianism, and redemocratization in Chile, on which this essay relies and by which it is framed. In addition to the works cited, see Manuel Antonio Garretón, Saúl Sosnowski, and Bernardo Subercaseaux, eds., *Cultura, autoritarismo y redemocratización en Chile* (Mexico City: Fondo de Cultura Económica, 1993); Subercaseaux, *Historia, literatura y sociedad* (Santiago: Centro de Indagación y Expresión Cultural y Artística, 1991); Horacio Riquelme, ed., *Era de nieblas: Derechos humanos, terrorismo de estado y salud psicosocial en América Latina* (Caracas: Nueva Sociedad, 1990); José Joaquín Brunner, *La cultura autoritaria en Chile* (Santiago: Facultad Latinoamericana de Ciencias Sociales, 1981); Brunner, *Políticas culturales para la democracia* (Santiago: Centro de Indagación y Expresión Cultural y Artística, 1985); Hernán Vidal, *Cultura nacional chilena: Crítica literaria y derechos humanos* (Minneapolis: Institute for the Study of Ideologies and Literatures, 1985); Vidal, *Fascismo y experiencia literaria* (Minneapolis: Institute for the Study of Ideologies and Literatures, 1989); and the magazine *Revista de Crítica Cultural*, ed., Nelly Richard, particularly the July 1992 special issue "Cultura, política y democracia."

absence of argument or evidence was key. Pinochet's was a discourse of pure statement, in which the words *thus* and *therefore* referred back not to facts or reasons but to essences and eternal laws—despatialized, not spatial, knowledge.[6] Against the drone of abstraction and essentialism, the literary practice of *testimonio* acquired force as a counterdiscourse. *Testimonios* lay bare the regime's practice of concealment, represented what was concealed, and reasserted the languages of evidence, bodily experience, and truth and falsehood, as well as the values of truth and falsehood.[7]

Ten years into the dictatorship, the experimental writer and video artist Diamela Eltit undertook something quite different. She produced, or rather encountered, a remarkable parody of the dictatorship's monologue, which by then had become "parody-able." Eltit taped a series of monologues uttered by what would in conventional terms be described as a madman, who lived outdoors in a vacant lot in a Santiago barrio and called himself "El Padre Mío" [My father]. The "complete state of delirium" in which, according to Eltit, El Padre Mío lived only reproduced many dimensions of the reality common to all Chileans: paranoia, uncertainty, a crisis of language in which words seemed unattached to referents, an omnipresent sense of victimization and death. At the same time, his discourse suggests the megalomania and paranoia of the dictatorship itself:

> You're taking me for a ride with this plan. How would I not know that? I'm the man who is going to give the orders here, me. I am going to give the orders in the country. Because I have no commitments either to them or to King George, who has been giving the orders lately and has that rank. El Padre Mío gives the illegal orders in the country. For many years he has been living off illegal bank deposits, from the money that belongs to the concession of the personnel of the administration. He is the accomplice of El Padre Mío in these matters. I would like to do you a service in exchange for

6. Archibald, class lecture on Pía Barros in the context of the Pinochet regime, Stanford University, May 1994. See also Giselle Munizaga, *El discurso público de Pinochet, 1973–1976* (Buenos Aires: Consejo Latinoamericano de Ciencias Sociales, 1983).
7. According to Grinor Rojo, *testimonios* circulated clandestinely in Chile as early as 1975 and openly after 1981 ("Casi veinte años de literatura chilena [1973–1991]," in Garretón et al.).

the sale of your rights. Because I was asked to take up these tasks, not El Padre Mío, nor Mr. Colvin, who is Mr. Luengo, who is a congressman and a senator.[8]

Ironic implications abound. Under the military regime, only the madman in the street can speak, and he does have something to say. Alternatively, the only man in the street who is speaking is mad. *El Padre Mío* exemplifies Eltit's commitment to marginality as a critical source of insight in any hegemonic structure. El Padre Mío seems to appropriate the disembodied oratory of the dictatorship and reflect it back in a form that the authorities cannot decipher.

El Padre Mío parodies in particular the abstraction of the regime's rhetoric, which created an unbridgeable, tectonic gap between what the regime said and what its citizens experienced. The "plans of the government and the new institutionality it proposes to establish in the future" were under way. The Pinochet regime had, as Giselle Munizaga calls it, a "foundational project."[9] People tend to think that military dictatorships aim simply to impose order, suppress opposition, and uphold established hierarchies, rather than to advance elaborate social and institutional agendas. But Pinochet had no problem at all with "the vision thing," and devastating the militant Left was only one small part of it (accomplished, as in all these dictatorships, in a matter of weeks). When he spoke, as he did all the time, of "the new institutionality" (*la nueva institucionalidad*), he meant a wholesale transformation of state and civil society, no fooling.

In terms of political economy, the project was to interrupt the historical trajectory of "development" in Chile by redirecting industrial production from national markets, which were driven by rising wages, to the world market, facilitated by substantial wage cuts.[10] (Resonances

8. Eltit, *El Padre Mío* (Santiago: Francisco Zegers, 1989). My translation.
9. Munizaga, "El sistema comunicativo chileno y los legados de la dictadura," in Garretón et al. See also Carlos Catalán and Giselle Munizaga, *Políticas culturales estatales bajo el autoritarismo en Chile* (Santiago: Centro de Indagación y Expresión Cultural y Artística, 1986).
10. See André Gunder Frank, *Economic Genocide in Chile* (Nottingham: Spokesman, 1976); Frank, *Reflections on the World Economic Crisis* (New York: Monthly Review Press, 1981); and Neil Larsen, ed., *The Discourse of Power: Culture, Hegemony, and the Authoritarian State* (Minneapolis: Institute for the Study of Ideologies and Literatures, 1983).

with the U.S. in the 1980s are clear.) As Hernán Vidal succinctly puts it, "Pinochet's job was to offer a cheap workforce to the world."[11] By 1975 Chile had 30 percent unemployment, and wages had dropped by 30–50 percent, leaving a huge proportion of the population destitute. Rapid, drastic immiseration mobilized Chilean women, who collectivized domestic life in every way they could. In vast impoverished neighborhoods, shopping, cooking, eating, sewing, child care, medical care, laundry, and artisanal production moved out of private houses into circles, clubs, and cooperatives, with support and help especially from the church, the only oppositional force the regime was obliged to tolerate. In the face of such extreme circumstances, the regime's pious rhetoric about women's roles became an insult.

Economic intervention was accompanied by a complete shutting down of civil society and its interfaces with the state. Political parties were abolished; a press blackout was followed by draconian censorship; curfews were imposed; public assembly was prohibited; universities were purged; presses were shut down; the judiciary was suspended; the opposition was annihilated; and a regime of terror based on torture and disappearance was installed. To understand how drastic this rupture was, one needs to recall the high, indeed acute, politicization of Chilean society at the time of the coup. The dramatic struggle between the Unidad Popular government and its opposition had been played out in huge daily demonstrations in streets and plazas, particularly in the central plaza in front of La Moneda palace, the seat of the presidency.[12] The Chilean military shredded the public script in the very staging of the coup: La Moneda, a pivotal site of political expression, was bombed by the air force—an extraordinary self-inflicted wound—and the national soccer stadium, the pivotal site of nonpolitical citizenship, was taken over and transformed into a detention and torture center where, among other horrors, the revered singer-guitarist Victor Jara was displayed, not dead but tortured and beaten, with his fingers cut off. The stadium had been converted into a plaza with walls. It is hard to exaggerate the symbolic and psychic force of

11. Vidal, "La Declaración de Principios de la junta militar chilena como sistema literario: La lucha antifascista y el cuerpo humano," in Larsen, 47. My translation.
12. These events are vividly captured in the documentary *La batalla de Chile*, produced by Patricio Guzmán and directed by Federico Elton in 1973.

the militarization of this canonized arena for the exercise of a secular, civilian, masculine nationality. (It is no accident that when elections were restored, the new president, Patricio Aylwin Azócar, made his acceptance speech there in 1989.)

The figure of the plaza with walls epitomizes the reimagining of the nation itself following the coup. Chile became Fortress Chile, its entrances and exits fiercely guarded, its dissidents expelled, the order of the seen and unseen reconfigured. Hence the powerful impact in film and writing of another experiment in representation, *The Adventure of Miguel Littín in Chile* (1986).[13] Littín, a prominent Left leader under Allende, had been exiled under an absolute prohibition from returning to Chile. In 1985, with a disguise and a false passport—and, of course, the extensive collaboration of the internal opposition—he slipped back in, accompanied by no fewer than three European film crews that traveled with him the length and breadth of Chile, also under false pretenses, filming what became an extraordinary documentary of the country under the dictatorship. A straightforward referential work, almost a travelogue, it represents a literal recovery of place and spatialized knowledge: generous footage of walks through the city streets and of the beloved Chilean landscape, viewed from the windows of moving trains. The film, and García Márquez's widely read narrative account, dramatize the porosity of Fortress Chile, the ubiquity and effectiveness of the clandestine opposition, and, more important, the fact that the dictatorship, with eyes everywhere, could be made to see without knowing what it was seeing. Time and again Littín directly encounters the police and escapes unrecognized. The film crews, which made no secret of their filming, even penetrated La Moneda. As Eltit later dramatized in *El Padre Mío*, the regime's claim to interpretive power could be contradicted *openly*. Littín's heroic infiltration was a seizing of agency that simply refused the culture of fear and appropriated—or intercepted—the tools of secrecy.

Ironically, Littín's adventure worked uncritically within the gendered construction of power that the dictatorship mobilized in its own

---

13. See Gabriel García Márquez, *La aventura de Miguel Littín, clandestino en Chile: Un reportaje* (Buenos Aires: Editorial Sudamericana, 1986). The footage was edited into a four-hour TV series and a two-hour film titled *Miguel Littín clandestino en Chile*.

acts of penetration, whether nocturnal invasions of homes or sexual tortures or university purges. (Indeed, within a year, opposition movements were crushed again following a failed assassination attempt against Pinochet by the Manuel Rodríguez Front.) Some theorists of democratization have asserted the need to abandon models of resistance based on this heroic model of agency. Abandoned they were, for the most part, at least in practice. By the time Littín slipped inside the fortress walls, other paradigms of resistant agency had been put into play, with great effectiveness, by dozens of oppositional groups overwhelmingly composed of women.[14] These groups likewise intercepted and redeployed the dynamics of the secret and the seen and unseen. The international community became familiar with images of demonstrations of women parading photos of the "disappeared," who were thus made to reappear. Other startlingly original forms of social drama were staged on national days of protest, which occurred monthly during a period of intense opposition between 1983 and 1986. In a mock election held in Santiago, for instance, ballot boxes mysteriously appeared on street corners, and people were invited to cast votes. In the neighborhoods, the apparently spontaneous banging of pots from inside houses at a certain hour of the day unnervingly recycled a strategy used by middle-class women against the Allende government. Out of nowhere, teams came to paint murals on buildings and then quickly photographed them, knowing they would be gone in hours or days. The literary sphere was sustained, at first clandestinely, by workshops. In her workshops, fiction writer Pia Barros responded to censorship by developing a new form of publication: the "book-object" (*libro-objeto*) disseminated short prose texts in the guise of other consumer objects, such as boxes of stationery, or concealed in little burlap bags. A marketing tool as well as an open disguise to avoid censors, the book-object pointed a parodic finger both at censorship and at the consumerism that neoliberal economics had brought to Chile.

Such innovations were meant to counteract the authoritarian

14. One uniquely informed resource on the Chilean women's movements of the period is Sandra Palestro, *Mujeres en movimiento, 1973–1989*, Serie Estudios Sociales, 14 (Santiago: Facultad Latinoamericana de Ciencias Sociales, 1991).

reorganization of citizenship that the Pinochet regime imposed in the most everyday ways. As the foregoing examples suggest, the rearrangement and resymbolization of public space were among its principal physical and psychic weapons. Two texts exemplify this resymbolization and the response to it. The first is a propaganda pamphlet, translated into English as *Chile Lights the Freedom Torch*, concerning the festivities held on the second anniversary of the coup, on 11 September 1975.

According to the pamphlet, they began in the military garrisons, which the regime defined as the core site of citizenship and where, we read, "solemn religious services were held."[15] The main event took place in the yard of the country's principal military academy—another plaza with walls—where the four-man junta, accompanied by "thousands of military and civilian men," prayed for Chile. At an evening rally held in a large square in Santiago, the junta took its place at a high podium backed by a huge map of Chile. To the light of thousands of torches, "giving to the night an unforgettable appearance," a gigantic national flag was raised in the center of the square; then, as the translation (hilariously) reads, "President Pinochet addressed to all the Chileans a brief harangue." Following the speech, "four anonymous civilians representing the women, the youth, the field workers and the city workers" approached the podium and lit four torches. These were handed off to four cadets, representing the four branches of the armed forces, who in turn took them up to the podium and handed them off to the four members of the junta. They together lit an enormous freedom torch that, by the photos, formed a ring the size of a large auditorium. At the end of September, the "month of the fatherland," this torch was moved "in a somber ceremony" to the hilltop where in 1541 the Spaniard Pedro de Valdivia had founded Santiago de Chile. "There it will remain forever as a symbol to a country that wants to be truthful to its origins."

An intriguing aspect of the ritual is the foursome chosen to represent civilian society, for the list excludes the very sector that, under civilian rule, constitutes the core of the citizenry: the adult men of property, who, in classical state theory, attend the assembly and vote.

---

15. *Chile Lights the Freedom Torch* (Santiago: Editorial Nacional Gabriela Mistral, 1976).

The youth, the women, and the workers make sense only as a set grouped around this absent center (a slot for teachers or intellectuals, for example, is unimaginable here). Of course, what replaces that center, and that image of citizenship, is the military, whose vertical relations are reproduced as the torches move up the podium. "Enlightenment" here refers to flames in the night.[16]

The second text, Diamela Eltit's daunting, avant-garde work *Lumpérica*, published in 1983, is likewise set at night in a Santiago plaza presided over by a figure called "El Luminoso" [The luminous one (masc.)].[17] El Luminoso turns out to be a flashing neon sign that projects light and words onto the bodies of those below, a potent image for the authoritarian state: light/power emanating from an unseen source. The protagonist is a woman named "L. Iluminada" [The illuminated one (fem.)] who, defying curfew, spends a long, hallucinated night bathed in the cold light of El Luminoso and engaged in what seems to be an epic struggle to find or achieve a convergence of selfhood, agency, language, and meaning.[18] Her quest, expressed in a surreal text virtually indecipherable at first, is for a reterritorialization. *Lumpérica* was written in the context of two demoralizing events: the 1980 plebiscite, probably rigged, in which Chilean voters approved a constitution legitimizing the Pinochet regime, and a crippling recession that marked a genuine crisis of neoliberal economics and coalesced opposition to the regime. One message of the book is that the new convergence of selfhood and agency must be found (or created) in the cold night of the plaza under the relentless semantic projections of El Luminoso. There is no elsewhere. The process the reader accompanies in the text is arduous and full of agony and desire.

The privileged witnesses and acolytes of L. Iluminada's struggle are another group that made no appearance at Pinochet's ceremony,

16. Vidal speaks at length of the medieval quality of the Pinochet dictatorship in "La Declaración de Principios de la junta militar chilena," in Larsen, 43–66.
17. Eltit, *Lumpérica* (Santiago: 1983). My translations. The title puns on the adjective *homérica* and the phrase *lumpen América*.
18. There is an obvious blank in L. Iluminada's name where the *a* of the article *La* should appear. Reminiscent of a neon sign in which one letter has gone out, the absent *a* perhaps designates what is to be recovered: a marker of gender and also of being—"the-ness"—itself.

the lumpen of Santiago, referred to in Eltit's book as "the pale ones" (*los pálidos*). They are the street people who trickle into the plaza, curfew or not, with nowhere else to go. (Eltit says that the idea for the book came to her late one night when she had permission to be out after curfew and drove past the empty plazas of Santiago, indicators of the interruption of public life that had taken place.) In the opening scene L. Iluminada, lying on her back on the cold cement at the center of the plaza, writhes in pain and desire as El Luminoso baptizes her with "the name of her citizenship" (*el nombre de su ciudadanía*), the label that "corresponds to her" (an echo of Pinochet's words). It is a "desolate citizenship," which involves stamping her and the pale ones "like commercial products." The question then becomes what sorts of agency and consciousness exist for those imprinted. The often indecipherable 150 pages that follow are a physical and imaginary odyssey to find an answer.

After her baptism by El Luminoso, L. Iluminada rebaptizes herself by sticking her hand into the bonfire around which she and the pale ones are sitting. "Just for the sake of giving herself a new identity," the narrator remarks derisively, "she turns to tradition like a quote" (29). Self-mutilation pays off, however: "New damage has been done, and a new circle opened in literature." It is hard to miss the scene's medieval resonance, apparently opposing the medievalism of Pinochet's rituals with an invocation of the counterculture of witchcraft. The hand in the fire is the test of truth, and the test gives L. Iluminada, as she tells us, the "power to disorganize language" (30). Bringing her burned hand to her mouth, she utters the sentence "I am thirsty" (*Tengo sed*), ritually "deconstruct[ing] the phrase, word by word, syllable by syllable." What is deconstructed or reorganized is not only the scene of Christ thirsting on the cross but also, more vividly, the scene of torture, with which the phrase *I am thirsty* is irrevocably linked in the vocabulary of this period in Chile. Physical pain itself must be reclaimed; within the national security state, the imagery of masochism can counteract the "secret" of state violence.[19] Indeed, the "I am thirsty"

19. The southern-cone regimes often described their work as that of healing a diseased national body. Communism, for example, was a cancer that had to be removed by self-inflicted surgery. This rhetoric obscured the sadism of state violence, which L. Iluminada's masochism brings to the surface.

episode is followed immediately by an interrogation, in which the interrogator asks, "What are the uses of a public square?" (37).

L. Iluminada takes the reader through a series of hallucinated and hellish metamorphoses and reconquests first of self, then of writing, in which autoeroticism and masochism remain key routes to the power of the word, to a hell of writing. The journey culminates in fifteen vignettes, called "cuts" (*cortes*), referring simultaneously to filmic or textual excerpts and to self-inflicted wounds (the section is introduced by a photo of a woman, probably the author, with her arms bound in bandages). The fifteen cuts take L. Iluminada through descending states of madness, from which she emerges, at dawn, lucid, serene, and alone in the light of El Luminoso, who seems now to be transmitting signals only for her. She recognizes herself as irrevocably vulnerable to his messages but able, by moving, to determine which letters strike her body and where. El Luminoso is limited by his "estatismo," a pun on "static-ness" and "statism." As the text draws to a close, L. Iluminada ambiguously recodes her own body. From a paper bag she takes out a mirror, a pair of scissors, and a necklace; then she cuts off all her hair and puts the necklace on over the gray dress that links her with the gray cement of the plaza. The reader is not sure what she has conquered.

In retrospect, L. Iluminada's quest seems to have prophesied a related struggle, five years later, in which mobility was also a weapon against the "estatismo" of the regime. The "Campaign of the No"—the political campaign in the fall of 1988 that won the plebiscite that ended Pinochet's rule—was also a concerted attempt to "open a new circle," not in literature but in politics, public life, and the social imagination of the Chilean citizenry.[20] An electorate as abject as L. Iluminada in the opening scene of Eltit's text had to be given confidence and hope in the possibility of recovering public life and the plazas after a "desolate citizenship" of fifteen years. The points of intersection between the representational strategies of the Campaign of the No (especially its use of TV cuts) and those of neo-avant-garde writers like Eltit constitute a unique and fascinating conjunction of literary,

20. For the use of television in the campaign, see Melquíades, ed. *La campa del no vista por sus creadores* (Santiago: CIS, 1989).

intellectual, and political history. The points of divergence are illuminating as well, for the neo-avant-garde practices backlight, as always, the limits of the possible even as they place at the disposal of the possible a powerful poetics of renewal. Here, then, is a conjuncture at which a literary history of the present opens out on the vital quest for a future.

The Historical Meaning of Cruelty in Machado de Assis

ROBERTO SCHWARZ

Sah ein Knab' ein Röslein stehn,
Röslein auf der Heiden.—Goethe, "Heidenröslein"

He is poor . . . , therefore he must be easily offended.
—José de Alencar, *Sonhos d'Ouro*

The lowly wildflower, whose charm is due to neither artifice nor lineage, is an image dear to the Enlightenment, romanticism, and the democratic sentiment. The expression appears as the title of a crucial episode in *Memórias póstumas de Brás Cubas* (164; 80), where it encompasses another, contrary meaning:[1] it disdainfully designates the young woman born out of wedlock, conceived behind the bushes, in the wild, so to speak. This conflict in meaning summarizes the ideological tenor of the episode, and the vulgarity of the opening pun gives us a taste of what is to come.

The events narrated (chaps. 30–6) are that of a short-lived bucolic

This essay first appeared under the title "A sorte dos pobres" [The fate of the poor], chapter 6 of *Um mestre na periferia do capitalismo: Machado de Assis*, by Roberto Schwarz (São Paulo: Duas Cidades, 1990). Translated from the Portuguese by Sabrina E. Wilson.

1. Machado de Assis, *Memórias póstumas de Brás Cubas* (Rio de Janeiro: Instituto Nacional do Livro, 1960). Page numbers refer first to this edition and second to the translation, *Epitaph of a Small Winner*, trans. William L. Grossman (New York: Noonday, 1952). When only one page number appears, it refers to the Portuguese text and indicates either the lack of corresponding lines in Grossman's version or the choice of a different translation. The expression used by Machado to refer to Eugênia is *a flor da moita*, translated by Grossman as "the flower of the thicket." "Wildflower" is more appropriate for the purposes of the present article. —Trans.

romance between Brás and Eugênia. She is the illegitimate daughter of Dona Eusébia, an unwed woman of lower social status who frequented the Cubas household; he is the wealthy, upper-class young man we are very familiar with at this point in the narrative. The episode takes place on the outskirts of Rio, in Tijuca, where the young Dr. Cubas has retreated after his mother's death. The protagonists, the circumstances, and the social obstacles create the expectation of a romantic involvement, which does indeed insinuate itself but is abruptly curtailed by considerations of a very different sort.

Eugênia greets her well-to-do visitor in an unusual fashion: garbed in a plain white dress, she wears no ornaments, no earrings, brooch, or bracelet. Pride determines this demanding and poetic gesture: by emphasizing the material differences between Brás and herself, Eugênia undercuts any fantasies of social parity and indicates that she knows her place. However, it seems clear that her actions can be read differently: by doing away with external ornamentation, she reminds her visitor that individuals are fundamentally equal and implicitly forbids him to treat her as an inferior. Such reasoning is not entirely devoid of seductive intent, for an enlightened sensibility will recognize that simplicity and natural charm are supreme adornments, superior to the circumstances of fortune.

Dr. Cubas, the veteran of some years of "practical romanticism and theoretical liberalism" in the Old World (150; 65), does not remain insensitive to the young woman's charms. He can appreciate her dignity, sustained despite the irregular circumstances of her birth and her precarious social status, and risks "really fall[ing] in love with her" (170; 87), that is, loving her as an equal and marrying her. On the other hand, he feels the urge to take advantage of her situation and confirm the dictum "Like mother, like daughter." In the first scenario, love would enable him to overcome family and class barriers and acknowledge equality among individuals (slaves excluded). In the second scenario, made all the more abject by his earlier recognition of Eugênia's dignity, the notion of equality would be rejected, and Brás would simply reap the benefits of his superior social status.

Eugênia's attitude, as exemplified in her choice of attire, reveals an analogous double movement: she both accepts the inferiority of her situation (leaving Brás in a superior position) and sustains, albeit more discreetly, her absolute personal dignity (thereby demanding respect and allowing for the possibility of marriage). In other words, there is a strict correspondence between Brás's conduct and Eugênia's situation, and their respective ambivalences engage with and feed on each other within a practical system both fictional and historical. Their relationship is caught up in a play of objective possibilities that are exploited by Brás and that in turn shape his character, formalized in the novel's diction: in effect, the narrator's deliberate fickleness— at every turn he postulates and then violates literary and other norms—produces an oscillation with ideologically similar references at the level of narrative structure. We thus find unity between social observation, dramatic scheme, character types, and the prose structure, shaped by a class perspective.

Literary form and unjust social relations correspond rigorously to one another, so that the examination of one leads to the fixation of the other's dimensions. Historical knowledge is here a requirement for proper critical scrutiny. It is essential that the sociological particularity of the "romance" not be dissolved in a simplistic poor girl– wealthy suitor archetype.

Actually, Eugênia is not exactly poor. Having grown up and been educated among the wealthy, she could marry into a good family. But she could also end up begging in a tenement house, as in fact she does. What determines the outcome? A rich man's—or his family's— fancy. In other words, Eugênia's fate depends on a whim of the dominant class. Herein lies the crux of the matter, a painful reality for anyone who had heard—and almost every nineteenth-century Brazilian had—of the Rights of Man, a reality all the more intolerable given the drastic difference between the outcomes of lady and beggar. As a result of slavery, there was no developed job market in Brazil; in other words, no practical structure existed in which an individual without means might gain autonomy. A person's value therefore depended on arbitrary (and humiliating, if inconsistent) recognition by a wealthy patron. In this context, it does not seem unreasonable to suggest that Eugênia, among other similar characters, embodies the general reality of the poor, free person in Brazilian slave society.

Neither proprietors nor slaves, these individuals were marginal elements in the system and faced a disconcerting ideological reality.

Given the absence of a free job market, their access to the goods of civilization depended on the fortuitous and discretionary benevolence of the wealthy. Without some form of patronage, the poor were left with no reliable means of survival and remained thoroughly cut off from contemporary material and institutional spheres. On the other hand, the contemporary world, patterned on the classic nations of the bourgeois revolution, disapproved of the very type of patronage that was mandatory for acceptance into Brazil's privileged sphere. In other words, in order to participate in modern culture, the poor person had to pay a high price: a considerable moral and ideological compromise, which might take many forms but was ultimately inescapable.

It is no exaggeration therefore to state that the country's social structure itself privileged the mechanism of the personal favor, including its inevitable—and by the late nineteenth century, unacceptable—component of whim. Unsurprisingly, the complex web of humiliation and hope engendered by this system became a primary source of material for the Brazilian novel. Indeed, to a great extent the novel in Brazil can be studied as the presentation and elaboration of dilemmas resulting from these social dynamics. At any rate, it is within this social setting that fickleness acquires its full significance, being perceived and perceiving itself as a form of social power that presents the other with few, and extreme, options: on the one hand, the "lucky break" of co-optation (in this case, an unequal marriage), possibly coupled with the humiliation of dependence; on the other, acceptance of the modern indifference toward fellow citizens (many of whom, however, are not true citizens and have no means of survival). While this range of possible fates is catastrophic for the poor, for the rich it is a fertile field for the exercise of caprice. Given such extreme imbalance, it is hardly surprising that the upper classes should develop an inflated sense of themselves and of their own importance. On the other hand, the poor's dependence on such a chaotic and unstable process, shaped by the absolute power of whim, indicates the extent of their vulnerability.

A few days after stealing his first kiss from Eugênia, Brás remembers his father, his professional obligations, the constitution, his horse, and so forth and decides to return to Rio. An internal voice triggers the change, whispering words from the Bible in his ear ("Arise, and go into the city" [Acts 9.6]) (170; 86). Brás interprets the divine counsel to suit his own needs, concluding that the city must be Rio and that he must leave Eugênia.

While the biblical Paul converted from persecutor into apostle of Christians, his Brazilian emulator reconverts from enlightened temptation back to the familiar ground of oligarchic injustice. He recalls his father's precepts: "You have to continue our name, continue it and make it even more illustrious. . . . Fear obscurity, Brás; flee everything that isn't big. Look here, there are different ways for a man to amount to something, but the surest of all is to amount to something in other men's opinions. Don't throw away the advantages of your position, of your background" (162; 78).

What is the meaning of this conduct? As far as the plot goes, the episode ends with the young man's departure, with no further developments or revelations. This absolutely commonplace ending could not have been more lackluster or more characteristic. Its critical effect lies in the reader's frustrated romantic desire, for Eugênia, fully aware of her position, represses all feelings and exits in silence. Given the asymmetry of relations, in which, as we have seen, the poor are powerless, all decisions lie in the hands of the dominant class: there is nothing to add to this state of affairs. From this perspective, the minimalist intrigue expresses a power relation and reproduces power's taciturn features. Nonetheless, the Rights of Man and the nineteenth century are not entirely silenced in the text. The options that Brás rejects in practice, thereby excluding them from the plot, subsist in his modern spirit and surface according to circumstances. When the moral repercussions logically experienced by Brás as a modern, enlightened man are added to the episode, a social portrait of unparalleled eloquence in Brazilian letters emerges.

The romance occurs under the sign of four butterflies. The first butterfly, a simile of the young man's idle fantasies, introduces the theme. The wealthy Brás imagines the second, gold-and-diamond butterfly (an insinuation?) flying around in Eugênia's head and making her eyes shine. The third one, large and black, flutters onto the veranda where D. Eusébia, her daughter, and their guest are gathered. Mother and daughter are frightened, perhaps superstitiously so, and Dr. Cubas feels manly and philosophical as he waves the insect away with his handkerchief. That same afternoon, he comes upon the young woman again and notices that she greets him comfortably, as an equal. He is disconcerted when she does not turn to look at him as she rides away. His disappointment irritates him and shapes the context in which the fourth butterfly becomes meaningful. It is large and black, too, and makes its appearance in the young man's room the following day. At first it is well received, for it reminds Brás of the veranda scene, of Eugênia's charming attempt to hide her fear, and especially of his own superior and gratifying role in the events. The butterfly's meaning soon changes, however, perhaps because it lingers in the room, showing no sign of fear as it gently moves its wings. For Brás it now represents the persistent memory of Eugênia, as well as the lack of the appropriate subaltern gesture, which so irritated him the day before. Brás feels a sudden "tug on his nerves" (165)—an acute form of fickleness—and puts an end to the matter with the flick of a towel.

The brutality of this solution foreshadows the end of the romance, which at this point has hardly begun. The mortal blow, dealt to a defenseless creature, reveals a methodically random aspect of class domination. The content of the social relation is extended to nature: Eugênia's *natural* (citizen) dignity, free of subordination to the oligarchy, makes any sort of spontaneity, including that of butterflies, unbearable to Brás. Further, as nature also exists within us, it is certain that the blow is aimed not only at the insect and the young woman but also at Brás's own internal, spontaneous respect for others.

At this point, the reader of *Memórias póstumas* will have no doubt noticed that I have omitted a decisive element of the episode, a factor that apparently accounts for Brás's ultimate decision in the matter: Eugênia's physical defect. Aside from being illegitimate and poor, she has a lame leg. Brás in fact notices the defect only much later in the narrative, after the poor woman's dignity has so irritated him that he is driven to symbolically destroy her. In other words, the logic of the episode and its resolution are determined by social inferiorities; the later, natural imperfection does not affect the course of events. Nonetheless, the physical inferiority becomes pivotal in Brás's reasoning. He projects whatever undesirable feelings the class difference provokes in him onto Eugênia's deformity. Moveover, and more important, a slippage occurs between physical and social inferiority, so that

Brás ends up viewing social inequality from the blameless and irrevocable perspective of nature and natural injustice.

How can we understand this substitution? The naturalization of historical relations is generically tied to conservatism. In this instance, the usefulness of such a move is evident, since Eugênia's social predicament poses a problem for the young man's conscience, whereas her physical defect is a concrete, and therefore comforting, fact. Unfortunately for Brás, things are more complicated, as it is clear that Eugênia could make an ideal wife despite her lame leg. Brás's reasoning is therefore not only untruthful but also unconvincing, and it reinforces the episode's general tone of deliberate falsehood and evasiveness, crucial to the calculated brutality of these chapters. The narrator's transparently false explanation is not intended to justify anything but is offered rather as a show of power, a base action among others. Indeed, the ten or so pages in which Eugênia, the only upright character in the novel, appears constitute a thorough exercise in abuse. The cruelty of these pages is so deliberate, layered, and detailed that readers hesitate before assimilating it. It is as though the extreme character of this narrative section distracted readers and kept them from noticing its strangeness. Let us not reduce it to a psychological study, a clear case of sadism, but rather analyze it as a likely manifestation of the social order we have been examining. It is the social conflict that lends transparency and artistic integrity to the narrator-protagonist's excesses.

We have already noted the derogatory use of the ostensibly innocent expression *wildflower*. Another chapter (chap. 32) is unkindly titled "Born Lame [*coxa*]." When Brás swears "by Diana's thigh [*coxa*]" (170; 86) that he meant Eugênia no harm, he is obviously making an effort to outdo himself, to surpass his own standards of brutality. In any case, what is at stake are Eugênia's rights and, by extension, the enlightened-liberal-romantic concept of the individual. It is precisely this concept that Brás methodically sets out to attack, not out of a satanic impulse (even if these pages do carry the mark of Baudelaire) but for specific class reasons. As a member of the dominant class, he cannot ignore the liberal model despite its nonexistence in Brazilian society; he (and his class) must therefore live with this grating contradiction. Brás's impudence climaxes in the chapter addressed "to a sensitive soul," in which the narrator-protagonist's cynicism is suddenly directed at the reader and turns into unmediated aggression: Brás orders the reader to clean his eyeglasses—"for sometimes the trouble is with one's eyeglasses" (170; 86)—which he suggests are uselessly tear-stained as the reader frets over poor Eugênia's fate. Thus liberal sentimentality is purged and the reality of privilege underscored through confrontation with the reader, who is forced to experience directly the insulting barb of Brás's narrative fickleness and of the power that sustains it.

"I give you my word of honor that there was nothing lame about the look with which she returned mine: it was direct and perfectly healthy" (168; 84). The maliciousness of this statement lies in the initial oath, which implies a dubious attitude on the reader's part (*mon semblable, mon frère*), as though the latter were inclined to believe that a lame leg must be accompanied by moral inferiority. This supposition of complicity aims to be insulting, and it reveals the aggressive intent behind the narrator's excessively informal attitude toward the reader throughout the novel. However, on further examination, it seems clear that reader persuasion is not the sole purpose of the oath. It is also self-directed, expressing discomfort rather than surprise, and functions as an internal exclamation. Why should Eugênia's resilient spirit be disturbing to the narrator-protagonist? The paragraph that follows the oath begins with an analogous exclamation, elaborating on the earlier one: "Worst of all, she was lame" (170). This indicates a problem among a set of inconveniences, which he hastens to enumerate: "Eyes so clear, lips so fresh, composure so ladylike" (170; 84).[2]

2. In *Sonhos d'ouro*, which Machado must have been quite familiar with, José de Alencar had already attempted to articulate class remorse and sadism. The novel's wealthy heroine cannot stand the spectacle of poverty, and it exacerbates her cruelty. In one scene she happily looks on, gleefully snapping her fingers, as her pet dog kills a poor family's chicks. She proceeds to enjoy herself by making her elegant English horse stomp on the same family's humble dishware. Having thoroughly humiliated them, she handsomely indemnifies the family. Her ill deeds, by the way, are motivated by a noble cause, for their purpose is to shock the family out of their defeatist frame of mind. See Alencar, *Obra completa*, vol. 1 (Rio de Janeiro: Aguilar, 1959), 744–8. The "poor but worthy" theme is also featured in Alencar's novel: Ricardo, who considers himself "a black butterfly" (!) in relation to the heroine, was an excellent student. "But what is the use if no one knows him? It would have been better for

These positive qualities, which attract the young man, become negative attributes when, accompanied by poverty, they create a moral and
sentimental dilemma for him. Let us keep three points in mind: (*a*)
the crux of the matter is class, and the physical defect is a mere after-
thought that functions as an alibi; (*b*) in the context of class domination, the inferior class's human achievements are seen as further
misfortunes; (*c*) the fickle character's temporary convenience is ideologically productive and engenders a particular discourse, a mode of
perception and expression, that, although absurd to an enlightened
conscience, articulates the character's (and social) processes with precision. This last point is exemplified in the questions "Why pretty, if
lame? Why lame, if pretty?" In other words, if the universe were organized according to reason, lame (poor) women would not be pretty,
and pretty women would not be lame (poor). It is a question of universal harmony, conceived from the narrow viewpoint of immediate
personal convenience, whereby any other point of view is suppressed.
In this vision of harmony, however, class domination is notably not
suppressed.

What to make of this display of cruelty? It continues at the level of
language, where the primitive urge to humiliate periodically takes
precedence over narrative and expository functions. Here and there,
for no particular reason but as a gratuitously malevolent contribution
to the general tone, the word *foot* and related terms pop up. Brás
places himself at Eugênia's *feet*; she is likewise at his *feet*; aside from
Diana's thigh, there is also mention of a *Lame Venus*, as well as of innumerable other *feet, boots, cobblers, calluses, legs* that *limp*, and, finally, a
human tragedy that *stamps* its *feet* in anger. In all, in the space of a few
pages, there are over thirty allusions of this dubious sort, seventeen of
which can be found in the short chapter 36, titled "Concerning

---

him to replace half his talent with an equal amount of patronage." And further on:
"So a poor person can't mingle with rich people without fawning over them? What a
doctrine!" With respect to the inconveniences of love across class barriers, the "mil-
lionaire's daughter" explains to the "obscure pauper": "Imagine what agreeable
entertainment for each of us: you, crushed by my wealth and generosity; I, pricked
by the thorns of your dignity. At the end of a month we could no longer bear each
other's company and would have the poorest idea of each other" (736, 753, 739,
776, 821).

Boots." Hardly a sophisticated approach, but it is articulated within a context subtle in the extreme: we might say that Machado tries to sublimate the vulgar joke. Through excessive repetition of this crass humor, other layers of meaning are progressively uncovered. Initially, the point is to bury Eugênia and all she represents under an avalanche of mockery. In addition, by indulging in ostensible vulgarity, the narrator provokes the reader and highlights his own impunity. Finally, the ferocity with which the process culminates exposes Brás's need to annihilate the "sensitive soul" within himself. In short, the thrust of the narrative is to crush any form of spontaneity that manifests itself outside the oligarchic order, whether it be on the part of the characters, the reader, or the narrator himself.[3]

"Then a blow from a towel ended the adventure" (166; 82). Brás thus curtly recalls the black butterfly incident, whose social content and significance we have already noted. Shortly thereafter, the chapter addressed "to a sensitive soul" concludes in an analogous manner: "And let us be done once and for all with the wildflower" (170; 72). This same categorical, truncating gesture can be found elsewhere in the text, in a number of different contexts and adopting a variety of forms, abruptly cutting off a paragraph or chapter or stifling a desire. Recalling how he bribed the reluctant but needy Dona Plácida into cooperating in his affair with Virgília, Brás concludes, "And that was how her aversion [to the adulterous affair] was overcome" (214). Reminding the leaves on the trees of their mortality, he declares, "You will fall" (251). He ends his reflections on his mother's death by pushing them aside: "A sad chapter. Let us move on to a happier one" (155;

3. Here, too, Alencar furnishes material that is reformulated by Machado. In *A pata da gazela* Alencar describes a crippled foot, with evident relish, as "an atrocity, a monstrosity, a hideous deformity," "a plank, a tree trunk." "This aberration of the human body, albeit in a single aspect, seemed to him to be the symptom, if not the effect, of a moral monstrosity." "This foot was covered with bumps, like a tuber. . . . it was a slab of meat, a stump!" (599, 602). Later we will consider Dona Plácida's unhappy fate, another example of critical revision of the Brazilian literary tradition: like the hero in *Memórias de um sargento de milícias*, the poor woman is the daughter of a "conjunction of lascivious urges," of "a knock and a nip." In the case of Machado's character, however, the irregular circumstances of her birth do not point to a carefree or accommodating attitude toward life; rather, they represent a great deal of difficulty and constant humiliation. See Manuel Antônio de Almeida, *Memórias de um sargento de milícias* (São Paulo: Editora Atica, 1980), chap. 1; and *Memórias póstumas*, chap. 75.

70). All these endings echo or foretell, more or less forcefully, the blow aimed at Eugênia. The spirit of the times celebrates individual rights and potentialities, particularly through the figure of boundless spontaneous expression, and only a flash of cruel determination, the "tug on his nerves," can wipe out this spirit, allowing the man in love to crush the insect. The subjective recurrence of barbarity is the price paid for the reaffirmation of a slavocratic, nepotistic will in the age of liberalism. Of course, there is nothing extraordinary about this reassertion; it is a routine aspect of Brazilian reality. Individual rights and aspirations—perceived, quite rightly in this context, as frivolous —are regularly curtailed in the text: this gesture becomes a cyclical constant, a linguistic tick that signals irritation and impatience with unfeasible desires. Disseminated throughout the book, it transposes the ideological precipitate of a social structure into a generalized narrative tone, an ideological configuration likewise mirrored in the various episodes' dramatic design. Such factors contribute to the novel's powerful unity, or perhaps we might call it "harmony," with proper Machadian sarcasm.

Brás meets Eugênia when he is taking stock of his life and preparing to enter a new phase—thus the particular significance of this section. The spoiled rich kid belongs to the past, to his childhood and adolescence. A trip to Europe, equally marked by inconsequence, makes an educated man of him: "Of history, jurisprudence and so on I preserved the phraseology, the shell, the ornamentation" (155–6; 71). His mother's death brings him back to Rio and, above all, to the "fragility of the things of this world" (159; 75). The young doctor takes refuge in Tijuca to meditate on life, death, and the emptiness of his prior existence. What happens to whim, to concern with external (European) appearances, when he is confronted with the abyss of nothingness? Within the context of this crisis, Brás's attraction for Eugênia signals the possibility of change. To fully understand the significance of this moment, we should consider the alternatives available to the narrator-protagonist.

After seven days in Tijuca, Brás is tired of "solitude" and is anxious to get back to the city's "hustle and bustle" (157; 73). The allusion is to Pascal, on man's need to be distracted from himself. In the Brazilian case, however, the terms of the dilemma are less Christian and are firmly rooted in class privilege. "Hustle and bustle" implies the social advantages available to the member of an important family: political show, mundane splendor, a "civilized," up-to-date lifestyle. The "solitude" Brás refers to is equally privileged: in Tijuca he "live[s] like the grizzly bear that [he is]" (159; 75), hunting, sleeping, reading, and relaxing, with the help of his personal slave. There is no merit to his life in the city, nor is there any in Tijuca, where he does no work. In both places what is lacking is *individual worth*, the only acceptable justification for social inequality (according to bourgeois values, whose articulation in the text is attested by the satirical tone of the portrait).

The elder Cubas, anxious to secure a position of social prominence for his son, encourages a marriage arrangement that would make the younger Cubas a congressman, thanks to his future father-in-law's political connections. The frivolity of this arrangement is twofold: from a metaphysical viewpoint, it contrasts jarringly with the mother's recent death; from a historical perspective, it rejects modern concepts of individuality, firmly inscribing marriage and politics in a system of patronage and exchange of favors. Life lacks meaning for Brás because on the horizon there is nothingness or, again, because his horizon is the Brazilian social structure. Both factors, to which a third one can be added, contribute to Brás's misanthropic tendencies. "I pressed my silent grief to my breast and experienced a curious feeling, something that might be called the voluptuousness of boredom" (157). His cynical and defeatist attitude includes a measure of contempt for the absurd roles society forces on a modern man like himself. In a daring move, characteristic of his capacity for inventive adaptation, Machado articulates the lexicon of Baudelairean tedium to express the Brazilian elite's melancholic satisfaction with their condition: "Voluptuousness of boredom . . . one of the most subtle emotions of which man is capable" (157). Of course, it is evident that the Cubas with spleen is no less arbitrary and no less property-conscious than the Cubas who dreams of becoming a minister. His oscillation between "melancholy" and "love of fame," between apathy and excitement, complementary sides of the same class experience, underscores the equivalence of these apparent oppositions and constitutes one of the novel's crucial patterns (157, 162; 72, 78). To partake or not to partake in the city's or, more generally, in the Europhile elite's senseless glitter ("the phraseology, the shell"), that is the question, which naturally does not go as far as to include a deeper inquiry into social privilege. Further, Brás's self-imposed isolation and rejection of the social spectacle might spring not from ideological scruples but rather from an urge to more freely enjoy the advantages of wealth, far from the constraints of liberal ideology. In short, as his father puts it: "Don't remain out here, useless, obscure, unhappy. I spent a lot of money, gave you the best care in the world, and got influential friends to do things for you, all in order to see you shine as you should" (162; 78). Thus when he is not being useless, Brás is frivolously "shin[ing]," and when he is not shining, he is being useless, moving from one state to the other according to the (in)conveniences of the moment.

His mother's death further highlights the inanity of this alternative and functions as a call for change. This is where the romance with Eugênia comes in, promising just such a change: the protagonist's complete moral transformation. In this hypothetical scenario, Brás's love for Eugênia would lead him to acknowledge individual worth and spontaneity, introducing a small measure of justice in the edifice of oligarchic injustice by recognizing equality between individuals, particularly between the wealthy and the educated poor. We have seen, however, how the protagonist furiously rejects this scenario—whose national and class significance I have tried to point out—as it would curtail his capricious excesses. Far from instigating change, his encounter with Eugênia only strengthens abusive social patterns, which are now further aggravated by the aborted transformation: after this failed peripeteia, things only change for the worse. The episode's underlying structure defines the narrative's general curve: the anti-climax underscores the futility of any liberation fantasy; it also exposes the mediocrity, due to this same futility, of Brás Cubas's later life, which constitutes the greater part of the novel. The liberal norm is both foolish expectation and unforgivable absence. This contradiction has a devastating effect and indicates the ideological dead end faced by educated Brazilians.

Years later, Brás can consider marrying Nhá Loló, even though she is not his social equal. Given that the protagonist has not changed, what might explain this action? Socially ambitious, Nhá Loló studies the refined ways of society and tries to "conceal the inferiority of her family background" (271; 177). At the opportune moment she repudiates her father, whose lower-class habits shame her. "This seemed to me a commendable and even a lofty purpose; it established another bond between us," recalls the bridegroom, who is determined to "pluck this flower from the swamp" (271; 191). An unequal marriage is thus admissible as long as it reaffirms the power of the upper class. Thoroughly inadmissible, because it threatens the arbitrary exercise of this power, is Eugênia's (i.e., the poor's) affirmation of her own dignity and rights. It is curious to note that although social privilege is vehemently defended, this defense is not accompanied by an ideology or conviction of superiority. The absence of a consistent ideological justification for social privilege might almost seem like a positive quality, given the candidness of such a stance. However, from another perspective, it indicates a brutal and absolute attachment to privilege— very characteristic of Brazilian society—that eschews the sort of justification and moral obligation that a more clearly defined self (and class) image might require.

In terms of its action, the Eugênia episode is an example of realism at its best. Frugal plot and detail, rigorously carved out of social contradiction, produce the poetic cadence characteristic of the great nineteenth-century novel. And yet the conflict remains largely undeveloped, or rather, it is developed not through the plot but through the male protagonist's moral contortions and the narrator's expository cruelty. Subjectivity and writing are privileged, while the practical dimension of the conflict remains in the background. This induces us to see Machado as an early postnaturalist. Without wanting to disagree, I would point out that the subjective thrust of the narrative, in the form of fickleness, is firmly rooted in and expressive of a concrete social structure. From this perspective, heterodox formal solutions can be read as a means of producing a deeper, more radical representation of a given practical reality. For example, the disparity between the brevity and the importance of the episode is an eloquent aspect of composition. In reality, Eugênia is the only worthy character of the book: she is lucid about social relations; she has a zest for life and high moral standards. And yet she plays a bit role, as if to say that in Brazilian society the best qualities of the poor are stifled and wasted. Narrative composition itself thus configures and evaluates a historical tendency. We have also seen that the social conflict is hardly developed at the level of plot but elaborated extensively in Brás's imagination, and it is he who has the last word, an insulting one at that. The one-sidedness of the narrative is scandalous and mirrors the social inequality inherent in the situation. This narrative procedure also possesses the merit of undoing the moralist perspective. Rather than focus directly on Eugênia's unjust predicament, which would be the tendency of an "egalitarian" narrator, the narrative plays out the episode's repercussions in the consciousness of the guilty party. In other words, it maliciously adopts the exclusive point of view of a conspicuous member of the upper class. From the very beginning, the narrative bias suppresses any kind of moral sentiment, voicing a ruthless dominant-class view. This is not to say that moral concern disappears—it may even acquire a more strident tone—but it loses all presumption of efficacy and surfaces as a narrow viewpoint. We are once again on terrain familiar to Baudelaire, who used deception and literary masquerades as fighting strategies. He would, for instance, take the side of the oppressors, only to unmask them through excessive zeal, while humiliating and provoking the oppressed in an attempt to shock them out of their passivity.[4] We might at first react indignantly to the narrator's excesses and biases in *Memórias póstumas*, but we soon realize that the alternative is simply a different biased perspective: in the modern world, narrative processes cannot but articulate in one way or another the generalized social conflict.

4. For so-called philanthropic reasons, Baudelaire suggested that street beggars be beaten. As he put it, this was the only way to make them recover their lost dignity, as it would instill in them a desire for revenge ("Assomons les pauvres!" [Let us eliminate the poor], in *Le Spleen de Paris* [1869]). For a political analysis of this *petit poème en prose* see Dolf Oehler, *Pariser Bilder (1830–1848)* (Frankfurt am Main: Suhrkamp, 1979).

Linguistic Maps, Literary Geographies, and Cultural Landscapes: Languages, Languaging, and (Trans)nationalism

WALTER D. MIGNOLO

The aim of my argument is to challenge the authority of the past by looking at languages and languaging in the context of Western expansion since 1500. I argue that theoretical models dealing with languages have been built in complicity (not necessarily planned, but perhaps resulting from a lack of awareness) with colonial expansion. The linguistic and philosophical models of the twentieth century, and most remarkably those popularized in the sixties and seventies, are of little use for dealing with the transnational dimension of language and languaging, since they appear in academic discourse as a universal speaking subject. This speaking subject, curiously enough, was modeled on the experiences and the idea of national languages that were, at the same time, imperial languages. My argument implies the legacies of the early modern and colonial periods (modernity and coloniality) and joins forces with efforts to demodernize and decolonize scholarship as well as discourse in the public sphere that emerged in postmodern and postcolonial theorizing after World War II. In this genealogy, modernity and coloniality presuppose the coexistence of the modern state and imperial domains in a way that was not yet articulated in the early modern period under the Spanish and Portuguese Empires. It is precisely in the junction between the early modern and colonial periods (sixteenth and seventeenth centuries) and modernity and coloniality (seventeenth century to 1945) that we witness a significant switch in the way languages are conceived and languaging is practiced, in relation both to colonial control and to the rearticulation of knowledge and reason, indeed two sides of the same coin. What we

are seeing now, as the examples discussed below illustrate, is a relocation of languages and cultures made possible by the very process of
global interconnection.

It is worth noting that the last stage of a process designed to
Christianize and civilize was transformed into a process whose aim is
to "marketize" the world and no longer to civilize or Christianize it.
Paradoxically, the emphasis on consumerism, commodities, and
increasing marketplaces plays against the control imposed by early
Christian and civilian programs. In the first place, non-Western languages such as Quechua and minority Western languages such as
Catalan are reemerging from the forceful repression to which they
were subjected during the national period in Latin America as well as
in Europe. Secondly, Western languages such as Spanish, French, and
English are being fractured by emergent languaging practices in formerly colonial domains. Finally, the processes resulting from the
internal hierarchy within Western expansion and from the displacement of Spanish to second-class languaging rank (as it was considered inadequate for philosophical and scientific languaging) find
their way of intervention prompted by migratory movements from
areas colonized by the Spanish and British Empires and their national
configurations during and after the nineteenth century. If a word is
needed to identify the locus of these phenomena and processes, it is
transculturation.[1] Transculturation subsumes the emphasis placed on
borders, migrations, plurilanguaging, and multiculturing and the
increasing need to conceptualize transnational and transimperial languages, literacies, and literatures.

Sociohistorical transformations demand disciplinary modifica-
tions as well. The challenges presented to language and literary scholarship by transnational and transimperial languaging processes are
epistemologically and pedagogically serious, for they impinge on the
very conception of the humanities as a site of research and teaching.
This is particularly the case when reevaluations are viewed from the
perspective of nations with colonial legacies rather than from the perspective of the European modernity. Such challenges alter the com-

1. Fernando Ortiz, *Cuban Counterpoint: Tobacco and Sugar*, intro. Bronislaw Malinowski,
new intro. Fernando Coronil (1940; Durham, N.C.: Duke University Press, 1995), x.

monly held belief that linguistic and literary studies deal only with texts and literary authors, with canon formation and transformation, and with aesthetic judgments and textual interpretations. Transnational languaging processes demand a theory and philosophy of human symbolic production predicated on languaging and transnational and transimperial categories, on a new philology, and on a pluritopic hermeneutics that will replace and displace "the" classical tradition in which philology and hermeneutics were housed in the modern period. The clouding of national frontiers also demands rethinking disciplinary boundaries, if not undoing them. In the past ten years, a substantial exchange has taken place among literary theorists, critics, and social scientists, chiefly in the fields of anthropology and history. Transimperial and transcolonial (and by *trans* here I mean beyond national languages and literatures as well as beyond comparative studies that presuppose national languages and literatures) cultural studies could serve as an emerging inter- and transdisciplinary space of reflection in which issues emerging from Western expansion and global interconnections since the end of the fifteenth century might be discussed and linguistic and literary studies redefined. Literacy, the missing and complicitous word between languages and literatures, and languaging, a concept difficult to grasp in the Western denotative philosophy of language, are moving to the forefront of this transdisciplinary discourse.

In the early modern world, languages were attached to territories, and nations were characterized by the "natural" links between them. After World War II, languages and territories were redefined when area studies emerged as a consequence of the hierarchical division of the World into First, Second, and Third. The linking of languages and territories to constitute a particular nation was essentially a move by intellectuals and the state striving for certain types of imagined communities. In contrast, area studies was a distribution of scientific labor among scholars located in the First World that was meant to secure (both in terms of war and in terms of production of knowledge) its primacy in the order of economy as well as of knowledge. Thus, insofar as the configuration of area studies coincided with the latest period of globalization, it brought into the foreground a new meaning for the expression *understanding other/foreign languages and cultures*. A fundamental question then becomes "understanding diversity and subaltern languages and knowledges," where *understanding* is used both as a gerund and as an adjective. When it is employed as an adjective, *understanding diversity* becomes part of the paradigm in which we encounter expressions such as *ethnic diversity* or *cultural diversity*. In such cases, *understanding diversity* can be read as equivalent to *diversity of understanding*, provided that we can make sense of expressions such as *ethnicity of understanding* and *cultures of understanding*. What follows is predicated on understanding diversity, where *understanding* is employed both as a gerund and as an adjective. I will first comment on some particular cases (Arguedas, Cliff, Anzaldúa) before coming back to languaging and understanding diversity.

José María Arguedas's introduction to his *Tupac Amaru Kamaq Taytanchisman/A nuestro padre creador Tupac Amaru* is titled "I Do Not Regret Writing in Quechua."[2] The introduction itself is devoted to an explanation of Arguedas's decision. Anticipating objections from "quechólogos," who would like to preserve the purity of the Quechua language, Arguedas points out that he has used Castilian words with Quechua declension as well as Castilian words written as Indians and "mestizos" pronounce them. He observes that in his text there is just one Quechua word that belongs to a sophisticated register of Quechua and that there are also words taken from the Huanca-Conchucos dialect. Despite these few obstacles, Arguedas states that the book of poems is accessible to the Quechua-speaking population in the linguistic map of Runasimi, from the Department of Huancavelica to Puno, Peru, to the entire Quechua zone in Bolivia. Furthermore, he believes that it could be well understood in Ecuador.

Arguedas also mentions that the Haylli-Taki was originally written in the Quechua he speaks, his native language, Chanca.[3] After writing the book of poems, he translated it into Castilian. In the introduction

2. Arguedas, *Tupac Amaru Kamaq Taytanchisman/A nuestro padre creador Tupac Amaru* (Lima: Salqantay, 1962).
3. With this expression Arguedas refers to his book of poetry, which he calls not poetry (a Greco-Latin derivation) but "Haylli-taki." In Quechua, *hally* means "victory, extreme success, triumph," and *taki* means "song, chant." So the expression translates as "victorious or triumphal chant." I am grateful to Juan Carlos Godenzi and Lydia Fossa for discussing this issue with me.

he notes that an "impulso ineludible" forced him to write the poems in Quechua:

> A medida que iba desarrollando el tema, mi convicción de que el quechua es un idioma más poderoso que el castellano para la expresión de muchos trances del espíritu y, sobre todo, del ánimo, se fue acrecentando, inspirándome y enardeciéndome. Palabras del quechua contienen con una densidad incomparables la materia del hombre y de la naturaleza y el vínculo intenso que por fortuna aún existe entre lo uno y lo otro. El indígena peruano está abrigado, consolado, iluminado, bendecido por la naturaleza: su odio y su amor, cuando son desencadenados, se precipitan, por eso, con toda esa materia, y también su lenguaje.
>
> Sin embargo, aunque quisiera pedir perdón por haberme atrevido a escribir en quechua, no sólo no me arrepiento de ello, sino que ruego a quienes tienen un dominio mayor que el mío sobre este idioma, escriban. Debemos acrecentar nuestra literatura quechua, especialmente en el lenguaje que habla el pueblo; aunque el otro, el señorial y erudito, debiera ser cultivado con la misma dedicación. *Demostremos que el quechua actual es un idioma en el que se puede escribir tan bella y conmovedoramente como en cualquiera de las otras lenguas perfeccionadas por siglos de tradición literaria. El quechua es también un idioma milenario.* (8; italics added)

[While I was developing my subject matter, my conviction that Quechua is a language better suited and more powerful than Castilian to express critical moments of the soul and, above all, critical moments of the mind, grew on me; became a source of inspiration and of growing excitement. Quechua words embrace the human and natural dimension in a density without parallel and, above all, the Quechua words also embrace the relationships that fortunately still exist between humanity and nature. Peruvian indigenous people are sheltered, comforted, brightened, blessed by nature: when their hate and love are unleashed, they hastily move toward grasping humanity and nature, with a force that also includes their language.

Nevertheless, and even if I would like to excuse myself for daring to write in Quechua, I have to confess that I do not regret

it at all; on the contrary, I would go even further and beseech
those who have a better command of Quechua than I to write
themselves. We must enhance our Quechua literature, particularly in the language spoken by the people, without forgetting the
other Quechua, the erudite and noble Quechua, that must also
be cultivated with the same intensity. We will prove that current
Quechua is a language in which it is possible to write with the
same beauty and moving effect achievable in any other language
that has been improved through centuries of literary tradition.
Quechua too is a millenarian language.]

In Latin America, different manifestations of the tensions between
linguistic maps, literary geographies, and cultural landscapes can be
linked with linguistic dismissal under colonial and Western expansion.
Arguedas's need and decision to write in Quechua, to translate his
poem into Spanish, and to write a justification comparing Quechua
with Spanish clearly articulate such tensions. Arguedas has struggled
both with the millenarian forces and the memories of a language
grounded in the body of those living and dying in the linguistic map
and literary geography of Runasimi (to whom he addresses his
poems), and with the centennial and institutional forces of a transplanted language grounded in the body and memories of Castilians
living and dying in Spain, as well as in a New World constructed on the
ruins of Runasimi.

There are other linguistic experiences complementing Arguedas's
and foreshadowing the question of language and colonialism, an area
in which linguistic maps, literary geographies, and cultural landscapes
collide and in which social and cultural transformations reinforce each
other. Let us now compare the Andes with the Caribbean and with the
Mexican-U.S. border by bringing into the discussion a Jamaican writer,
Michelle Cliff, and a Mexican American author, Gloria Anzaldúa.[4]

Cliff, who underlines the differences between metropolitan English and the colonial English of the West Indies, is more concerned
with the political and cultural dimensions of language than with mat-

---

4. Cliff, *The Land of Look Behind: Prose and Poetry* (Ithaca, N.Y.: Firebrand, 1985);
Anzaldúa, *Borderlands/La frontera: The New Mestiza* (San Francisco: Spinsters/Aunt
Lute, 1987).

ters of accent or lexicon. Of the several types of creole languages in the Caribbean, I would like to remind the reader of the main varieties: the Creole of French lexicon spoken in French Guyana, Martinique, Guadaloupe, and Haiti; "Papiamentu," the Creole language of Castilian and Portuguese lexicon spoken in the Dutch Caribbean; and the English Creole spoken in Barbados, Jamaica, Trinidad, Tobago, and elsewhere.[5] Cliff refers to this last variety in her text.

The daughter of an affluent family, Cliff pursued graduate studies at the Warburg Institute in London. Her dissertation on game playing in the Italian Renaissance took her to Siena, Florence, and Urbino, a journey that ended in her participation in the feminist movement and in her rediscovery of an identity she had learned to despise. I will let Cliff speak for herself by quoting extensively from the preface to *The Land of Look Behind*:

> I originated in the Caribbean, specifically on the island of Jamaica, and although I have lived in the United States and in England, I travel as a Jamaican. It is Jamaica that forms my writing for the most part, and which has formed, for the most part, myself. Even though I often feel what Derek Walcott expresses in his poem "The Schooner Flight": "I had no nation now but the imagination." It is a complicated business. Jamaica is a place halfway between Africa and England, to put it simply, although historically one culture (guess which one) has been esteemed and the other denigrated (both are understatements)—at least among those who control the culture and politics of the island—the Afro-Saxons. As a child among these people, indeed of these people, as one of them, I received the message of anglocentrism, of white supremacy, and I internalized it. As a writer, as a human being, I have had to accept that reality and deal with its effect on me, as well as finding what has been lost to me from the darker side, and what may be hidden, to be dredged from memory and dream. And

---

5. Luca Citarella, "Problemas de educación y modelos de desarrollo: El caso de los criollos del Caribe," in *Pueblos indios, estados y educación: 46o Congreso internacional de americanistas*, ed. Luis Enrique López and Ruth Moya (Puno: Programa de Educación Bilingüe de Puno; Quito: Proyecto de Educación Bilingüe Intercultural del Ecuador; Lima: Programa de Educación Rural Andina, 1989), 167–88.

it is there to be dredged. As my writing delved longer and deeper into this part of myself, I began to dream and imagine.

One of the effects of assimilation, indoctrination, passing into the anglocentrism of the British West Indian culture is that you believe absolutely in the hegemony of the King's English and in the form in which it is meant to be expressed. Or else your writing is not literature; it is folklore, and folklore can never be art. Read some poetry by West Indian writers—some, not all—and you will see what I mean. You have to dissect stanza after extraordinarily Anglican stanza for Afro-Caribbean truth; you may never find the latter. But this has been our education. The Anglican ideal— Milton, Wordsworth, Keats—was held before us with an assurance that we were unable, and would never be enabled, to compose a work of similar correctness. No reggae spoken here. (12–3)

Cliff makes it clear that colonial literature will always be viewed as inferior when confronted with the practice defined and exemplified by the metropolitan literary canon. The same language, the same syntactic rules; but the game played under different conditions results in diverse verbal practices: folklore is not literature, just as myth is not history. In both cases, the "wisdom of the people" was invented to distinguish "taste and knowledge of genius and educated fews," establishing a hierarchy of cultural practices parallel to economic and political regulations and government.

It is *languaging*, rather than language, that Arguedas and Cliff allow us to emphasize, moving away from the idea that language is a fact (e.g., a system of syntactic, semantic, and phonetic rules) toward the idea that speaking and writing are moves that orient and manipulate social domains of interaction. Both Arguedas's and Cliff's linguistic conceptualization and literary practices create fractures within languages (Spanish in Spain and in Peru; English in Jamaica) and between languages (Spanish on the Iberian Peninsula in contact with Spanish "dialects" and in the Andes in contact with "Amerindian languages"; English in England, and in the Caribbean, in contact with creole languages), revealing the colonial aspects of linguistic, literary, and cultural landscapes. The very concept of literature presupposes the major or official languages of a nation and the transmission of the cultural literacy built into them. Therefore it is not sufficient to recognize the links between the emergence of comparative literature as a field of study and literature's complicity with imperial expansion; nor is it adequate to denounce the pretended universality of a European observer, who does not recognize the regionality of other literatures.[6] It is the concept of literature that, like the concept of languages, should be displaced from the idea of collecting facts (e.g., literary works; masterpieces) to the idea of languaging as cultural practice. Furthermore, colonial expansion and colonial legacies (since the sixteenth century) have created the conditions, on the one hand, for languaging across cultures and, on the other, for inventing a discourse about languages that placed the languaging of colonial powers above other linguistic and cultural practices.

Let me further explore the question of languaging and colonialism by moving to Anzaldúa's *Borderlands*. To read *Borderlands* is to read three languages and three literatures concurrently, which is, at the same time, a new way of languaging. It would be helpful to bear in mind Alton Becker's articulation of the idea of languaging, based on his experience of dealing with Burmese and English:

> Entering another culture, another history of interactions, we face what is basically a problem of memory. Learning a new way of languaging is not learning a new code, into which the units of my domain of discourse are re-encoded, although the process may begin that way; and if the new way of languaging shares a history with my own, the exuberances and deficiencies may not get in the way of simple interactions. However, at some point the silences do get in the way and the wording out gets slow and hard. A new code would not be so hard and painful to learn; a new way of being in the world is.[7]

I would like to make it clear that I am quoting Becker not as a linguistic authority (even if he is) but next to the experiences of Arguedas, Cliff, and Anzaldúa: theorizing is a way of languaging, just as languaging implies its own theory; theorizing languages within social struc-

6. Edward W. Said, *Culture and Imperialism* (New York: Knopf, 1993).
7. Becker, "A Short Essay on Languaging," in *Research and Reflexivity*, ed. Frederick Steier (London: Sage, 1991), 230.

tures of domination is dealing with the "natural" plurilingual condi-tions of the human world "artificially" suppressed by the monolingual ideology and monotopic hermeneutics of modernity and nationalism. In *Borderlands* Anzaldúa remaps linguistic and literary practices, artic-ulating three linguistic memories (Spanish, English, and Nahuatl). Chapter 6, for example, is titled "Tlilli, Tlapalli: The Path of the Red and Black Ink." Anzaldúa explains:

> For the ancient Aztecs, in tlilli, in tlapalli, la tinta negra y roja de sus códices (the black and red ink painted on codices) were the colors symbolizing escritura y sabiduria (writing and wisdom). . . . An image is a bridge between evoked emotion and conscious knowledge; words are cables that hold up the bridge. Images are more direct, more immediate than words, and closer to the unconscious. Picture language precedes thinking in words; the metaphorical mind precedes analytical consciousness. . . .
>
> I write the myth in me, the myths I am, the myths I want to become. The word, the image and the feeling have a palatable energy, a kind of power. Con imágenes domo mi miedo, cruzo los abismos que tengo por dentro. Con palabras me hago piedra, pájaro, puente de serpientes arrastrando a ras del suelo todo lo que soy, todo lo que algún día seré.
> Los que están mirando (leyendo),
> los que cuentan (o refieren lo que leen).
> Los que vuelven ruidosamente las hojas de los
>   códices
> la tinta negra y roja (la sabiduría)
> y lo pintado,
> ellos nos llevan nos guián,
>
>   nos dicen el camino.

> [With images I tame my fear, crossing my innermost abyss. With words I become stone, bird, bridge of snakes dragging along to the ground level all that I am, all that someday I will be.
> Those who are looking at (reading),
> Those who are always telling (or narrating what they read).
> Those who noisily unfold the leaves of the codices

the black and the red ink (wisdom),
and what is painted,
They are who carry us and guide us,

they show us the way.]

These two paragraphs bring to the foreground the juxtaposition of several memories. The Spanish quotation in verse form comes from the *Colloquios y doctrina christiana*, a dialogue between the first twelve Franciscan friars—who arrived in Mexico in 1524, after the fall of Mexico-Tenochtitlán—and representatives of the Mexican nobility. The dialogue was recorded in Nahuatl, collected, and then translated into Spanish by Bernardino de Sahagún toward 1565. Originally, then, this quotation, which reports the answers of the Mexican nobility to the Franciscan presentation, requesting that they adopt the Christian doctrine, was in Nahuatl. The excerpt quoted by Anzaldúa narrates the moment in which the Mexican noblemen refer to the Tlamatinime (the wise men, those who can read the black and the red ink written in the codices). Anzaldúa's languaging entangles Spanish, English, and Nahuatl (the first two with a strong "literary" tradition kept alive after the conquest; the third, which was and still is an oral way of languaging, was disrupted during and marginalized after the conquest), and her languaging invokes two kinds of writing: the alphabetic writing of the metropolitan center and the pictographic writing of pre-Columbian Mexican (as well as Mesoamerican) civilizations.

The scenario sketched above is embedded in a larger picture where colonial legacies and current globalizing processes meet, which I introduced in the first part of this essay. The increasing process of economic and technological global integration and some of its consequences (massive migrations) are forcing us to rethink the relationships between (national) languages and territories. The rearticulation of nations, as a result of the global flow of economic integration, is forming a world of connected languaging and shifting identities. As people become polyglots, their sense of history, nationality, and race becomes as entangled as their languaging. Border zones, diaspora, and postcolonial relations are daily phenomena of contemporary life.

How migration modifies languaging is related to its geopolitical direction. While migrations during the nineteenth century moved from Europe toward Africa, Asia, and the Americas, at the end of the twentieth century they proceed in reverse directions. Thus, migratory movements are disarticulating the idea of national languaging and, indirectly, of national literacies and literatures, in Europe as well as in the U.S. On the other hand, the rise of indigenous communities and their participation in the public sphere (such as the recent events in Chiapas, or the cultural politics of the state in Bolivia) complement migratory movements in their challenge to the idea of national languaging and to the one-to-one relation between language and territory. The notion of homogeneous national cultures and the consensual transmission of historical and literary traditions, as well as of unadulterated ethnic communities, are in the process of profound revisions and redefinitions. We need to think seriously about the processes by which languaging and the allocation of meaning to groups of people presumed to have common features (e.g., "ethnic culture," "national culture," etc.) are being relocated and how linguistic maps, literary geographies, and cultural landscapes are being repainted.

The current process of globalization is not a new phenomenon, although the way in which it is taking place is without precedent. On a larger scale, globalization at the end of the twentieth century (mainly occurring through transnational corporations, the media, and technology) is the most recent configuration of a process that can be traced back to the 1500s, with the beginning of transatlantic exploration and the consolidation of Western hegemony. Paradoxically, the early modern and early colonial periods (roughly 1500–1700, with the predominance of the Spanish and Portuguese Empires), as well as the modern and colonial periods (roughly 1700–1945, with the predominance of the British Empire and French and German colonialism), were the periods during which the consolidations of national languages took place concurrently with migrations promoted by transatlantic exploration and improved means of transportation. This progress created the conditions necessary to undermine the purity of *a* language that unified *a* nation. The construction of the first giant steamer (between 1852 and 1857) made possible transatlantic migrations unimaginable until then. Millions of people migrated from Europe to the Americas between 1860 and 1914, complicating the linguistic colonial map and placing increasing demands on national literary geographies. In Argentina, for example, intellectuals were uneasy at the end of the nineteenth and the beginning of the twentieth centuries, when the national and linguistic community was shaken up by massive Italian immigration.[8] Migrations of people and the internationalization of capitals during the second half of the nineteenth century impinged on the spread of print culture and general education, emphasized by nation builders in both Americas. Thus, by the end of the nineteenth century, Amerindian legacies were becoming museum relics, more a reality of the past than a critical force of the present. Nahuatl, among others, became a language (i.e., an object) of the past, rather than a languaging activity of millions of people, suppressed by national languag(ing)es.

Migratory factors introduced an element of disorder at the otherwise quiet national horizon of linguistic, literary, and territorial homogeneity. While Arguedas's landscape presents the conflict between languaging practices prior to Spanish colonizing migrations and the introduction of new practices brought by the colonizing migratory movements, Cliff and Anzaldúa draw a map of reverse migration, from colonial territories relabeled *Third World* (after 1945) toward the First World (Cliff to Europe; Anzaldúa's ancestors to the U.S.). One could say that the cases of Arguedas, on the one hand, and Cliff and Anzaldúa, on the other, are the end of a spectrum whose chronological beginning I locate around 1500. Arguedas experienced the legacies of the linguistic conflict created by migrations from the metropolitan centers to the colonial domains, and the fractures of local languages introduced by colonial ones. For Cliff and Anzaldúa, in contrast, languaging practices fracture the colonial language. In Cliff's texts, these fractures result from the linguistic transformation of imperial languaging practices in colonial domains. In the case of Anzaldúa, such fractures occur due to the languaging practices of two displaced linguistic communities: Nahuatl, displaced by the Spanish expansion, and Spanish, displaced by the increasing hegemony of the colonial languages of the modern period (English, German, and French).

8. Roberto Cortéz Conde and Ezequiel Gallo, *La formación de la Argentina moderna* (Buenos Aires: Paidos, 1987).

Anzaldúa's observations about the future geographies of languaging practices, are relevant to my argument: "By the end of this century, Spanish speakers will comprise the biggest minority group in the U.S., a country where students in high schools and colleges are encouraged to take French classes because French is considered more 'cultured.' But for a language to remain alive, it must be used. By the end of this century English, not Spanish, will be the mother tongue of most Chicanos and Latinos" (59). Cherríe Moraga's *Last Generation* articulates a similar idea: English, not Spanish, will be the languaging practice of Chicano/as and Latino/as.[9] I am not in a position either to mistrust or to contradict such predictions. I would, however, like to present some doubts based on other experiences. These doubts support the implicit desire (expressed by Anzaldúa and Moraga) not to see happen what they both predict. Anzaldúa's fear, for instance, that English will become the national languaging of Chicano/as and that French will be the foreign languaging of distinction may not look in 1994 as it looked in 1987. I have two reasons to cast such doubts: one is the decreasing number of students taking French at the college level in recent years; the other is the increasing interest in *la francophonie*, with the changing linguistic maps and literary geographies of French outside France and the growing significance in social and academic discourse of the relationship between language and race. Francophone languaging has as much in common with French languaging in France as Hispanic languaging in the U.S. has with Castilian languaging in Spain: the same *languages* allow quite different languaging priorities, feelings, and knowledge.

Frantz Fanon articulates the colonial legacies and linguistic politics of French outside France and the complicities between linguistic ideology and race.[10] If nineteenth-century Europe invented the concept of race in order to bridge the gap between a "purity of blood" and a twentieth-century "color of your skin," the complicity with linguistic ideology has been effortlessly traced. The method of classifying animal species provided the basis for the hypothesis that the "human races" were founded on an inheritance that transcended social evolu-

9. Moraga, *The Last Generation* (Boston: South End, 1993).
10. Fanon, *Black Skin, White Masks*, trans. Charles Lam Markmann (New York: Grove, 1967), 17.

tion.[11] At the same time, the new science of linguistics found its inspiration for classifying languages in the method of the biological sciences, associating, by the same token, the supposedly unique character of peoples with the characteristics of their languages. The gaps between Indo-European and Semitic (Hebrew and Arabic) languages were constructed as linguistic oppositions with racial implications. This statement is familiar to those educated in Spanish colonial discourse and the evaluation (with few exceptions) of Amerindian languages. Ernst Renan, for example, talked about the monstrous and backward character of Semitic languages, as opposed to the perfection of European languages, in a way that echoed early Spanish missionaries and men of letters.[12] Today the belief in a hierarchy of human intelligence based on languaging-as-ethnicity is well and alive, even in academic circles.

Fanon's first chapter, an indirect response to Renan, is titled "The Negro and Language." There he states: "I ascribe a basic importance to the phenomenon of language. That is why I find it necessary to begin with this subject, which should provide us with one of the elements in the colored man's comprehension of the dimension of the other. For it is implicit that to speak, is to exist absolutely for the other" (17). Fanon's speculations revolve around the black people in the French Antilles with respect to the metropolitan language and, further, with respect to the distinctions, among languages, between those of Martinicans and Guadaloupeans in the Caribbean and those of Antilleans and Senegalese in the context of African diaspora. Colonial mimicry consisted, in the first context, of achieving white status by speaking good French. In the second, Martinicans felt that they were "better" than Guadaloupeans and blacks in the Antilles and "better" than Senegalese, owing to the ways in which they related to the French language. This is why Fanon states at the beginning that "the Black man has two dimensions. One with his fellows, the other with the White man." Thus, Anzaldúa's fear that French distinction will prevail over Spanish

11. See Wilhelm von Humboldt, *On Language: The Diversity of Human Language Structure and Its Influence on the Mental Development of Mankind*, trans. Peter Heath (Cambridge: Cambridge University Press, 1988).
12. Renan, *Histoire générale et systèmes comparés des langues sémitiques* (Paris: Imprimerie Impériale, 1863).

subalternity in the U.S. may have an interesting turn if we consider the growing force of French out of France (i.e., the so-called Francophonie, although France itself is also a Francophone country), similar to Spanish out of Spain and to English out of England and the U.S. But, in any event, the modern aura of territorial French is being paralleled by Francophone linguistic maps, literary geographies, and cultural landscapes.

From Morocco, Abdelkebir Khatibi rearticulates the early (somewhat dogmatic, although clearly justifiable) positions adopted by Fanon.[13] Khatibi's concept of "l'amour bilangue," and his preference for "bilanguage" over "bilingual," locates him closer to Anzaldúa than to Fanon. To a certain extent, the transculturation of French with Arabic enacted by Khatibi has inscribed in it the silent presence of the early Castilian expulsion of the Moors from the Iberian Peninsula and the philosophical rearticulation of Arabic and its place in the early modern and colonial periods. By so doing, Khatibi makes an explicit connection between linguistic geographies and not only literary but also philosophical landscapes. His criticism of the social sciences, particularly sociology, could be applied to the disciplinary construction of philosophy in the modern period and to the subsequent suppression of the links between Greek and Arabic metaphysical reflections from the seventh to the fourteenth centuries.

Let me conclude by coming back to diversity of understanding and saying that insofar as linguistic maps are attached not only to literary geographies but also to the production and distribution of knowledge, changing linguistic cartographies imply (implies) a reordering of epistemology. "Serious" knowledge and "serious" literary production have been enacted, since the sixteenth century, in the colonial languages of modernity and their classical foundations (Greek and Latin). Global interconnections are now bringing us back to the relevance of millennial languaging (such as in Chinese, Arabic, Hindu, and Hebrew) relegated to second-class status by the epistemology of European modernity, to a critical examination of the "purity of languages," and to the relevance of languages suppressed under the ban-

13. Khatibi, *Love in Two Languages*, trans. Richard Howard (Minneapolis: University of Minnesota Press, 1990).

ners of the nation (such as Quechua and Aymara in Bolivia and Peru, and Nahuatl and Maya in Mexico and Central America). Thus languages, languaging, and diversity of understanding go hand in hand with subaltern knowledge and with understanding diversity. But this is a topic for another argument, focused on languages and epistemology rather than on languages and the politics of languaging.

The Lightning Bolt Yields to the Rainbow: Indigenous History and Colonial Semiosis in the *Royal Commentaries* of El Inca Garcilaso de la Vega

JOSÉ ANTONIO MAZZOTTI

Among the many studies of El Inca Garcilaso de la Vega and his work, it is still all too common to find simplified images of Garcilaso as an acculturated mestizo and master of Spanish prose whose narrative models were all drawn from classical and Renaissance historiography. Certainly, the reason that the *Royal Commentaries* enjoyed great success in Europe from the moment it appeared was that it broadly manipulated European themes to erect a framework of familiarity for its learned readers in the Old World. The text was written in two parts: part 1 is the history of life under Incan rule; part 2 describes the first four decades of the Peruvian Conquest (1532–72).[1] Garcilaso's work is the first response published by an author born in the New World to the historical versions of the same past written by such prestigious Spanish historians as Cieza de León, Zárate, Gómara, Diego Fernández, Acosta, and Román. The *Royal Commentaries*, even in its title, thus presupposes a dialogue with a European reading of the Incas. Indeed, Garcilaso relies on many of the same rhetorical weapons wielded by the Spanish historians, which is why the authority of his text was nearly indisputable until the late nineteenth century.[2]

Translated from the Spanish by G. J. Racz and B. M. Corbett.

1. References are to part, book, and chapter of the first edition of the *Comentarios reales* (pt. 1, Lisbon, 1609; pt. 2, Córdoba, 1617).

2. Among the works that cast doubt on the veracity of the *Royal Commentaries*, the most important were the Jiménez de la Espada editions—Joan de Santacruz Pachacuti Yamqui Salcamaygua's *Relación de antigüedades deste Reyno del Pirú* (1879), Pedro de Cieza de León's *El señorío de los Incas* (1880), and Juan Díez de Betanzos's *Suma y narración de los Incas* (1880)—and, above all, Waman Puma's *Primer nueva corónica*, discovered by Richard Pietschmann in the Royal Library of Copenhagen in 1908

Nonetheless, I propose an alternative reading of the *Royal Commentaries* that centers on its dialogue with a potential Andean public. In particular, I argue that Garcilaso uses the knowledge of indigenous history that he acquired in Cuzco (before permanently departing for Spain at age twenty) to reinvent Incan history in order to invest his Incan mother's lineage with greater legitimacy than other noble Incan families enjoyed in Cuzco.

From this perspective, the reliability of Garcilaso's history matters little. What is important is identifying the symbolic, metaphorical, and stylistic configurations that unfold in the text and that permit us access to the subtextual Andean dialogue, which has understandably escaped critics whose analyses are limited to intertextual canonical references. My analysis relies on the kind of gnoseological, symbolic, and discursive exchanges that Walter Mignolo calls "colonial semiosis."[3] Mignolo's work can inform an Andean reading of Garcilaso's text by shedding light on the relationship between an indigenous referential universe and Garcilaso's account of it.

In this essay, I analyze some passages from the *Royal Commentaries* both to reveal the Andean subtext and to underscore the inefficacy of reading such an intercultural work armed only with the instruments of conventional literary criticism.[4] The passages are descriptions of the

---

and published in a new edition by Paul Rivet in 1936. A wealth of other archaeological, anthropological, and linguistic studies from this century offer irrefutable evidence about Incan imperial expansion, as well as more complex versions of Incan rituals and categories of knowledge than the *Royal Commentaries* seems, on the surface, to provide.

3. Mignolo employs the concept of "colonial semiosis" because, he argues, "colonial discourse" is insufficient to the study of the cultural exchange that occurred in the wake of the European arrival, due to the indigenous systems of representation (*quipus, quilcas,* codices, etc.) ("Colonial and Postcolonial Discourse: Cultural Critique or Academic Colonialism?" *Latin American Research Review* 28 [1993]: 120–31; "Afterword: From Colonial Discourse to Colonial Semiosis," *Dispositio* 14 [1989]: 333–7).

4. Elsewhere I have used the term *subtext* to refer to the aspects of Garcilasian discourse that the narrative does not make explicit and that can be recognized only against the backdrop of the Incan cultural world ("En virtud de la materia: Nuevas consideraciones sobre el subtexto andino de los *Comentarios reales*," *Revista Iberoamericana* 61 [1995]: 171–2). The concept stems from Gérard Genette's elaboration of the category of *hypotext* (*Palimpsestes: La littérature au second degré* [Paris: Seuil, 1982]).

Incan fortress of Saqsawaman, at the northern border of the imperial city of Cuzco. I will show how Garcilaso uses the lightning bolt and the rainbow, primordial Andean symbols peculiar to the Incan royal court, to structure the meaning and strategy of his narration. In this way the *Royal Commentaries* escapes the rhetorical limits of contemporaneous European accounts and acquires a hybrid form that corresponds quite well to its mestizo writing subject.

An Andean Referent

One premise is that Garcilaso's text bears the stamp of his Incan lineage. As we know, his mother belonged to the royal family, or *panaka*, of the eleventh Inca, Tupaq Yupanqi. This family played an important role in the bloody war of succession following the death of Wayna Qhapaq, the twelfth Inca, late in the 1520s, about when the Spanish first arrived on the shores of Tawantinsuyu. Such wars were common among the Incas. Historians such as Franklin Pease and María Rostworowski de Diez Canseco have argued that violent ritual procedures were needed to consecrate one of the contending parties and legitimate its claim to rule.[5] Wayna Qhapaq's two sons, Waskhar and Ataw Wallpa, were both claimants but also half-brothers born to mothers from rival *panakas*. War broke out between Waskhar's side, the Tupaq Inka Yupanqi, and Ataw Wallpa's, the Pachakutiq Inka Yupanqi.[6] In the end, Ataw Wallpa's troops captured Cuzco and massacred all branches of the nobility that had supported Waskhar, beginning with the Tupaq Inka Yupanqi. Among the few members of that family who escaped was Chimpu Uqllu, the niece-granddaughter of the late Inca and the future mother of Garcilaso (*Comentarios* 1.9.14).

These events help explain Garcilaso's treatment of the rise of the Incan empire in the *Royal Commentaries*. By championing the eighth Inca, Wiraqucha, as the leader of his nation's final triumph over the

5. Pease, *Los últimos Incas del Cuzco* (Lima: Villanueva, 1972), 5–15, Rostworowski de Diez Canseco, *Estructuras andinas del poder: Ideología religiosa y política* (Lima: Instituto de Estudios Peruanos, 1983), 172–3.
6. Modern historians tend to ignore the extremely important role that women played in power struggles. On the role of women in Andean society in general see Rostworowski de Diez Canseco, 9–17, 72–96.

rival Chanca nation and as the great reforming hero of the Incan state, Garcilaso overturns Spanish versions that give the credit to the ninth Inca, Pachakutiq, whose descendants supported Ataw Wallpa three generations later.[7] Such a reading rests on the certainty that representatives of noble families in Cuzco manipulated the virtues and shortcomings of Incan governors in their histories to advance the immediate political interests of their own *panakas*.[8] As Garcilaso's version is at least partially based on oral histories told him by his great-uncle Kusi Wallpa and other elders (*Comentarios* 1.9.14), it makes sense that he should champion Wiraqucha to favor Waskhar's bid for the succession, which for all intents and purposes was lost just when Pizarro's troops appeared.[9]

Saqsawaman's Duality

The *Royal Commentaries* states that the great northern fortress of Saqsawaman is located on a hill whose southern slope hangs perpendicularly over Cuzco. On that side the Incas built a single wall two hundred fathoms long; no greater protection was needed, given the chasm. On the other side, however, we find "three walls, one in front of the other, ascending the hill, each wall more than two hundred fathoms in length. They are made in the shape of a half moon so as to enclose and join with the other burnished wall, which faces the city."[10]

7. One suspects that "Yupanqui," the mysterious tenth Inca referred to in the *Royal Commentaries* but not elsewhere, came to be through Garcilaso's attempt to diminish the importance of Pachakutiq, Ataw Wallpa's great-grandfather, by splitting him in two.
8. The so-called historical poems of the Incan court were initially described by chroniclers such as Pedro de Cieza de León, *El señorío de los Incas*, ed. Manuel Ballesteros (1552; Madrid: Historia 16, 1985), chaps. 11–2. Recent researchers describe them in greater detail (see Francisco Lisi, "Oralidad y escritura en la crónica de Pedro de Cieza de León," *Hispamérica* 56–7 [1990]: 175–85; and Martin Lienhard, *La voz y su huella: Escritura y conflicto étnico-social en América Latina (1492–1988)* [Havana: Casa de las Américas, 1990], chap. 7).
9. I argue that in style also the *Royal Commentaries* is modeled to some extent on its oral Quechua sources. For an in-depth examination of its formula, syntactic structures, semantic couplets, and, of course, primordial images of life and death, see José Antonio Mazzotti, *Una coralidad mestiza* (Mexico City: Fondo de Cultura Económica, forthcoming), chap. 2.
10. "Tres muros, vno delante de otro, como va subiẽdo el cerro, tẽdrá cada muro mas de dozientas braças de largo. Van hechos en forma de media luna, porq̃ van a cerrar y

The half-moon imagery used to describe the walls is striking, both because the symmetry of its three concentric semicircles provides an ideal spatial plane and because its relation to the actual architecture is debatable, as we shall see. Garcilaso's text, on the other hand, contains one of the only references we have to three interior towers, whose existence was in doubt until 1934, when Luis E. Valcárcel found them buried in the earth.[11] The Spanish had apparently begun to dismantle them shortly after the Conquest, both to get stones for the rebuilding of Cuzco and to obliterate any religious power that native *cuzqueños* still vested in the towers. By the end of the sixteenth century, they had been destroyed. Garcilaso claims that the three towers form "an extended triangle, conforming to the shape of the fortress,"[12] that is, proportionally distant from the walls, and that he saw their ruins as a boy playing among the fortress walls and rooms with friends. The central, circular tower is called Moyoc Marca; the lateral, squarish ones are Paucar Marca and Sallac Marca (fig. 1). The similarity between Garcilaso's visualization of Saqsawaman and a stylized rainbow is clear.

We will examine the symbolic significance of the similarity later. For now it is important to note that the archaeological evidence partially contradicts the outlines we find in the *Royal Commentaries*. The three front walls do run parallel to each other and are connected to the southern wall at both ends, but they are not curvilinear, as Garcilaso's half moon suggests. Rather, they follow a zigzag pattern. Furthermore, the remains of the towers show that they were not positioned triangularly at all, so that the fortress in fact lacks an ideal symmetry (fig. 2).[13]

---

juntarse con el otro muro pulido, que està a la parte de la ciudad" (*Comentarios* 1.7.28, f. 193v).

11. See Valcárcel, "Sajsawaman redescubierto," *Revista del Museo Nacional* (Lima) 4 (1935): 161–203; and Víctor Angles Vargas, *Sacsayhuaman: Portento arquitectónico* (Lima: Industrial Gráfica, 1990).

12. "Un triángulo prolongado, conforme al sitio" (*Comentarios* 1.7.29, f. 194v).

13. See John Hemming and Edward Ranney, *Monuments of the Incas* (1982; rpt., Albuquerque: University of New Mexico Press, 1990), 69. The aerial map of Saqsawaman is taken from Graziano Gasparini and Luise Margolies, *Inca Architecture*, trans. Patricia J. Lyon (Bloomington: Indiana University Press, 1980), 78. I thank Gasparini for his permission to reproduce it.

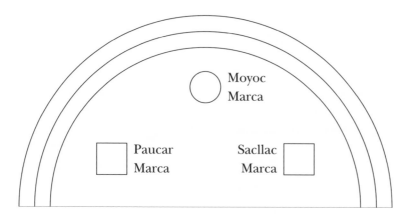

Figure 1   Saqsawaman, according to the *Royal Commentaries*.

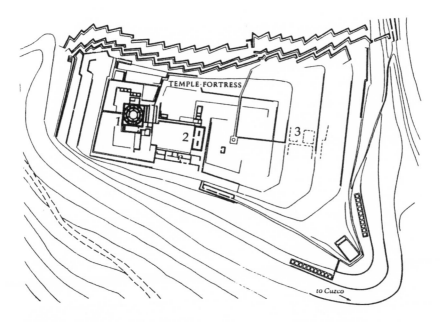

Figure 2   Aerial map of Saqsawaman, according to Hemming and Ranney. Note especially the location of the towers: (1) Moyoc Marca, (2) Sallac Marca, and (3) Paucar Marca.

It is unfortunate that most Spanish chroniclers emphasize Saq-sawaman's military attributes only. Yet some, Cieza de León, in particular, note early on that the indigenous people referred to it as Inti Wasi, "House of the Sun" (Hemming and Ranney, 65). Indeed Angles Vargas claims that its ritual function would have been the primary one, since it made little sense for an expanding empire to construct such a fortress at the city gates (43–8). R. Tom Zuidema suggests that Moyoc Marca represents the connecting point between the forces of the underworld and of this world. The very design of the tower, composed of underground levels analogous to its above-ground ones, made it possible to find "the squareness of the circle in Ancient Peru," since this vertical, cylindrical center had the power to rule the four quadrants of the Incan earthly universe.[14] Some early chroniclers like Pedro Sancho even describe the towers as having five floors,[15] and a passage from the *Royal Commentaries* adds that "beneath the towers, another had been wrought equal to the one above."[16] Garcilaso bestows to the subsoil a labyrinthine character that the indigenous people themselves dare not penetrate unless, he insists, they are guided by "a ball of yarn" (ibid.). (Here Garcilaso evokes the Greek myth of Ariadne and Theseus to reach a European public.)

The three zigzag walls on the northern side of Saqsawaman may have been built to represent three bolts of lightning extending from east to west, or vice versa. The Spanish chronicler Cristóbal de Molina points out that the cult of the god of thunder and lightning was inaugurated by the ninth Inca, Pachakutiq, who ordered the construction of Saqsawaman and other temples dedicated to that deity.[17] Sarmiento de Gamboa, a leading expert on the *wawqi*, or brother symbols of noble lineages, affirms that "Chuquiylla" or Chuki Illa, the lightning, was adopted by Pachakutiq as his family totem, and the examinations of *panaka* iconography undertaken by Horacio Urteaga, Arthur Demar-

14. Zuidema, "La cuadratura del círculo en el antiguo Perú," in *Reyes y guerreros: Ensayos de cultura andina*, comp. Manuel Burga (Lima: Fomciencias, 1989), 283–5.
15. See Pedro Sancho, *Relación de la conquista del Perú* (1550; Madrid: Porrúa, 1962), chap. 17.
16. "Debaxo de los Torreones auia labrado debaxo de tierra otro tanto como en cima" (*Comentarios* 1.7.29, f. 195).
17. Molina, *Fábulas y mitos de los Incas* (1573; Buenos Aires: Futuro, 1959), 26; see also John Hyslop, *Inka Settlement Planning* (Austin: University of Texas Press, 1990), 55.

est, and Zuidema indicate the same.[18] Chuki Illa was most likely a version of the pre-Incan deity Tunupa, also known in Quechua as Illapa, who lorded over all manifestations of the sky and was an important, though subsidiary, divinity (Demarest, 35).

In the *Royal Commentaries*, however, Garcilaso calls Illapa only an instrument of the Sun, not an independent deity. Given his importance to Pachakutiq's *panaka*, one suspects that the selectivity so characteristic of historical tales from the Cuzco nobility explains Garcilaso's downgrading of him. Such an Andean reading does not preclude the more traditional approach of noting European classical and Renaissance tautologies at work in Garcilaso's text; rather, the transformation of the lightning bolt into an instrument of the Sun, the greatest visible Incan deity (*Comentarios* 1.3.21), conjures up Jupiter and his lightning bolt. Garcilaso's "Romanization" of the Incas is quite explicit in part 1's "Proemio al lector," where Cuzco is compared to ancient Rome. Obviously, Garcilaso is dialoguing with two very different publics simultaneously.

Garcilaso also speaks of Kuychi, the rainbow or "sky arch" (*arco del cielo*), as a minor figure in the Incan pantheon, yet its importance in the Andean universe is evident in many texts. In a myth frequently cited by Spanish historians, for example, the rainbow appears as a sign of a new era shortly before the founding of Cuzco, when the Ayar brothers arrive at the peak of the hill known as Huanacaure. Molina mentions the rainbow's importance, but critics have argued that his descriptions of the Andean world are permeated with European themes, in this case with the rainbow as the sequel to a flood.[19] Molina and other Spanish chroniclers may indeed interpret evidence of a devastating flood in Incan history as proof of the Bible's universal truth; however, in pre-Columbian Andean mythology, too, destruction by water is a sign of cosmic renewal.[20] (The rainbow that follows is typi-

18. Sarmiento de Gamboa, *Historia índica*, vol. 135 (1570; Madrid: Atlas, Biblioteca de Autores Españoles, 1960), chap. 31; Urteaga, *El imperio incaico* (Lima: Museo Nacional, 1931), 153; Demarest, *Viracocha: The Nature and Antiquity of the Andean High God* (Cambridge, Mass.: Harvard University, Peabody Museum of Archaeology and Ethnology, 1981), 35; Zuidema, "Cuadratura del círculo," 243.

19. See Ernesto Morales, "Notas," in Molina, 28.

20. See Cieza de León, chap. 3 (see n. 8); Molina, chap. 1; Josep de Acosta, *Historia natural y moral de las Indias*, ed. Barbara G. Bedall (1590; Valencia: Valencia Cultural,

cally represented with four stripes rather than seven.) Other evidence of the Andean origins of the rainbow image can be found in ceramic and pictorial works.[21] In the Andean universe the rainbow represents a privileged natural element positioned on the axis of two worlds, imparting heavenly order to earthly chaos.

After the 1520s war of succession, the rainbow was emblazoned on the coat of arms of the *panakas* that had survived Ataw Wallpa's massacres, that is, Garcilaso's mother's *panaka* and its allies. Later, because they had opposed Ataw Wallpa during the Conquest and had submitted to Spanish rule, they were able to negotiate the privilege of blazonry and continued to bear their coat of arms.[22] In part 1 of the *princeps* edition of the *Royal Commentaries*, Garcilaso includes a personal coat of arms, in which the left side is an Andean field. There, under a sun and a moon, a rainbow emerges from the mouths of two sacred serpents (*amaru*), and a royal crêpe (*llawtu*) hangs between them.[23]

In Garcilaso's text, the imperial city of Cuzco is enclosed by two confluent rivers and, at its northern border, Saqsawaman, by a rainbow (*Comentarios* 1.7.8–11; fig. 3). If one imagines the intersection of

---

1977), 6.19; Anello Oliva, *Historia del reyno y provincias del Perú* (c. 1620; Lima, 1895), 1.2; Betanzos, *Suma y narración de los Incas*, ed. María del Carmen Martín Rubio (Madrid: Atlas, 1987), chap 1; Francisco López de Gómara, *Historia de las Indias y conquista de México* (1552; Mexico City: Centro de Estudios de Historia de México, 1977), chap. 122; Sarmiento de Gamboa, chap. 6; and *Comentarios* 1.3.25.

21. See Teresa Gisbert, *Iconografía y mitos indígenas en el arte* (La Paz: Gisbert, 1980), figs. 121, 123, 125, 201, 203–5.

22. See David de Rojas, "Los tocapu: Un programa de interpretación," *Arte y Arqueología* (La Paz) 7 (1981): 119–34; and Rojas, "Los tokapu: Sistema de graficación del parentesco inca" (Thesis, Biblioteca de Ciencias Sociales, Universidad Nacional San Antonio Abad del Cuzco, 1978).

23. That Garcilaso's coat of arms had Spanish elements on the right and Incan on the left is unexceptional for Andean iconography. Rolena Adorno studies this distribution in Waman Puma engravings and establishes its syncretic correspondence to relations of dependence or adoration even in drawings with Christian elements and characters (*Cronista y príncipe: La obra de don Felipe Guamán Poma de Ayala* [Lima: Pontificia Universidad Católica del Perú, Fondo Editorial, 1989], 159–68). Constance Classen argues that in Incan iconography, the right side represents day, dryness, masculinity, and spatial superiority; the left side, night, wetness, femininity, and spatial inferiority (*Inca Cosmology and the Human Body* [Salt Lake City: University of Utah Press, 1993], chap. 2).

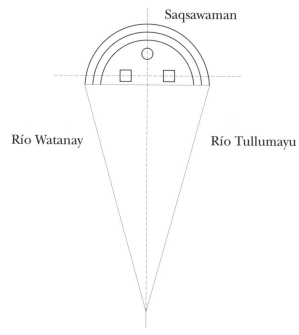

Figure 3 Projection of Cuzco based on descriptions
in the *Royal Commentaries*.

the city's north-south and east-west axes, it becomes clear that Garcilaso projects Cuzco as a cross crowned with the Incan "sky arch." I
suggest that this triangular image is one of many Andean referents
implicitly transformed in the *Royal Commentaries*. They do not contradict the text's explicit discourse but endow it with a subtext that reveals
itself only in relation to an Andean iconographic tradition.

Not surprisingly, Garcilaso's syncretic projection of Cuzco differs
from John Howland Rowe's archaeological hypothesis, according to
which the city was laid out in the shape of a puma facing northwest.
Whether it was or not has been debated at length by Zuidema and others.[24] However, even if we accept Zuidema's argument that Cuzco's bor-

24. Rowe, "What Kind of a Settlement Was Inca Cuzco?" *Ñawpa Pacha* 5 (1968):
59–76; cf. Zuidema, "El león en la ciudad," 306–85. For variations of the puma
shape of Cuzco see Gasparini and Margolies, 48. For a summary of the discussion see
Hyslop, 50–1. Classen accepts Rowe's hypothesis concerning the importance of the
puma as an Incan symbol of power and divinity (101–6). For his part, Carlos Milla

ders extended beyond its center to include the many outlying communities whose purpose was to tend to the forty-one concentric lines (*seq'e*) linking more than 340 sacred places (*wak'a*),[25] Garcilaso's image of Cuzco significantly alters this conception of sacred space and many symbolic aspects of the Incan capital.

Just as Garcilaso incorporates Christian elements, such as the cross, into his description of Cuzco, so too does he imply the Christianization of the city's virtuous rulers, who insist on peaceful conquest and wise and just governance. Garcilaso's Incan utopia represents a New World translation, not so much of Thomas More's *Utopia* (1516), already somewhat out-of-date by 1609, as of *El príncipe cristiano*, by the Jesuit Pedro de Rivadeneira, and of *Del rey y de la institución de la dignidad real*, by another Jesuit, Juan de Mariana.[26]

One might read such "accommodations" of the Andean world to a European universe *only* as an apology for Incan civilization. After all, Garcilaso neglects to mention the Incan practice of *qhapaq ucha*, or burying children alive as sacrifices to the gods. Furthermore, he constructs a history in which the rulers of Cuzco gradually and methodically expand Tawantinsuyu to the colossal size it has when the Spanish arrive; whereas archaeological evidence shows that the expansion of Tawantinsuyu was much less orderly and abruptly occurred during the last hundred years of Incan rule, starting with the ninth Inca, Pachakutiq. However, Garcilaso is not interested in some "truthful" version of the past and its symbolic attributes. His text purposefully interweaves indigenous and Europeanized versions of the past to create a complex, ultimately coherent vision of the Andean future.

Villena suggests that the generative figure of the llama served as the model for the urban space of Cuzco (*Génesis de la cultura andina* [Lima: Colegio de Arquitectos del Perú, Fondo Editorial, 1983], 219–25).

25. See Zuidema, *The Ceque System of Cuzco: The Social Organization of the Capital of the Inca*, trans. Eva M. Hooykaas (Leiden: Brill, 1964).

26. So argues Carlos Araníbar in the "Glosario" of his edition of the *Comentarios reales* (Lima: Fondo de Cultura Económica, 1991), 769–70. For a reading of the *Royal Commentaries* as modeled on More's *Utopia* see Juan Durán Luzio, "Sobre Tomás Moro en el Inca Garcilaso," *Revista Iberoamericana* 42 (1976): 349–61; and Margarita Zamora, *Language, Authority, and Indigenous History in the "Comentarios reales de los Incas"* (Cambridge: Cambridge University Press, 1988), chap. 6.

Garcilaso's image of a Cuzco "crucified" and crowned with an Incan rainbow seems to represent an idealization based on virtues that Garcilaso himself establishes as foundational. Since the rainbow symbolizes the dawn of the productive season following the destructive but renewing rains, the Cuzco laid out in the *Royal Commentaries* displaces certain Incan icons, including the lightning bolt, in favor of ones more amenable to Garcilaso's sources and his vision of the Incan past.

Another reading of the idealized Cuzco centers on its surprising coincidence with representations of Incan power found on certain coats of arms. If the rainbow symbolizes Saqsawaman and the serpents the convergent rivers Watanay and Tullumayu, then Garcilaso's own coat of arms would seem to depict the sacred, fertile space of Cuzco. In Gisbert's description of the coat of arms of the first Inca, Mankhu Qhapaq, found in the Yábar Collection in Lima, the image of serpents and rainbow reappears in one of the heraldic fields (158). One of the oldest known coats of arms, preserved in the National Institute of Culture in Cuzco, bears the same symbols of the Incan capital. The coincidence of the image with that of Garcilaso's Cuzco attests to the need to explore the *Royal Commentaries* armed with knowledge of the city's cultural reference points, which are as important to the text as those of the European Renaissance.

The Writing of History and the Colonial Subject

I hope to have shown that the gnoseological exchange in the *Royal Commentaries* can be discerned only with wide knowledge of the Andean cultural world. One can deconstruct Garcilasian discourse on at least two levels: the surface and the subtext. Just as baroque churches in colonial Cuzco were erected atop Incan stone walls, so too does the *Royal Commentaries* constitute meaning from the layering of European classical and Renaissance models with transformed primordial images attributed to the indigenous world. Given its complex dual configuration, the narrative presupposes that someone will emit its discourse and grant it unity. That someone is the writing subject, who performs distinct narrative, ethnographic, descriptive, and even recita-

tive functions (as, for example, in the speeches attributed to indigenous nobles). Only when narrative breaches occur—only when the
subtext is read against the backdrop of the sixteenth-century Andean
universe—do we encounter the subject's hidden face.

Within the learned world of late-Renaissance Spanish historiography, referring to oneself as a "Mestizo Indian," as Garcilaso did,
challenged the norm that only wise, white, pure-blooded men quali-
fied as authorities.[27] José Rabasa has argued that in an earlier work,
titled *La Florida del Inca*, Garcilaso resolved his dilemma by writing
from the borders of a universalizing culture, thus expanding the criteria that had traditionally defined the possession and wielding of the
historical word.[28] Because he was mestizo, illegitimate, and born in
the Andes, Garcilaso had to overcome immense obstacles to advance
both his ideas and the cause of the surviving Incan elites of Cuzco,
who faced impoverishment after the Conquest.[29] But his specific
political and social motives in publishing the *Royal Commentaries* may
well lie, alongside the aesthetic intention of idealizing the Andean
past, in the abundant biographical sources that have yet to be rigorously examined.

Whether or not the biographical facts of Garcilaso's life support
his having known "the whole truth" about Incan history and symbolism
(he surely knew more than his Spanish counterparts), the writing subject of the *Royal Commentaries* uses narrative (both content and style) to
distance himself from European historians, even though he has mas-
tered their culture and has adopted many ideas of Italian Neoplaton-

27. In the prologue to his *Historia general de las Indias* (1552; Caracas: Biblioteca
Ayacucho, 1976), 6, Bartolomé de Las Casas states that historians should be learned,
religious men; the responsibility of writing history cannot be left to the spiritually or
intellectually unfit. Cabrera de Córdoba agrees in his *De Historia: Para entenderla y
escribirla*, ed. Santiago Montero Díaz (1611; Madrid: Instituto de Estudios Políticos,
1948), 31–2.
28. Rabasa, "On Writing Back: Alternative Historiography in *La Florida del Inca*," in
Latin American Identity and Constructions of Difference, ed. Amaryll Chanady (Minneapolis: University of Minnesota Press, 1994), 130–48.
29. See Manuel Burga, "El Inca Garcilaso de la Vega: Exilio interior, ambigüedad y
segunda utopía," in *Nacimiento de una utopía: Muerte y resurrección de los Incas* (Lima:
Instituto de Apoyo Agrario, 1988), 271–309.

ism. Thus, Garcilaso's contradictory practice of exalting Christian values while infusing his subtext with "pagan" Andean symbols needs examination.

David Brading has argued that Garcilaso's work should be interpreted as a political proposal for the establishment of a Holy Incan Empire in the Peruvian viceroyalty.[30] The text is ultimately very critical of the Spanish colonial regime, particularly of the reforms of the viceroy Toledo (1569–81), who curtailed privileges that had been granted to Incan descendants and attempted to undermine the local power base of Spanish *encomenderos*, of whom Garcilaso's father had once been among the most important in Cuzco. Clearly, a thorough understanding of the authority the *Royal Commentaries* enjoyed in its own day must rest on the text's political and moral dimensions. Likewise, by deciphering some aspects of its subtext, I hope to have shown that Garcilaso's "history of the Incas" forged a new historiographical form, whose complexity of meaning stems precisely from its intersemiotic (indigenous as well as European) character. We must abandon critical approaches that presuppose a purely European public, since Garcilaso's rhetorical strategy also targeted a New World public that eventually decoded the Andean referents found in the passages on Saqsawaman and elsewhere in the *Royal Commentaries*.[31]

Inasmuch as Garcilaso's text sets in relief conflicting versions of Cuzco's indigenous past and transforms it in accordance with the ideological and stylistic forms of sixteenth-century Spanish historiography, it allows us to bear witness to the emergence of a new voice: the dominated yet privileged colonial subject. Garcilaso has already been read as a completely Europeanized writer by the majority of contem-

30. Brading, "The Incas and the Renaissance: The *Royal Commentaries* of Inca Garcilaso de la Vega" *Journal of Latin American Studies* 18 (1986): 1–23.

31. Although there is no evidence of an indigenous reception in the 1600s, the *Royal Commentaries* is known to have greatly influenced the Incan national movement, and one of its most important rebels, Tupaq Amaru II, in 1780–81. It was banned in Peru after the rebellion. See John Howland Rowe, "El movimiento nacional inca del siglo XVIII," *Revista Universitaria* (Cuzco) 7 (1954), rpt. in *Túpac Amaru II—1780: Sociedad colonial y sublevaciones populares*, comp. Alberto Flores Galindo (Lima: Retablo de Papel Ediciones, 1976), 13–66.

porary *Garcilasistas*; he has also been read as a faithful representative of Andean indigenous values.[32] What remains is the much more difficult task of understanding Garcilaso's internal complexity, which demands a novel, interdisciplinary approach to this foundational text in Latin American literature.

32. See José de la Riva-Aguero, "Elogio del Inca Garcilaso," *Revista Universitaria de la Universidad Mayor de San Marcos* 11, no. 1 (1916), in *Comentarios reales de los Incas*, vol. 1 (Lima: Librería e Imprenta Sanmarti y Cía., 1918); Valcárcel, *Garcilaso el Inca: Visto desde el ángulo indio* (Lima: Imprenta del Museo Nacional, 1939); and César Delgado Díaz del Olmo, *El diálogo de los mundos: Ensayo sobre el Inca Garcilaso* (Arequipa: Universidad Nacional San Antonio Abad, 1991). For the European sources of the *Royal Commentaries* see especially Luis Arocena, *El Inca Garcilaso y el humanismo renacentista* (Buenos Aires, 1949); Enrique Pupo-Walker, *Historia, creación y profecía en los textos del Inca Garcilaso de la Vega* (Madrid: Porrúa Turranzas, 1982); Zamora (see n. 26); and Claire Pailler, "Estructura y fuentes de una historia incaica: Una lectura 'romana' de Garcilaso," in *Conquista y contraconquista: La escritura del Nuevo Mundo: Actas XXVIII Congreso del Instituto Internacional de Literatura Iberoamericana*, ed. Julio Ortega and José Amor y Vazquez, with Rafael Olea Franco (Mexico City: Colegio de México; Providence, R.I.: Brown University, 1994), 61–74.

The True History of Early Modern Writing in Spanish: Some American Reflections

MARY M. GAYLORD

This essay's scene of writing is a morning walk along the Charles River. I thread my way through narrow streets and set out on the path nearest the water, leaving to the spur of the moment the decision—when, on which bridge, even whether—to cross over. From the Cambridge bank I can see the neo-Georgian business school, copied from the older campus and transplanted on the opposite shore in shining, tidy rows. I know there is "another world" over there; often I retrace my steps without crossing the river at all. Yet, when I do follow one of the bridges and am thus translated to the other side, I look back on "my town." On all but the most blustery days, Cambridge is doubled by the Charles, its skyline sketched twice, in paired worlds above and below the bank, like something from a baroque poem. On sunny days the old buildings beam at themselves with self-satisfaction; on misty mornings the town eyes its face dreamily in the mirror of the water. I suppose it must do so every day, or glower gray when it can't. But *I* can see the mirroring of my town's self-image only when I am on the other shore, when my there has become a here, and my old here a there. So as I walk along, a self-translating subject, I am mentally in both places at once.

Anecdotes like this one carry big risks. Not only has self-indulgent self-reference ever been a handy vehicle for irony, but Cambridge, Massachusetts, and its residents have earned for themselves a sure niche, right alongside Sleeping Beauty's stepmother, in the "Mirror, Mirror" Hall of Famous Self-Contemplators. I take on the risks here, with some trepidation, in order to use my exercise route as a parable of the two-world itineraries of writing in Spanish during the sixteenth and seventeenth centuries, particularly the writing of texts advertised as "true histories." I believe that it can also serve as a revealing figure for the itineraries of criticism and literary history focused on those centuries in the Hispanic world, that is, for the very paths and crossings that bring scholars of Peninsular Golden Age literature and Latin American colonial literature together in the 1990s.[1]

The *deambulatio animae* as a figure for mental itineraries was familiar to Golden Age readers from the *Examen de ingenios para las ciencias* (1575), where Juan Huarte de San Juan used it to trope the meanderings of that most vagabond of human faculties, Imagination or *Imaginativa*.[2] The link between physical movement and the processes of thought and imagination becomes particularly suggestive in the very mobile world of sixteenth- and seventeenth-century cultures.[3] As the "compañera del Imperio" of the grammarian Antonio de Nebrija's famous formulation, the Castilian language produced much of its speech and its writing in actual motion.[4] Many Hispanic writers, like the New World chroniclers, "came to writing" (in the wonderful expression of Hélène Cixous) literally on the move, either outward bound, roaming abroad, or on the journey home.[5] A very large portion of the canonical literature of what is called Spain's Golden Age bears, along with the obsession with the *transitory* routinely ascribed to the baroque, the conspicuous thematic mark of *transience*. A host of the period's celebrated literary transients, both authors and char-

1. An earlier version of this essay was presented to the MLA Division on Latin American Colonial Literature, in a session on "intersecting narratives" of Golden Age and colonial literatures. I thank both the chair of the session, Kathleen Ross, and my colleague Doris Sommer for pressing me to develop these reflections on the interconnectedness of our fields.

2. Huarte de San Juan, *Examen de ingenios para las ciencias*, ed. Esteban Torre (Madrid: Editora Nacional, 1976).

3. Georges van den Abbeele, *Travel as Metaphor: From Montaigne to Rousseau* (Minneapolis: University of Minnesota Press, 1992), and Steven Hutchinson, *Cervantine Journeys* (Madison: University of Wisconsin Press, 1992), take up the connection between literal and figurative movement.

4. Nebrija, *Grammatica Castellana, 1492; El Orthografia Castellano, 1517*, facsimile ed. (Yorkshire: Scolar, 1969), a.ii..

5. Cixous and Clément, *The Newly Born Woman*, trans. Betsy Wing (Minneapolis: University of Minnesota Press, 1986), 69.

acters, come readily to mind: imperial soldiers (two Garcilaso de la Vegas, Hernando de Acuña, Alonso de Ercilla, Miguel de Cervantes) and itinerant clergy (Bartolomé de Las Casas, John of the Cross, Teresa of Avila); fictional knights, *pícaros*, shepherds, poet-pilgrims like Góngora's, wandering Byzantine lovers. Nor is it surprising that the thematics of transience should have bred what might be called a poetics of transgression. The period's penchant for overstepping classical boundaries is proverbial: literary history offers us the record not of single transgressions, one-time events, but of multiple crossings and recrossings as borders continued to be redrawn and literary bloodlines mixed. These "golden centuries" surely owe much of their dazzling richness both to their writers' literal transits and to their literary transgressions, in short, to the generalized cultural practice, real and imagined, of distances and of difference.

No body of writing from the early modern Spanish-speaking world offers more telling evidence of chronic transgressiveness than the texts that cluster together under the promising and suspect name of "true history," *historia verdadera*. Why is it, I propose to ask briefly, that this rubric turns up in so many texts and in such an extraordinary range of situations and kinds of writing in Spanish? My threefold aim is to pull out of a familiar topos a new, historical understanding of the early modern Hispanic fascination with the truth-telling capacities of narrative; to suggest that an engagement with either "serious" or fictional history is necessarily an engagement with the other; and to propose Cervantes' *Don Quixote* as the *summa* of his age's double obsession. The last proposal entails two unorthodox claims that I cannot support fully here but that are essential indicators of where my meditation on "true history" comes from and where it is leading.[6] First, I take the *Quixote* to be a book not only about fiction and the writing of fiction but also about history and about the *serious* historiography of its time. Second, I believe that it is bound up, not just in a general sense but in concrete textual ways, with historical writing in Spanish about the New World. If this is true, then Cervantes' master-

6. The reflections in this essay belong to a book nearing completion, titled *Tropics of Conquest*. One of its chapters studies the narrative trope of *historia verdadera* in Cervantes' *Don Quixote*, where I take it to mirror the many varieties of early modern historiographical writing in Spanish.

piece belongs as much to "Latin American colonial" discourse as to Spain's Golden Age.

Historia verdadera, as an itinerant motif, crops up in an astonishing variety of texts. Predictably, the name of "true history" is applied to narratives that make serious, responsible, even plausible claims to credibility. Bernal Díaz del Castillo's *Historia verdadera de la conquista de la Nueva España* (posthumously titled for publication in 1632) is the most familiar, but in the Hispanic world of the 1500s and 1600s their name was legion.[7] Their subjects range from Spain, Europe, and the Mediterranean to the Holy Land, the Far East, and the Indies. If we agree to bracket for a moment the historiographical distinction between the terms *historia* and *relación* (the latter ordinarily reserved for more local narratives), we can draw into this group of "factual histories" the huge number of chapbooks that provided accounts of contemporary historical events.[8] Another kind of "true history" is found in the more suspect narratives that play to and on the general reader's curiosity, recounting fictional events alleged, more or less convincingly, actually to have happened. Into this category go Antonio de Guevara's pseudochronicles of Roman emperors and Spanish royalty, the *falsos cronicones*, the *Libros plúmbeos*, and the *Historia verdadera del Rey don Rodrigo*, which royal interpreter Miguel de Luna claimed to have translated from the eighth-century Arabic original of an eyewitness recorder of Spain's mythical scene of origins. Although their playful intent seems clear enough to us, some of these "true histories" were

7. Díaz del Castillo, *Historia verdadera de la conquista de la Nueva España*, ed. Miguel León-Portilla, 2 vols. (Madrid: Historia 16, 1984). In addition to the famous *Historia verdadera del Rey don Rodrigo* of Miguel de Luna (Granada, 1592, 1600), clearly fraudulent, the rare book collection of the Houghton Library at Harvard contains a host of sixteenth- and seventeenth-century historical texts that advertise themselves as "true," chronicling travels to the Holy Land, major battles, the births and deaths of royalty, the reception of Spanish ambassadors abroad, natural catastrophes, apparitions of the Virgin Mary, and so on. Although the label *relación verdadera* (true account) is applied with a liberal hand during this period to much eyewitness documentary writing, analogous in function to modern print and television journalism, the term *historia verdadera* is applied less frequently and thus would still have made a provocative title for a larger-scale work of historical interpretation.
8. On generic distinctions among kinds of historical writing about America see Walter D. Mignolo, "El metatexto historiográfico y la historiografía indiana," *MLN* 96 (1981): 358–402.

considered authentic by many—the eighteenth-century protests of Nicolás Antonio notwithstanding—as late as the nineteenth century, especially outside Spain.[9] A third group of texts that press serious claims of truth are the histories in verse, epic poems grounded more or less firmly in historical events known to have taken place. Among them we find Ercilla's *Araucana* (1569, 1578, 1589), Juan Rufo's *Austríada* (1584), Juan de Castellanos's *Elegías de varones ilustres de Indias* (1589), Gabriel Lobo Lasso de la Vega's *Mexicana* (1594), and many more.[10] Finally, we come to the "true histories" that all readers take to be so in name only: fictions that, like *Don Quixote*, hang their plots on the scaffolding of their authors' "historiographical" enterprises and make "true history" the central metaphor for the construction of a fictional narrative.[11]

In the early modern Hispanic world, "true history" is both a broad umbrella and an uncommonly protean rubric, playing a variety of discursive roles, introducing widely divergent subjects, moving across multiple chronologies and geographies. Its shifty tag covers everything from serious, supporting concept, to advertising ploy, to paradox (for example, a history written in verse), to pure figure. It visits the sweeping times and places of what might be called a European Renaissance chronotope, swinging between ancient and modern times, traversing the continents and oceans of a post-1492 geography, crossing the borders of classical and modern genres, flourishing on the frontiers between reality and fantasy. As a ubiquitous label, the term did everything but what it ostensibly aimed to do: in the words of Charlie Brown, *historia verdadera* made it harder and harder to tell the "reallies" from the phonies. "True history" was the great linguistic crossdresser of the day: it went everywhere in drag; its name delivered not an essence but a guise. Yet in Cervantes' lifetime, the label *historia verdadera* sold books. This fact cannot be explained simply, either by pub-

---

9. A classic survey of the particulars of sixteenth-century Spanish pseudohistoriography is Bruce W. Wardropper, *"Don Quixote*: Story or History?" *Modern Philology* 63 (1965): 1–11.

10. Frank Pierce's canonical study of Golden Age epic, *The Heroic Poem of the Golden Age* (Oxford: Oxford University Press, 1947), presents evidence that an astonishing 150 epic poems were written in Spanish during the early modern period.

11. This theory is advanced by Wardropper (see n. 9).

lic credulity or by the enduring popularity of a good joke. Like those of other forms of cross-dressing, the vagaries of "true history," even when it is being spoofed, point to an underlying cultural anxiety about the very nature of historical truth and the capacity of written language to know it and to transmit it.[12]

Whether it means to or not, the label *true history* opens a can of worms left untouched by the simpler *history*. To invoke *historia verdadera* is at the very least to activate a dynamic of curiosity. It associates history with discovering, witnessing, recording. As the story of a cognitive or epistemological adventure, "true history" draws attention to the scene of its writing and to the subject position of the historian. "True histories" are always double-plotted: they are "historias de una historia," as Carmelo Saenz de Santa María says in another sense of Díaz del Castillo's text.[13] They necessarily recount two stories: one, the story of events; the other, the story of how the author has come to know what he knows and to write it, that is, of how the historical text has come into being. And as stories of history, "true histories" thus paradoxically call into question, along with the verisimilitude of the people, places, and events they detail, the very authorial privilege they invoke.

With its progeny scattered over vast real and fictional geographies, the textual history of *historia verdadera* reads like a family romance of knowing and writing, in the course of which the authority of representation is passed back and forth between history and poetry, poetic history and historical fiction, Old World and New, often planting its feet in more than one place at once. Many voices bear witness to the discomforts and uncertainties experienced by this shifty tribe: theorists of fiction like Jacques Amyot, Torquato Tasso, and Alonso López Pinciano enjoin their sixteenth-century contemporaries who would write romances to stay away from known worlds, to spare themselves the caviling of pedants.[14] Pinciano concedes (with shades of Borges) in the *Philosophia Antigua Poética* that it would be possible for

12. See Marjorie Garber, *Vested Interests: Cross-Dressing and Cultural Anxiety* (New York: Routledge, 1992).

13. Saenz de Santa María, *Historia de una historia: La crónica de Bernal Díaz del Castillo* (Madrid: Consejo Superior de Investigaciones Científicas, 1984).

14. Alban K. Forcione, *Cervantes, Aristotle, and the Persiles* (Princeton, N.J.: Princeton University Press, 1970), 80.

two authors to produce one and the same written account of an event and that one would be historical and the other fictional.[15] The lexicographer Sebastián de Covarrubias Horozco, brooding in his 1611 *Tesoro de la Lengua Castellana o Española* that real Spanish exploits in the New World were so fabulous that they would not be recognized as true by future readers, especially foreigners, would even legislate that history must be composed exclusively in prose.[16]

Here and elsewhere, we are reminded insistently that the frontier separating the historical from the fictional was anything but clear. Representation, these voices seem to say, is a no-man's-land, where it is easier to pass from one camp to the other without realizing it than to draw a line between them. And it is far easier for the writer of fiction to have his story pass for history than it is for the earnest chronicler of unfamiliar worlds to clear his "true history" of the charge of lying.

We have long assumed that the sixteenth and seventeenth centuries' engagement with now-tired binaries like reality and fantasy, fact and fiction, history and poetry, is either neo-Aristotelian or "naturally" baroque. But it was not only the humanist, academic rediscovery of Aristotle's *Poetics* that made verisimilitude and the marvelous the burning questions of the day.[17] Rather, the lived experience of astonishingly new worlds, and the urgent need of Spaniards in Europe and America to write about them, put the earnest historian and the literary liar in the same boat. Indeed, most early modern writers, whether of fiction or of history, wrestled with one and the same set of representational paradoxes. For both, after all, had to make things "never before heard or seen" present in the here and now of their audiences' imaginations. Both had to deal in and with things "not here": fiction, with scenes and characters that weren't here by definition, that didn't and never would exist outside the pages of books; contemporary history,

15. Pinciano, *Philosophia Antigua Poética*, ed. Alfredo Carballo Picazo, 3 vols. (Madrid: Consejo Superior de Investigaciones Científicas, 1973), 2:9–10.
16. Covarrubias Horozco, *Tesoro de la Lengua Castellana o Española*, facsimile ed. (Madrid: Turner, 1979), 580.
17. Bernard Weinberg identifies Giorgio Valla's 1498 Latin translation as the first major step in the reintroduction of the *Poetics* into European literary thought (*A History of Literary Criticism in the Italian Renaissance*, 2 vols. [Chicago: University of Chicago Press, 1961], 1:361).

with radically new scenes "not here," because dramatically increased physical distance precluded the widespread sharing of experience. It appears that spatial distance so close to the present was much more unsettling than temporal distance from the remote past, perhaps because the newly revealed geographic expanse had not yet been spanned by an established chain of authoritative witnesses, perhaps also because its startling realities could never be thought of as tucked safely away in some venerable text, since they were ongoing and likely to impinge in unpredictable ways on one's own experience. Each writer of history had to invent his own chain of witnesses and documents and to work actively to maintain his authority in the face of his readers' incredulity, of the possible appearance of other witnesses with other stories, or of chance turns of event that would require the rewriting of the entire narrative. This pervasive anxiety of transmission moved the Sevillian Fernando de Herrera, poet and historian of the great 1571 Christian victory over Islam in the eastern Mediterranean, to disarm possible critics of his account of the battle of Lepanto by asking them to consider "cuán incierta es la voz de la verdad, traída de partes tan remotas y de lenguas tan varias" [how uncertain is the voice of truth, brought out of such remote regions and such diverse languages].[18]

As they struggle with the question of how to distinguish "true history" from poetic fable, Pinciano and Covarrubias come very close to the modern recognition that the difference between historical and fictional narratives lies not in some formal essence capable of separating real sheep from imagined goats but in a set of conventional agreements governing the relation of language to the world in each mode of writing.[19] Historical representation usually leans heavily on what has already been acknowledged as fact, in other words, on the "twice-told."

18. Herrera, *Relación de la guerra de Chipre y Suceso de la batalla naval de Lepanto*, vol. 21 of *Colección de documentos inéditos para la historia de España* (Madrid: Sociedad de Bibliófilos Andaluces, 1852), 248. My translation.

19. Some central contributors to this discussion in our day are Roland Barthes, "The Discourse of History" and "The Reality Effect," in *The Rustle of Language*, trans. Richard Howard (Berkeley: University of California Press, 1989), 127–40, 141–54; Michel de Certeau, *The Writing of History*, trans. Tom Conley (New York: Columbia University Press, 1988); Barbara Herrnstein Smith, *On the Margins of Discourse: The Relation of Literature to Language* (Chicago: University of Chicago Press, 1978); and

Working without benefit of prior tellings, the first Spanish historians of the New World had to build the conventions of the real and the true virtually from the ground up, with precious little shared ground. Their writings testify above all to an obsession with grounding in the world that is essential to history. Yet as their enterprise called attention to the means by which any representational authority is constructed, it inevitably called the same authority into question.

It took Cervantes' genius to see in the story of historiography both a blueprint for the fabrication of fictions and a deeply troubling mirror for his culture's prevailing angst. In the quests of his personified authors and his vainglorious protagonist to write the real, to write the "true history" of the Spanish self and its others, he sums up the triumphs and the trials of his age's great cognitive adventure and its overdetermined political agenda. Cervantes undoubtedly learned much about the historical paradoxes he engaged from Lucian of Samosata. This second-century Greek author, better known for his satires, produced two historiographical meditations, one straight (*How to Write History*) and one a tease (*A True Story*), mirror how-to and how-not-to manuals that enjoyed enormous popularity through translation and imitations in their Renaissance revival. After opening the *Verae historiae* with the provocative declaration that it will contain not an ounce of truth, Lucian trots out the entire arsenal of historiography's standard devices: the self-references of a first-person author-witness, geographic detail, physical description, even "notarial certification" from other witnesses to his passing. In the culminating episode of his journey, he elicits from no less an authority than Homer a *poem* that "certifies" that he has reached the point of their meeting and has left his mark on an actual tree.[20] Cervantes incorporates many of the same tricks into the *Quixote*, largely through such surrogate authorial fig-

Hayden White, *Metahistory: The Historical Imagination in Nineteenth-Century Europe* (Baltimore, Md.: Johns Hopkins University Press, 1973).
20. Lucian, *A True Story*, trans. A. M. Harmon, in *Lucian I*, and *How to Write History*, trans. K. Kilburn, in *Lucian VI*, Loeb Classical Library, (Cambridge, Mass.: Harvard University Press, 1913–59). The tree-engraving episode is found in *Lucian I*, 333. For the fortunes of Lucian in Spain and Italy during this period see the late Michael O. Zappala's exhaustive *Lucian of Samosata in the Two Hesperias: An Essay in Literary and Cultural Translation* (Potomac, Md.: Scripta Humanistica, 1990).

ures as Cide Hamete Benegeli and the "second author." The last ploy finds its way into the episode in which the novel has its closest brush with historical reality: the interpolated tale of the *Capitán cautivo*, whose accuracy is finally "validated" not by historical documents but by a pair of sonnets and whose eyewitness narrator evokes a shadowy figure one is invited by name ("un tal de Saavedra") to associate with the historical Miguel de Cervantes Saavedra.[21] In the *Araucana* Ercilla, too, appropriates the Lucianesque motif of writing on trees to certify his presence in the South American places he describes.[22]

Enthusiasm for Lucianesque, fictional play with the notion of historical truth was the period's way of turning a pervasive source of cultural anxiety—how to know the real truth about the newly discovered territories, how to gauge the truth-value of contemporary accounts, how to speak and write credibly about the world—into merriment. With a wry wit tinged with cultural melancholia, Cervantes engages these burning questions by endowing his characters as well as his own fictional authorial persona with a historiographical obsession about the truth of their stories and, moreover, by letting them tell their stories with the counterfeited words of actual historians, some of them New World conquistadors.[23]

In the textual fusions and confusions of historical and fictional worlds under the name of "true history"—in the very texts (*Don Quixote* and the New World chronicles) that have so often been held up as emblematic of their cultural moment—lies an important lesson for us as critics. Until quite recently, the map on which studies of early modern Peninsular and American writing in Spanish are located has looked like a formula for distributing textual territory between poetry and history. We have called one province "Golden Age" studies and have assumed that its particular business was literature: art for art's sake, literature spun out of literature, fiction about the making of fictions, imagination dangerously divorced from a crumbling reality.

21. Cervantes, *El ingenioso hidalgo don Quijote de la Mancha*, ed. Luis Andrés Murillo, 3 vols. (Madrid: Castalia, 1978), 1:486.
22. Ercilla, *La Araucana*, ed. Isaías Lerner (Madrid: Cátedra, 1993), 942–3.
23. One of the central theses of my book in progress is that Cervantes puts the first- and secondhand words of Columbus, Cortés, Las Casas, and others into the mouths of his characters, chiefly Don Quixote and Sancho Panza.

To the other province, dubbed "Latin American colonial," has been assigned history. Indeed, on both the European and the American sides, national interests have long favored the patriotic reading of even remotely historical colonial texts as documents, either of imperial exploits or of new national origins. As critics, we have often found it difficult to inhabit two realms apparently so different; most of us have found it more comfortable to remain centered in just one of them.

But the "truth" about our literary-historical vision is that we have drawn a map that obscures as much as it reveals. Many are the texts that have been temporarily lost to the comforts of scholarly provincialism. Texts that straddle two hemispheres and two (or more) cultures, like texts that try to locate themselves in more than one genre (some do all of the above!), tend to fall into the cracks between orders, to be judged irrelevant or imperfect in relation to established categories and norms. Even Ercilla's extraordinary *Araucana* is still not standard reading in Golden Age poetry courses, which have traditionally found it more convenient to focus on the lyric and to leave politics and history to prose—or to the colonialists. A first and obvious response, in the late twentieth century, to the prevailing scholarly "politics of the center" on both sides has been to attune our ears to early modern voices that issue from the margins of either the Peninsular or the American Hispanic world. In Spain, the decentering of focus, which has its roots in Marcelino Menéndez y Pelayo's work on the *heterodoxos españoles* and in Américo Castro's celebration of the cultural diversity of modern Spain's formative centuries, means attending to writing "beyond literature," such as the Inquisition testimony of newly converted Christians of Jewish and Muslim origin, or the diaries of nuns.[24] For colonialists, it has lately meant pushing past the rows of

24. See Menéndez y Pelayo, *Historia de los heterodoxos españoles*, 3 vols. (Madrid: Librería Católica de San José, 1880); and Castro, *De la edad conflictiva: Crisis de la cultura española en el siglo XVII*, 4th ed. (Madrid: Taurus, 1976). On women's and nuns' voices see Electa Arenal and Stacey Schlau, eds. *Untold Sisters: Hispanic Nuns in Their Own Works*, translations by Amanda Powell (Albuquerque: University of New Mexico Press, 1989); Ruth Anthony El Saffar, *Rapture Encaged: The Suppression of the Feminine in Western Culture* (London: Routledge, 1994); Richard L. Kagan, *Lucrecia's Dreams: Politics and Prophecy in Sixteenth-Century Spain* (Berkeley: University of California Press, 1990); and Alison Weber, *Teresa of Avila and the Rhetoric of Femininity* (Princeton, N.J.: Princeton University Press, 1990).

colonial baroque copies into the unexplored expanses beyond the limits of Romance-language communities, and even beyond the European culture of books, into territory previously reserved for anthropologists.[25]

Yet, if it is true in Hispanic writing of the period that transgressions are a way of literary life, even in works issuing from the very center of the center of the dominant cultural world, then it is urgent for us to reread the entirety of what we are used to thinking of as the Golden Age literary canon, scanning it for traces of the literal and figurative crossings made inevitable by the double nature of the Hispanic world. Every culture gazes at itself dreamily in the reflection of its fictions. Genres like the chivalric, the pastoral, the picaresque, the epic, the lyric, and the *comedia* all were engaged in dramatizing the self-understanding and ideal self-image of Spaniards who were obliged to locate themselves on the map of a much-changed world. If we want to fathom the full impact of the discovery and its aftermath on the Hispanic consciousness, it is not enough to look at what Spaniards wrote about the New World and its natives; we must look for ways in which Europeans' image of themselves changed in the bargain.[26] As students of literature, we need to ask what we can learn about the cultural work embodied in the genres and masterpieces of the Spanish canon when we look at it from the other side. *All* Golden Age texts, after all, were written not, as the term might imply, in some "time before time" but after Columbus's voyages, and largely after the march on Tenochtitlán. It is only common sense to suggest that their mirrors of reality cannot *not* have reflected the expanded, newly doubled horizons of their authors' worlds.

25. Important contributors to this work are Rolena K. Adorno, *Guaman Poma: Writing and Resistance in Colonial Peru* (Austin: University of Texas Press, 1986); Regina Harrison, *Signs, Songs, and Memory in the Andes: Translating Quechua Language and Culture* (Austin: University of Texas Press, 1989); Mercedes López-Baralt, *Icono y conquista: Guamán Poma de Ayala* (Madrid: Hiperión, 1988); Elizabeth Hill Boone and Walter D. Mignolo, eds., *Writing without Words: Alternative Literacies in Mesoamerica and the Andes* (Durham, N.C.: Duke University Press, 1994); and Mignolo, *The Darker Side of the Renaissance: Literacy, Territoriality and Colonization* (Ann Arbor: University of Michigan Press, 1995).

26. J. H. Elliott, in a classic study, has called this "the uncertain impact" (*The Old World and the New, 1492–1650* [Cambridge: Cambridge University Press, 1970], 1–27). I believe that the impact is quite certain, if still largely unexplored.

Whether we choose to remain focused on the Old World or on America, or try to have one foot on either side of the water, we do well to remind ourselves regularly that *here* and *there* are particularly slippery deictics for the period we study. Both literally and in their "paseos del alma," sixteenth- and seventeenth-century Hispanics did a lot of bridge crossing, and in both directions.[27] Cervantes' most eloquent emblem for the bi-directional itinerary is perhaps the Clavileño, Imagination's steed, who takes you one day to France, the next to Potosí (2:341). If I were an astronaut, my emblem might be the twentieth-century lunar expeditions, whose images have irrevocably altered the way we envision our world. But as an academic pedestrian, I take for my homespun trope the view from the other side of the river, the view you can have only once you have crossed the water. It is the place from which you can see not just your own world but the way it reflects (on) itself, the place from which you can see your world and yourself "otherwise" and where you are likely to be "altered" by the recognition. Any future "true history" of early modern writing in Spanish will have to take in that doubled image.

27. See James D. Fernández, "The Bonds of Patrimony: Cervantes and the New World," *PMLA* 109 (1994): 969–81.

The Burden of Modernity

CARLOS J. ALONSO

During the last few years I have examined the rhetoric of cultural discourse in Spanish America in the context of the region's conflicted relationship with the ideology and experience of modernity. We are now beginning to recognize that Spanish American postindependence was singularly different from other postcolonial situations, and I believe that only by addressing its specificity head-on will we be able to understand the continent's cultural production in all its depth, ramifications, and contradictions. My argument is precisely that the particularities of the Spanish American condition—and by extension those of its cultural discourse—are best understood in the context of the continent's radically ambiguous relationship with the program of modernity.

Political independence did not so much mark the end of colonialism for Spanish America as it did its entrance into a neocolonial arrangement under the hegemony of nineteenth-century imperialist expansion. Very soon after emancipation European powers penetrated Spanish America swiftly and effectively, in a script all too familiar to need rehearsing here. Neocolonial penetration had the insidious advantage of being seemingly invisible, since it took the form of accords, loans, and guarantees between supposedly sovereign nations and thus dispensed with overt colonial takeover, contemporaneously exercised by metropolitan countries in other areas of the world. The economic results for Spanish America were, nevertheless, virtually the same: the region was quickly relegated to the periphery of a global commercial system with territorial ambitions to match.

The spatial arrangement of center and periphery was buttressed by a collection of ideological narratives that sought to naturalize the hierarchy created by economics. Perhaps the most important and all-encompassing narrative was the myth of modernity: the belief that there were metropolitan foci from which the modern emanated and through which its rippled and delayed expansion across time and space would transform the material and cultural orders of societies that languished in the outer confines of the system. In every colonial and neocolonial situation the indigenous ruling class, displaced or forced into the diminished role of mediator by the metropolitan power, eventually develops strategies to challenge progressively more openly the legitimacy of hegemonic authority. This is the development that historically results in the final expulsion of the metropolitan power after a protracted and multilevel anticolonial struggle.

However, in Spanish America the situation was much more complicated and ambiguous, for the tenets of the myth of futurity that the cultural foundation of the new countries rested on, and that had been especially effective in the anticolonial struggle against "backward" Spain, harmonized rather than conflicted with the narrative of modernity that sustained the legitimacy and prestige of metropolitan rule. Hence, at the precise moment that Spanish American intellectuals asserted their specificity or made a claim for cultural distinctness, they did so by using a rhetoric that inevitably reinforced the cultural myths of metropolitan superiority. This contradiction resides at the root of Spanish American cultural discourse and has dictated until very recently the contorted intensity of its rhetorical force.

The condition of being economically and culturally peripheral to the metropolis created yet another difficulty for the Spanish American writer: given the objective material and social circumstances of the new continent—semifeudal agricultural economies with flourishing slavery in some instances; masses of illiterate Indians, blacks, and "mixed-breeds"; precarious urban life; political instability— Spanish American reality was always at risk of becoming the negative object of modern Western knowledge, that is, the consummate example of a deviation from a norm established by the same metropolitan

discourses that were themselves confidently wielded by Spanish
American writers and intellectuals. For the latter, the threat of being
no longer the brandishers but the objects of a discourse instead constituted a permanent danger. Thus the rhetoric of modernity was
both the bedrock of Spanish American cultural discourse and the
potential source of its most radical disempowerment.

To address the persistent undermining of their own rhetorical
authority, Spanish American writers and intellectuals devised ways in
which to subvert the authority of the discourse of modernity even as
they wielded it. In the most general terms, they opened a textual
dimension in which the chosen rhetorical mode was contravened or
thwarted. While invoking the values, goals, and ideology of modernity,
Spanish American writers defined for themselves a space outside it: in
their works they adopt a rhetorical mode identified as "modern" yet
simultaneously argue that it is incommensurate with Spanish American circumstances. At the center of every Spanish American text, then,
lies a turning away, because at some level every Spanish American text
attempts to effect a cultural claim to exception from the demands of
modernity that is expressive of a discursive will to power, a staving off
of rhetorical disenfranchisement. The particularity of the Spanish
American postcolonial cultural condition is traceable to just such a
radical ambivalence to modernity.

The study of Spanish American cultural discourse therefore
demands critical discernment of the various strands of its contradictory textual maneuvering; it requires, in fact, a conception of cultural
resistance on a different basis from the symmetrical, zero-sum interaction between metropolis and colony that severely limited the applica-
bility of dependence theory to the study of cultural relations between
center and periphery. Recent debates in anthropology and cultural
studies have shown us that resistance is never a simple oppositional
strategy but a complex dialogic negotiation among parties in a multi-
layered relationship of constant and mutual reaccommodation. But a
formulation of resistance that is apposite to the Spanish American
context must account also for the quite explicit desire of appropriation and quotation of metropolitan discourses that is intrinsic to it; in
other words, it has to be a formulation capable of incorporating the
passionate commitment to a modernity understood in hegemonic

terms that is very much a part of Spanish American cultural discourse as well. This is why attempts to describe the relationship between Spanish American cultural production and metropolitan models according to some conception, however imaginative, of parodic appropriation necessarily offer an incomplete view of its subject. Parody implies a process of distancing from an original model that does not accurately represent the relationship that obtains between the Spanish American work and its hegemonic models. I use "parody" here to refer to any critical perspective for which colonial discourse is ultimately a "savage" appropriation and repetition of metropolitan paradigms, however much ideological resistive value one may wish to place on that deviation from the original.

This critique extends particularly to the concept of *transculturación* in several creative acceptations advanced recently. Since the coining of the term by Cuban anthropologist Fernando Ortiz in the forties, transculturation has presupposed a detachment manifested in the peculiarities of the colonial subject's appropriation of the metropolitan original.[1] Ortiz may have had it in mind, as Mary Louise Pratt has argued, "to replace the paired concepts of acculturation and deculturation that describe the transference of culture in reductive fashion imagined within the interest of the metropolis"; but as Pratt makes clear, transculturation seeks to change our perspective of cultural exchange between the metropolis and the periphery by simply allowing us to look at it from the standpoint of the subordinate cultural party.[2] Of course, the exercise always leaves the avowed original intact in order to then describe its decomposition, reshaping, reincorporation, or cannibalization into a novel cultural object produced by the colonial "savage" mind.[3] Hence there is no possibility of exploring

1. Ortiz, *Contrapunteo cubano del tabaco y el azúcar* (Caracas: Ayacucho, 1987).
2. Pratt, *Travel Writing and Transculturation* (New York: Routledge, 1992), 228 n. 4.
3. To my mind, the best critique of the use of the concept of *transculturación* in the Latin American context is by the Cuban anthropologist Manuel Moreno Fraginals, "Aportes culturales y deculturación," in *Africa en América Latina* (Mexico City: Siglo XXI, 1977), 13–33. Speaking about the experience of Africans brought to the Americas as slaves, he argues: "In our view, one cannot arrive at the essence of this problem if we take as our point of departure the established anthropological scheme that regards transculturation as a phenomenon of opposition and synthesis that occurs when a group of immigrants is inserted into a society founded on European cultural

the plurivocal, self-contradictory, and open-ended dimension of metropolitan discourse, left to stand as the selfsame, monolithic authority
it purports to be. Moreover, in its desire to identify an active strategy of
resistance in the appropriation of the original, transculturation does
not account sufficiently—and this is especially limiting in the Spanish
American case—for the desire that led to the original in the first
place. Instead we must formulate a critical discourse faithful to the
simultaneous embracing of and distancing from modernity that are
specific to cultural discourse in Spanish America.

This characterization of cultural discourse in Spanish America
has implications for any chronological or formalist approach to it. If
we conceive of the double movement at the core of every Spanish
American text as a displacement toward modernity, "followed" by a
recoil from it, for example, we can metaphorically project a temporal dimension onto every oeuvre. Each Spanish American work
would then possess an internal "chronology" that may or may not be
consonant with the developments or currents in a proposed larger
frame of cultural history. Indeed, one can envision the need to
reconstruct the received cultural history of Spanish America from a
perspective discerning of, and deriving its categories and major
points of articulation from, this textual dynamics.

The dialectics of the connection between Spanish American cultural discourse and modernity recalls the similarly ambiguous relationship between modernity and the concept of literature, widely
acknowledged to have arisen in response to an awareness of the experience of modernity toward the end of the eighteenth century.[4] Liter-

---

models. The reality of what one could tentatively call 'Black areas of the Caribbean'
is totally different. From the beginning these were *new* societies, to which both
Africans and Europeans arrived simultaneously: the former as people subjugated in
a capitalist war of spoils, and the latter in their role of exploiting agents. There was
no preexisting European-like society that was then inflected by African contributions. Hence, the search for Africanisms that inscribed themselves in the established
patterns constitutes a false working methodology" (31; my translation).
4. See Alvin B. Kernan, "The Idea of Literature," *New Literary History* 5 (1973):
31–40; and Tzvetan Todorov, "The Notion of Literature," *New Literary History* 5
(1973): 5–16. The first two chapters of Luiz Costa Lima, *Control of the Imaginary:
Reason and Imagination in Modern Times*, trans. Ronald W. Sousa (Minneapolis: University of Minnesota Press, 1988), are also relevant.

ature may be profoundly antimodern, but as it has devolved it has incorporated into itself a version of modernity, which becomes evident when one realizes, for instance, that the appearance of "literature" was accompanied by the demand for originality. If the business of literature was to challenge and question modernity, it would nonetheless be ruled by the requirement of doing so in ever newer ways. Hence, from its beginnings literary discourse, too, has been constituted around an ambivalence to modernity that rends it to the core. This internal split is the very same that I have tried to show exists in the Spanish American rhetorical tradition. Or more precisely, what could be said is that both literature and cultural discourse in Spanish America exist as a simultaneous rejection and affirmation of the modern. One might propose that literature and Spanish American cultural rhetoric describe the same movement between opposing poles, but starting from opposite ends: literature begins with an understanding of itself as engaged in a struggle with the modern and then moves in ways that are inconsistent with its avowed rejection of modernity. By contrast, Spanish American cultural rhetoric proceeds from its identification with modernity to a surreptitious turning away from it. Each trajectory is the other's specular opposite, which may help us understand the ambiguous relationship that the Spanish American discourse of cultural specificity has always entertained with the more explicitly literary discursive modalities against which it customarily purports to define itself.

The space that any postcolonial discourse must negotiate is constructed of myriad exigencies and openings, all of them shaped as exquisite double binds. In a recent essay Homi Bhabha offers a very useful summary of the difficulties both of postcolonial discourse and of the critic addressing it. Bhabha, along with such critics as Gayatri Spivak and Tejaswini Niranjana, is attempting a synthesis of poststructuralist positions concerning the instability of the subject's insertion into language and the ideological critique at the center of postcolonial studies:

> The reason a cultural text or system of meaning cannot be sufficient unto itself is that the act of cultural enunciation—the place

of utterance—is crossed by the *différance* of writing. This has less to do with what anthropologists might describe as varying attitudes to symbolic systems within different cultures than with the structure of symbolic representation itself—not the content of the symbol or its social function, but the structure of symbolization. It is this difference in the process of language that is crucial to the production of meaning and ensures, at the same time, that meaning is never simply mimetic and transparent. The linguistic difference that informs any cultural performance is dramatized in the common semiotic account of the disjuncture between the subject of a proposition (énoncé) and the subject of enunciation, which is not represented in the statement but which is the acknowledgment of its discursive embeddedness and address, its cultural positionality, its reference to a present time and a specific space. The pact of interpretation is never simply an act of communication between the I and the You designated in the statement. The production of meaning requires that these two places be mobilized in the passage through a Third Space, which represents both the general conditions of language and the specific implication of the utterance in a performative and institutional strategy of which it cannot "in itself" be conscious. What this unconscious relation introduces is an ambivalence in the act of interpretation. The pronominal I of the proposition cannot be made to address—in its own words—the subject of enunciation, for this is not personable, but remains a spatial relation within the schemata and strategies of discourse. The meaning of the utterance is quite literally neither the one nor the other. This ambivalence is emphasized when we realize that there is no way that the content of the proposition will reveal the structure of its positionality; no way that context can be mimetically read off from the content.[5]

Bhabha is in reality describing a problematic present in any linguistic utterance, but expanded to encompass the discursive situation

5. Bhabha, "The Commitment to Theory," in *The Location of Culture* (London: Routledge, 1994), 36. See also Spivak, *In Other Worlds: Essays in Cultural Politics* (London: Methuen, 1987); and Niranjana, *Siting Translation: History, Post-Structuralism, and the Colonial Context* (Berkeley: University of California Press, 1992).

of the postcolonial subject. To the poststructuralist ambiguities about the inscription of meaning and subjectivity into language, Bhabha adds the ambiguities that arise from the cultural positionality of the speaker and his or her immersion in an institutional network responsible for the construction of cultural meaning. The significant factor in this dimension, though, is that what Saussure would call the "value" of the sign is not only relative, and therefore identical in every case, but also informed by a set of hierarchical relations. Just as in the Saussurian linguistic model, they are always there, inasmuch as their totality determines the value of the individual utterance; yet they can never be fully articulated or apprehended. For the interpreter of cultural discourse, position—not simply meaning—is always in need of precision and simultaneously in centrifugal flight.

In the Spanish American scenario, furthermore, there has always been a truly radical ambiguity and ambivalence about the very position of Spanish American culture. Time and again it has been possible, for instance, to propose that to bring about the culmination of Spanish American historical development, one must import European settlers, technology, philosophical systems—choose your product. In most postcolonial situations cultural positionality may not be fully apprehensible to the speaker, but any awareness of it is clearly filtered through a hierarchical model that constantly seeks to invert what used to be the colonial state of affairs. In Spanish America, by contrast, the problems begin with the difficulty of drawing even the most basic distinctions that would allow a subject to attempt a definition, however tenuous, of his or her cultural location.

Indeed, *positionality* may be the most economical term to describe the central concern not only of Spanish American cultural production but of any theory of it: its status and authority and its relation to cultural activity in the metropolitan centers. A few years ago Fredric Jameson was roundly criticized for asserting that all postcolonial texts were ultimately national allegories of the relationship between the postcolony and the metropolis.[6] Yet, in an awkward way, Jameson had rec-

6. Jameson, "Third-World Literature in the Era of Multinational Capital," *Social Text* 5, no. 3 (1986): 65–88. The best-known critique of Jameson's thesis is Aijaz Ahmad, "Jameson's Rhetoric of Otherness and the 'National Allegory,'" *Social Text* 6, no. 2 (1987): 3–25, rpt. in *In Theory: Classes, Nations, Literatures* (London: Verso, 1992), 95–122.

ognized and attempted to find a place in his thinking for the category of positionality that is indeed present in most postcolonial literature, and especially in Spanish American cultural production. Where I believe he erred was in reducing this internal exploration of positionality vis-à-vis metropolitan modernity to an allegorizing intention, leaving his argument open to the reproaches that allegory has consistently evoked since the romantic period, on the one hand, and to charges of ahistoricity, on the other. But Jameson's reductionism should not obscure his having identified the core need of postcolonial discourse to demarcate a space, a position from which to speak authoritatively in a horizon of discursivity that assigns a precarious authority to the postcolonial interlocutor. The difficulty is wrenching in Spanish American cultural discourse, since its explicit point of departure is often the desire to erase the specificity of its location, that is, to argue that its here and now should be the metropolis's there and tomorrow. But its avowed intention can never erase the locational incommensurability that led to the project in the first place.

Jameson's allegorical figuration of authority and position may be reductive, but it is symptomatically accurate. There is in Spanish American cultural discourse a persistent will to shore up an authority felt to be threatened by the rhetorical dynamics described above. Nevertheless, this structure manifests itself not necessarily or uniquely as an allegory but as an internal disjunction that can occur at all levels and in all dimensions of a text. The Spanish American text's swerve away from itself, the foundation of its rhetorical authority, is in its creative aspect reminiscent of the Lucretian *clinamen*: the deviation from the expected that makes possible the beginning of the shaped world. For the Spanish American text the *clinamen* represents both the search for and the impossible rhetorical predicament of discursive authority. That they cannot, finally, be dissociated makes it exceedingly difficult to advance a concrete formulation about cultural discourse in Spanish America, unless in a fashion that duplicates the delicate, fragile balance that characterizes the object described.

My current work represents an attempt to read an admittedly idiosyncratic collection of texts from the Spanish American canon in order to call attention to the complex rhetorical structure in their midst. Guided by my desire to arrive at an interpretation of Spanish

American cultural production that is neither seduced by the naïveté of autonomy or the dead end of resistance, nor overwhelmed or paralyzed by the continent's obvious debts to European models and forms, I believe that the most accurate understanding of the phenomenon will give all of these qualities their due, since they all manage to coexist at the heart of every Spanish American work.

Salvador Brau: The Paradox of the *Autonomista* Tradition

ARCADIO DÍAZ-QUIÑONES

The end of a tradition does not necessarily mean that traditional concepts have lost their power over the minds of men. On the contrary, it sometimes seems that this power of well-worn notions and categories becomes more tyrannical as the tradition loses its living force and as the memory of its beginnings recedes.—Hannah Arendt, *Between Past and Future*

Our origins stem from the conquistadors and not the conquered. . . . We are Spaniards: give us the laws that apply in Spain. Destroy the *here* and *there* which poisons spirits and inflames sentiments.—Salvador Brau, *Ecos de la batalla*

During the last decades of Spanish domination something new seemed to take place in Puerto Rico. Despite the subaltern condition of colonial life, an emerging group of intellectuals managed to establish a tradition of their own. Salvador Brau (1842–1912) and other *hommes de lettres* (among them José Julián Acosta, Manuel Alonso, Manuel Fernández Juncos, and Manuel Zeno Gandía) sketched out the beginnings of a new intellectual and political life. They saw themselves as bearers of a modern cultural identity, but they were fully aware of their marginality. Unlike José Martí, Eugenio María de Hostos, and other radical revolutionaries in exile, these journalists, politicians, doctors, and poets resisted identification with armed rebellion. Instead they demanded liberal, progressive reforms and seemed committed to mediate between modernization and imperialism.

Brau placed himself at the center of a tradition that echoed throughout twentieth-century cultural and political discourse. In turn-of-the-century Cuba and Puerto Rico a movement surfaced that ambiguously opposed metropolitan power and created new grids of identity and difference. The defenders of political autonomy hoped to resolve the colonial problem from within the Spanish state. In spite of their loyalty to the metropolis and their opposition to violent rebellion, the *autonomistas* went further than any previous movement in favor of self-government. They raised moral objections to the entire colonial project, took up the causes of reform, and established a tradition that became a center of political validation even for those who opposed it.

Brau, Luis Muñoz Rivera, José Celso Barbosa, Román Baldorioty, and other liberals experienced both a variety of conflicts with respect to the Spanish metropolis and cultural and racial tensions in the colony. They shared with the Spaniards a profound sense of continuity, but they also had a sense of belonging to a new, distinctive, "Puerto Rican" people. Brau's writings reflect the ambivalence between painful awareness of colonial marginality and desire for unity with the Spanish nation. He wrestles with the advance and retreat of colonial coercion and gives voice to the anxieties of internal critics. Such contradictions and exclusions were experienced in the colony much more intensely than in the metropolis. Although not always expressed in writing, they were firmly established in the colonial consciousness.

This essay examines some of Brau's texts and focuses on the meanings of *autonomy* that, in my judgment, emerge as an epistemology and a program deeply embedded in the social practices and colonial forms of institutionalization.[1] The definition of *autonomista* political and cultural tradition may be summarized as an affirmation of a nation without the state. The defense of a national project does not necessarily imply the creation of an independent state; rather, it stands for stricter collaboration and common citizenship with the metropolis.[2] In a parallel move, however, *autonomistas* systematically contested

1. I would like to thank Professor James Irby, Christopher Britt, and Dušan Djurić for their comments and suggestions on an earlier, Spanish version of this essay and for their assistance in the translation of Brau's texts quoted in it. I would also like to thank Chris Mazzara for his capable copyediting.

2. Concerning Brau and his work, as well as the Puerto Rican *autonomistas*, see the following: Antonio S. Pedreira, *El periodismo en Puerto Rico: Bosquejo histórico desde su iniciación hasta 1930*, vol. 1 (Havana: Ucar García y Cía., 1941); Eugenio Fernández Méndez, introduction to *Disquisiciones sociológicas y otros ensayos*, by Salvador Brau (Río Piedras: Ediciones del Instituto de Literatura de la Universidad de Puerto Rico, 1956), 9–120; Angel Acosta Quintero, *José Julián Acosta y su tiempo* (San Juan: Instituto de Cultura Puertorriqueña, 1965); Pilar Barbosa de Rosario, *El ensayo de la autonomía en Puerto Rico, 1897–1898* (San Juan: Editorial La Obra de José Celso Bar

authoritarian imperial practices. This project, as we shall see, was articulated throughout Brau's work.

Brau's writings are complex antecedents of a symbolic order
and a long tradition to which he gave coherence and intelligibility.
A nationalist narrative was taking shape. He wanted to promote the
professionalization of history in order to attain public recognition
of subaltern subjects. From this perspective, *autonomy* and *conquest*
were crucial, but not mutually exclusive, terms. Conquest was necessary, paradoxically, so that the "civilized" descendants of the conquerors might better construct their autonomy over and against
"barbarism." Such constitutive ambivalence marked practically all of
Brau's essays, poems, and plays. In his own way, he was able to reconcile the two traditions that fought for preeminence toward the
turn of the century.

Subaltern colonial consciousness wages a constant epistemological struggle for and against the metropolitan definitions of the
nation. The framework elaborated in Edward W. Said's *Culture and
Imperialism*, for example, emphasizes the "connectedness" between
the empire and the colonies. Partha Chatterjee has also convincingly shown the deep ideological links between them. The dialecti-
cal relation between the imperial model of the nation and its colonial copy generates new and contradictory meanings. The successive
stages of the contestation of the political and intellectual premises
of empire can be historicized.[3] In an anticolonial struggle, the colo-

---

bosa, 1975); José Luis González, *Literatura y sociedad en Puerto Rico: De los cronistas de
Indias a la generación del 98* (Mexico City: Fondo de Cultura Económica, 1976);
José María Muriá, "Salvador Brau y la historia," *Latinoamérica* (Mexico City) 9
(1976): 211–30; Gervasio L. García, *Historia crítica, historia sin coartadas: Algunos
problemas de la historia de Puerto Rico* (Río Piedras: Ediciones Huracán, 1985); and
Angel G. Quintero Rivera, "Apuntes para una sociología del análisis social en
Puerto Rico: El mundo letrado y las clases sociales en los inicios de la reflexión
sociológica," in *Patricios y plebeyos: Burgueses, hacendados, artesanos y obreros: Las rela-
ciones de clase en el Puerto Rico de cambio de siglo* (Río Piedras: Ediciones Huracán,
1988), 189–279. See also María de los Angeles Castro, "De Salvador Brau hasta la
'novísima' historia: un replanteamiento y una crítica," *Op. Cit.: Boletín del Centro de
Investigaciones Históricas* (Río Piedras), no. 4 (1988–89): 11–55.
3. Said, *Culture and Imperialism* (New York: Knopf, 1993); Chatterjee, *Nationalist
Thought in the Colonial World: A Derivative Discourse?* (London: United Nations University, 1986). For the concept of *subaltern* see also the valuable exposition in Rajanit

nial spirit is both present in and absent from the discourses that oppose it.

The struggle for authority in Puerto Rico took place in the context of modern cultural and political traditions. Spain, however, wanted to preserve the center and resisted *autonomista* initiatives. Spaniards claimed that the empire itself was the entry into modernity. Hence during the final years of the Spanish domination, both imperial and anticolonial notions were caught in the rhetoric of progress and the search for historical laws. The teleological discourse of "civilization" and "barbarism" dominated colonial debates. Progress had to be recognized as the structure and force of history, with which *autonomista* intellectuals sought to align their thoughts and actions. The battles echoed without pause well into the twentieth century.

Brau aimed his struggle at several fronts at once. He laid the intellectual groundwork for a "native" literary and historiographical tradition. The origins of the intellectual space he hoped to institutionalize lay in an enlightened cultural model. At the same time, his historiography narrates reunification and advocates full citizenship for subaltern subjects. Brau imposed on himself the task of celebrating the many virtues he saw in progress and commerce. In 1884 he wrote a preliminary study for the second edition of Manuel Alonso's *El gíbaro* (1849), a foundational text for Puerto Rican literature. Brau's version of the basis for the nation, and his theory of cultural identity, persisted in Puerto Rican historiography. His vision was disseminated, more emphatically, in the discursive tradition renewed by Antonio S. Pedreira (1899–1939), in his persuasive *Insularismo* (1934). Spanish and Latin American historiography of the twentieth century has nevertheless frequently overlooked or inadequately addressed Cuban and Puerto Rican *autonomista* traditions. The colonial context of their intellectual development and the ways they imagined history and culture deserve serious attention.

Guha and Gayatri Chakravorty Spivak, eds., *Selected Subaltern Studies* (New York: Oxford University Press, 1988); and Shahid Amin, *Events, Metaphor, Memory: Chauri Chaura, 1922–1992* (Berkeley: University of California Press, 1995). There are relevant essays by Said, Homi K. Bhabha, and others in Gyan Prakash, ed., *After Colonialism: Imperial Histories and Postcolonial Displacements* (Princeton, N.J.: Princeton University Press, 1995).

Salvador Brau was a staunch critic of Spanish imperial abuses, as his adherence to the liberal tradition of abolition and autonomy makes evident. Yet although Spain as a homeland was highly problematic, Brau proudly asserted his Spanish heritage: "I loved Spain because my Spanish parents taught me how to love her; I despised her despotism and tyranny because in those who gave me life I had no recourse but to recognize two of its victims."[4]

In a colony without universities, Brau acquired ample culture by reading and studying in the private libraries owned by the immigrants who managed to elude Spanish censorship. Such intellectual contraband was one way of developing and shaping a viable self. The "importation" of ideas and texts gave Brau a connection to other metropolitan centers. He also reminded his readers constantly of the contributions made by nineteenth-century immigrants to both the material and the spiritual transformations of the colony.[5] Indeed, his thought reflects the influence of Spencer, Stuart Mill, Comte, Henry George, and Victor Schoelcher and the rich and substantive work of Frédéric Bastiat and Jules Simon. Comparing Spain with other modern centers, Brau wrote:

> All attempts to suffocate the manifestation of thought proved vain. The island of Saint Thomas facilitated the contraband of books, opening the doors wide to a universal communication of ideas; and merchant ships of the United States and England, which in their incessant search for sugar and honey dealt as well in newspapers and magazines written in English and Spanish, also assisted in maintaining epistolary correspondence with places where the intellectual activity of the cultured world was intense.[6]

4. Brau, *Ecos de la batalla* (Puerto Rico: Imprenta y Librería de José González Font, 1886), 6. The article, titled "En plena luz" and dated October 1885, serves as a prologue to the book; in it Brau explains the positions taken by the newspaper *Integridad Nacional* while he was the principal contributor to *El Clamor del País*.

5. The Cédula de Gracias of 1815 had opened the doors to foreigners. Its principal aspects are discussed in Francisco Scarano, ed., *Inmigración y clases sociales en el Puerto Rico del siglo XIX*, 2d ed. (Río Piedras: Ediciones Huracán, 1985), and in Astrid Cubano Iguina, *El hilo en el laberinto: Claves de la lucha política en Puerto Rico, siglo XIX* (Río Piedras: Ediciones Huracán, 1990).

6. Brau, *Historia de Puerto Rico* (1904), facsimile ed. (Río Piedras: Editorial Coquí, 1966), 258.

Brau came to be "the living historian and the budding sociologist of Puerto Rican studies."[7] Nevertheless, the search for national origins and affiliation to an intellectual tradition became problematic. Many of Brau's efforts were dedicated to legitimizing his double origin: son of a Catalan immigrant and Puerto Rican; *autonomista* and defender of the Hispanic European culture. Trapped between a sense of belonging and a feeling of exclusion, Brau wanted to establish a basis of continuity. At the same time, he emphasized a distance from that foundation. It is likely that he sometimes felt greater attraction to one pole than to the other, but what remains characteristic is the tension and ambiguity. His celebrated poem "¡Patria!" embraces both the duality of his self-conscious marginality and the centrality of this legacy:

In the colony I was born; but the fiery blood
which like a narrow trench my veins does invite
I inherited along with my name and flag. (*Disquisiciones*, 93)

What is more, Brau did not consider himself simply a successor; he was an agent of historical necessity. His 1881 series of essays "La política y sus fases" justifies the colony's Spanish origins and the right to conquest. He writes with passionate admiration: "Spaniards were the ones who tore from the profound depths of the ocean this unknown corner of the earth; the aboriginal races who populated it have disappeared forever; our origins stem from the conquistadors, not from the conquered; we are as Spanish as those who, in the fields of Yagüeca, aided Ponce de León in consolidating the power of Castille over this privileged land."[8] The right to conquer "barbarians" guaranteed the fruition of the "civilizing" seed and was, in fact, the source of colonial authority.[9]

7. Gordon K. Lewis, *Main Currents of Caribbean Thought* (Baltimore, Md.: Johns Hopkins University Press, 1983), 270.
8. Brau, "La política y sus fases," in *Ecos de la batalla*, 35–6. In a studied examination of colonial politics, Brau defines nationality in familial terms: "Human societies, constituted within the limits of whatever nationality, are formed like a single and expansive family. More to the point: the natural organization of the family must have served as the basis of organization for the tribe. The grouping together of tribes resulted in the formation of the nation, as such" (32).
9. See, for example, the series of essays titled "Allá y acá," in *Ecos de la batalla*, 248–82. There Brau writes: "That the American people were barbarians, that the

From 1866, when the commissioned representatives of Cuba and Puerto Rico were invited to attend informative legislative conferences in Madrid, to 1887, Brau's generation witnessed many political ups and downs. Freedom of the press was suddenly followed by terrific repression. The renewed promise of reforms preceded the tortures inflicted by the *compontes*, which served to eradicate "by means of terror, forced confessions, or accusations" the members of the Autonomista Party (Brau, *Historia de Puerto Rico*, 285). Although slavery was abolished in 1873, the climate of political repression was continually denounced by the *autonomistas*, chiefly through their representative in Madrid, Rafael María de Labra. Despite the unity proclaimed by the metropolis, Labra made manifest the subordination and vulnerability of the colony: a world without political liberties.[10]

During that period Brau wrote two of his most important essays: "Las clases jornaleras en Puerto Rico" (1882) and "La campesina" (1886). The polemical articles reprinted under the title *Ecos de la batalla* (1886) are also representative. As the title indicates, "Echoes of the Battle" is a document of particular importance to the study of the development of a liberal consciousness in the midst of the extraordinary censorship imposed by the colonial government. The bookish *battle* is tantamount to the constitution of a space: the desired intellectual and political autonomy. The battle was a polemical act, a rhetorical gesture, and a practical fact. In view of the increasing political and economic hegemony of the United States, Brau emphasized the

---

Spaniards brought to this people the saving doctrine of the Redeemer of humanity, is true. To Spain—says one historian—is due the glory of having put two races in contact, races which at the time were said to come from two separate worlds which in fact were only one world; in this way the Law of Providence, which destines humans to exchange knowledge, was obeyed" (265). Conquest of the "barbarians" is for Brau one of the modern laws transformed into a destiny that holds the promise of liberty.

10. See Labra, *La cuestión colonial* (Madrid: Tipografía de Gregorio Estrada, 1869), 90–1. On censorship in Cuba see Larry R. Jensen, *Children of Colonial Despotism: Press, Politics, and Culture in Cuba, 1790–1840* (Tampa: University Presses of Florida, 1988); and Louis A. Pérez Jr., *Cuba: Between Reform and Revolution* (New York: Oxford University Press, 1988). For more information and interpretations concerning this period in Puerto Rico see Blanca Silvestrini and María Dolores Luque de Sánchez, *Historia de Puerto Rico: Trayectoria de un pueblo* (San Juan: Cultural, 1987); and Francisco Scarano, *Puerto Rico: Cinco siglos de historia* (San Juan: McGraw-Hill, 1993).

incompatibility of Spain's imperial system with the imperatives of modern society. Brau took a stance within a peculiarly double imperial perspective:

> Does Spain, in fact, after having come face to face with the seductive and cosmopolitan Saxon democracy, aim to maintain its influence over America by preventing the *spirit of democracy* from taking root and flourishing in its overseas colonies? Is it not more and more obvious that Spain should strengthen its intellectual and material ties with the republics that violently separated themselves from its dominion and thus constitute a great league of Latin American nations that could offset the power of the colossal republic to the north? No; faced with North American democracy, faced with the influence of that nation whose strength is grounded in freedom, there is no room for suspicions or tyrannies or traditional doctrines. Freedom is fought with freedom. (8)[11]

Even though Brau would not defend Spain's "anachronism," it would be misleading to read his admiration for the "democratic" United States as a rejection of Spain's cultural authority. On the contrary, while developing historiography in order to inscribe a Puerto Rican identity, he relied on the sustaining quality of Spanish culture. The founding of an archive was not, therefore, only the result of a pure and erudite will; it was a moral and historical idea. The remaking of history, the diligent publication and analysis of sources, was a political task imperative to the "nation imagined" by the *autonomistas*. Brau's books *Puerto Rico y su historia: Investigaciones críticas* (1892), *Historia de Puerto Rico* (1904) and *La colonización de Puerto Rico* (1907) were the

11. Here Brau comments on a phrase used by the politician Emilio Castelar in reference to the peninsular "spirit of democracy." The battle is also the genre of polemic, which I discuss later. In the prologue to *Ecos de la batalla* Manuel Fernández Juncos, a critic, points out Brau's rhetorical talents: "In this genre, which could well be characterized as a *lyrical polemic*, Salvador Brau is without rival in Puerto Rican journalism. One must admire him when he sets his mind to one of those discussions which here so vividly grab one's attention, so much so, in fact, that his work may be said to define an era in our local journalism. Our gladiator becomes a giant in the face of opposition; he adopts a cultured and knightly attitude and makes generous declarations in honor of his adversary; he is not even frugal with regard to the choice of place and weapons, and then the battle begins with some of the dimensions and aspects of an extraordinary tournament" (xiii).

fruits of his inquiries in the Archivo de Indias in Seville. They are fragments of a historical discourse that demanded to be heard but barely
had an echo in the metropolis. Brau faced a dilemma: he was eager to
criticize Spain's lack of democracy but had to avoid subverting its cultural authority.

The tension is reiterated in Brau's reflections on the very idea of
a national archive. His journeys to the Archivo de Indias were finally
made possible within the context of the fourth centennial of the discovery of America. He found much to admire in Spain, and his writings bear witness to the close attention he paid to cultural and social
life there. Brau's historiographical quest for a telos was a means to
conquer autonomy, but he also felt connected, emotionally and intellectually, to Spain. The Archivo was for Brau a monument to the
ancient grandeur of Spain and a compelling emblem of unity. But
there was also a colonial reason for his enthusiasm: Puerto Rico
lacked archives of its own. In 1896, in the midst of the Spanish-
Cuban-American war, Brau praised the institution in a peculiar fashion. He used a homogenizing "we" to differentiate himself from other
independent nations and to distance himself, yet again, from the
armed rebellion against the mother country. The Archivo represented "a mute but eloquent testimony to that titanic struggle for the
colonization of a land which is today divided into free states, our
independent Latin American nations, but which will perpetually con-
serve, as a revelatory sign of their origin, our language, our religion,
and our customs."[12] The Archivo itself was surrounded by a sublime
aura, and Brau stood entranced before the edifice. Such exalted celebration permitted Brau to position himself in a time identical to that
of the metropolis, to negotiate his place at the center and to speak as
a citizen.

In spite of his vulnerability, Brau was capable only of historically conceiving an intellectual origin that was both Spanish and European. In
his classic essay "Las clases jornaleras en Puerto Rico" he views the "civilizing" presence of the Spaniards as the axis about which the whole of
Puerto Rican history revolves. Based on the authority of Spanish cul-

12. Brau, *Puerto Rico en Sevilla* (San Juan, 1896), 307.

ture, he defends the need of the working classes to be morally edu-cated by the landed and enlightened elite. He furthermore advocates "mutual cooperation between capital and workers" as well as the incul-cation of a "horror of vices" and "respect for private property" in order to create an industrious, modern working class.

Cultural and political authority merge in Brau's version of the origins of Puerto Rican society. Cultural and racial hierarchy in "Las clases jornaleras" confers on Spaniards and their descendants the virtue of representing civilization and power, as well as the right to educate. Order and reason, equated with Spanish ancestry, stand at the top of this narrative, which is intimately linked to the notions of Hispanic cultural superiority so preeminent in the twentieth-century thought of Tomás Blanco and Antonio S. Pedreira.

In "Las clases jornaleras" Brau acknowledges the existence of three "races"—the Indian, the African, and the Spanish—which form "our character." Yet their legacies are different. Brau's hierarchy privi-leges the Spanish "civilizing element." Implicitly, his text formulates an essential "us" and an orientalized "them," which seem to have no common intellectual ancestry.[13] He denies both the Indian and the African races any rational attribute. In his representation, they appear formless and violent, lacking self-discipline. The political need to define and to introduce hierarchies is evident in Brau's text, which is based on the classifying language that makes racist discourse possible. The thrust of his argument is linked to the liberal, and imperial, con-viction that only "rational minds" should participate in political life. Along with its many other virtues, colonial rationality is rooted in His-panic European origins:

> There you have the primordial sources of our character. From the
> Indian we inherited his indolence, his silence, his disinterest, and

13. Binary oppositions are characteristic of colonial experience, as Gyan Prakash reminds us in a very perceptive introduction to *After Colonialism*: "Modern colonial-ism, it is now widely recognized, instituted enduring hierarchies of subjects and knowledges—the colonizer and the colonized, the Occidental and the Oriental, the civilized and the primitive, the scientific and the superstitious, the developed and the underdeveloped. The scholarship in different disciplines has made us all too aware that such dichotomies reduced complex differences and interactions to the binary (self/other) logic of colonial power" (3).

his hospitable sentiments; from the African we inherited his spirit
of resistance, his vigorous sensuality, superstition, and fatalism;
and the Spaniard inculcated in us his knightly pride, his characteristic high-spiritedness, his festive spirits, his austere devotion,
his constance when faced with adversity, and his love of country
and independence. If one of the three was meant to hold sway
over the others it had to be that which held in its heart the powerful seeds of intellectual culture.[14]

"Lo que dice la historia" (1893), another text key to our understanding of Brau's ambiguities and strategies, resulted from his passionate commitment to the *autonomista* cause. In the form of six letters
written contemporaneously with the fourth centennial, Brau questions
the legitimacy of the empire and begins to outline the basis of Puerto
Rican citizenship. He relentlessly criticizes the minister of Ultramar,
whose disparaging statements had reduced Puerto Ricans to "third-
class Spaniards" and had restricted their political participation. In
1892 the Autonomista Party had withdrawn from the electoral process, because the Puerto Ricans were required to pay a higher poll tax
than the Cubans.

Still, Brau envisioned a broader horizon. He introduced the colonial debate in an attempt to develop an alternative history, which
required the transformation of marginal spaces into central sites. In the
letters he challenges the humiliating notion of Spanish superiority. The
great lesson of history, highlighted in their very title, is that the dis-
dained and disdainful imperial version of history should be questioned
through marginal historical interpretations. Brau's historiography is
born as a counterattack that ambiguously assumes the geographic and
cultural distance of a forgotten history. An examination of "Lo que dice
la historica" lays bare the fundamental concepts of his historical narrative and the original ways in which the writing of history interacted with
colonial politics.

From the first pages Brau sets a tone of resentment, mocking the
Spanish ministers who keep confusing one island with another. Brau's
moral claim for Puerto Rican citizenship is prefigured in the colonists'
defense of the island against continual French and English invasion.

14. "Las clases jornaleras en Puerto Rico," in *Disquisiciones*, 128–9.

The island had been "left behind" by the Spaniards, and the power vacuum was filled by subaltern colonial subjects who became proper guardians of the frontier:

> The economic law of change is inescapable, and the metropolis, by having failed to satisfy its demands, left the colonists of San Juan, who were favored by the foreign owners of nearby islands, with no recourse but to reestablish, of their own accord, commercial equilibrium between producers and consumers; this was done by placing their wood and livestock in the hands of English, Danish, and Dutch ships in exchange for farming materials, cloth with which to cover their nudity, and arms and bombs for their own personal defense.[15]

Brau boldly inverts the usual understanding; now the colony generates and guarantees nationality. "Given the indifference of the metropolis," he writes, "the colony responded by purifying nationalist sentiment" (283). Brau attributes the greatness of the Spanish nation to the heroism of the colonists, who cleared the border country of foreign enemies. His alternative interpretation places the colonists in a paradoxical situation: they proved to be courageous and self-reliant, yet they were humiliated by colonial powers. The days when the colony patiently awaited instructions from Madrid, Brau suggests, were gone. The polemical relationship between the colony and the metropolitan national model discussed by Chatterjee could not find clearer expression than in this central scene.

Farther on, Brau denounces the sugar colony sustained by the brutal violence of slavery. The textual space turns into a veritable battlefield. Brau clearly believes that there is already an enlightened tradition whose filiation is "foreign," not Spanish, and that it has been constituted by horrified young men returning to the colony from "cultivated and free nations" (289). A significant turn is taken: Puerto Ricans whose moral and intellectual loyalty lay with a rival nation—France, England, or the United States—are portrayed as viable histor-

---

15. "Lo que dice la historia" (Cartas al Sr. Ministro de Ultramar, por el director de *El Clamor del País*), in *Disquisiciones*, 281. The letters were first published in *El Clamor del País*, under a pseudonym. At the time, Brau was general secretary of the Autonomista Party of Puerto Rico. See also "La política y sus fases" (n. 8).

ical subjects, capable of modernizing and moving ahead. In this vanguard of creole culture, much more familiar with modern life and another cultural space, Brau discovers a new identity and his own requisite authority. In a striking passage, he proposes a provocative "genealogy": the colony represents moral depravity and a restricted public space, barbarism disguised as civilization.

> Without schools, without books whose introduction to the colony was obstructed by censorship, without metropolitan newspapers whose circulation was intercepted, without political representation, without municipalities, without ideas or awareness, there was only one goal which was to absorb the physical and psychological functions of our people: the production of sugar, lots of sugar, in order to sell it to the United States and England. Nothing more than a colony exploited to the fullest. Lots of gold for the large plantation owners who, along with the sugar, sent their sons to foreign lands in search of academic degrees they could not obtain in their own country and then, after their many long years of residence in cultivated and free nations, brought them back home only to participate in all those cockfights that the military governors freely allowed. (289)

Brau's search for autonomy—the mixture of ties and antagonisms characteristic of colonial traditions—assumes several perspectives. The perplexing dilemma of opposition and allegiance, shared by more than one *autonomista*, can be read in light of Homi Bhabha's observation that the location of difference and otherness is not completely "outside"; rather, it is a "pressure and a presence, that acts constantly, if unevenly, along the entire boundary of authorization."[16] Brau and the *autonomistas* sought a partnership with Spain even as they resisted its domination.

In Brau's texts the fissure is dramatic. In spite of his general indifference, he yearned for recognition by the metropolis. His texts gather a multitude of complaints by which he hoped to draw attention from a power that always remained deaf to his demands. In 1881 Brau demanded full citizenship, acclaimed the Spain of "civilization," and,

16. Bhabha, "Signs Taken for Wonders," *The Location of Culture* (London: Routledge, 1994), 109.

above all, required the annihilation of the difference of locality, of the here and there. The proximity to and the distance from the imperial Other was devastating, and Brau hoped for a time when there would be no divisions. "We are Spaniards," he writes. "Give us the laws that apply in Spain. Destroy the *here* and *there* which poisons spirits and inflames sentiments" (*Ecos de la batalla*, 36).

Brau did not want to dissolve the links with Spanish colonial origins. In his most ambitious work, *La colonización de Puerto Rico*, which condenses his readings and research during the years of the fourth centennial, the colony continues to hold an intense attraction for him. Brau concluded this volume after the North American invasion of 1898, a crucial period of reassessment of life under Spain. The ideal reader of *La colonización* is located in the future; Brau compares himself to an architect who offers "usable raw material." In the prologue he refers to the lasting and profound changes that the "ideas of economic progress, free critical examination, and social emancipation" caused in the "sedentary, patriarchal island," and he reiterates one of the enlightened principles that justified them: "Conquests by the sword are ephemeral, while those executed by thought live perpetually in the universal soul."[17]

Similar ambivalence prevails in Brau's final works. Under North American domination, he was able to write a history textbook with far-reaching influence. In the remarkable *Historia de Puerto Rico* he addresses a young audience and praises the steps taken by the new military government: the end of official religion, the creation of an insular census, and the reform of public finances and education. For Puerto Ricans disengaged from the long-standing tutelage of Spain, everything seemed to lead toward a program of unlimited progress (*Historia de Puerto Rico*, 305–8). Brau even explicitly regretted that the North American military regime had not lasted longer. His was no mere strategic retreat from the imperatives of liberalism; it was a requirement of progress. For Brau, military discipline was a necessary educational step: "Perhaps the prolongation of the military regime

17. Brau, *La colonización de Puerto Rico: Desde el descubrimiento de la Isla hasta la reversión a la corona española de los privilegios de Colón*, 3d ed., ed. Isabel Gutiérrez del Arroyo (San Juan: Instituto de Cultura Puertorriqueña, 1966), 14, 275.

would have been propitious to moderating the sudden shift from the old colonial system"—associated with ignorance—"to the ample methods of democracy" (310). After 1898 the real threat to democracy came from the Spanish colonial past.

Brau makes it clear that Spanish colonization of America was as legitimate as North American colonization. The former sowed seeds, but only the latter could bring forth the fruits of modern civilization. The end of the Spanish Empire therefore signaled a new beginning: the reconciliation of tradition and progress. The new North American colony of 1898 was a result of the harsh but triumphant march of "civilization." Brau welcomed military intervention and had high hopes that the new wave of "civilizing" violence from the United States embodied an inexorable law of history.[18]

The power of a tradition, as Hannah Arendt has observed, may be felt with greater intensity when it has reached its end and seems forgotten. One of the most profound meanings of *autonomía* is embedded in the paradox that the subaltern colonial subject appropriates and revitalizes the withering tradition of the imperial Other. In this social imaginary, *autonomía* must be redeemed through an external power and through the law of history, with its logic of progress. For this reason, Brau and many other *autonomistas* found "civilized" Spanish imperial origins perfectly compatible with the reality of North American empire.

18. There is a passage in "Allá y acá" worth noting here: "The right to conquest is the right of force; it is based on war, and we know that in battles warriors do not shoot democratic precepts and legal arguments back and forth at each other in the midst of bullets and other projectiles. But if Hernán Cortés, in Otumba, had recited one of the papal bulls or some fragment of the Fuero Juzgo, he would certainly have come away a more enlightened man" (*Ecos de la batalla*, 280).

Nation and Mockery: The Oppositional Writings of Simón Rodríguez

SUSANA ROTKER

In the years that followed independence, Latin American literati served the power structure by participating in the process of nation building in several significant ways: not only did they design government programs, draft laws, and spread patriotic mottoes, but they fixed the norms of language. But this picture is not as homogeneous as it appears at first glance. It contains a few important fissures, which rarely have received the attention of the few literary studies dedicated to the early nineteenth century. The most noteworthy "irregularity" is Simón Rodríguez.[1]

Rodríguez fit so uneasily in his period that, as he himself declared, he was dismissed as crazy.[2] Likewise, literary historians, aligned with the liberal model that eventually triumphed, preferred to wash their hands of his presence, "normalizing" him by reducing his significance to that of teacher of liberator Simón Bolívar. They then simplified his role by labeling him a Latin American Rousseau or Pestalozzi.[3]

1. Angel Rama's reflections in *La ciudad letrada* (Hanover, N.H.: Ediciones del Norte, 1984) are indispensable for understanding the relationship between the "city of letters" and power. Rama also focuses on Rodríguez's extraordinary contributions. Curiously, the most recent publications about Rodríguez in Venezuela have been works of fiction: Isaac Chocrón, *Clipper; Simón* (Caracas: Alfadil, 1983), and Gregorio Bonmati, *Rodríguez* (Caracas: Fundarte, 1988), both plays; and Arturo Uslar Pietri, *La isla de Róbinson* (Barcelona: Seix Barral, 1987), a novel. Rodríguez appears as a secondary character in another novel, Carlos Fuentes, *La campaña* (Mexico City: Fondo de Cultura Económica, 1990).
2. Rodríguez, *Obras completas*, 2 vols. (Caracas: Universidad Simón Rodríguez, 1975), 1:225, 2:161, 511, 517.
3. These qualifications do not take into account the differences between the projects of these writers and Rodríguez, or the abyss between the European context

Rodríguez's writing may be viewed as an interruption of official discourse, a short circuit that renders evident the distorting machine of ideology. In his texts he espouses the idea that to witness is to denounce the betrayal of the promises of social change that provoked the wars for independence; his conceptualization also means to write in such a way that language itself exposes the saturation of meaning and value commonly employed by the "republic of letters" (2:286). By uncovering and bringing attention to this linguistic manipulation, Rodríguez demonstrates how the republic of letters tried to hegemonically control symbolic order and national subjectivity.

Rodríguez's writing introduces heterogeneity; his representation of society contrasts significantly with the version that was officially imposed. By giving space to another view or, rather, by constructing another discourse in other sectors of reality, he displaces traditional boundaries and definitions of culture, expands the horizon of discussion, and includes in the realm of thought a reality that the official word silenced, saturated, manipulated, and tried to erase. Or, in his

---

and the effervescent reality of the New World. Johann Heinrich Pestalozzi, the eighteenth-century Swiss educational reformer, earned a reputation as a champion of neglected children and founder of an industrial school for the poor. But I would venture that the similarities between Rodríguez and the author of *How Gertrude Teaches Her Children* lie only in their interest in the education of poor children. The differences between them are obvious and can be seen in Rodríguez's *Consejos de amigo dados al Colejio de Latacunga* [Friendly advice given to the Latacunga School] and the texts of Pestalozzi. For example, Rodríguez argued that teachers should be professionals; Pestalozzi, on the other hand, believed that, given a model for education, mothers could reproduce the proper environment at home. See Pestalozzi, *How Gertrude Teaches Her Children: An Attempt to Help Mothers to Teach Their Own Children and an Account of the Method*, ed. Ebenezer Cooke, trans. Lucy E. Holland and Frances C. Turner (Syracuse, N.Y.: Bardeen, 1989); and Pestalozzi, *The Education of Man: Aphorisms* (New York: Philosophical Library, 1951). See also Alonso Rumazo Gonzalez, "Introduction," in Rodríguez, *Obras completas* 1:105–7. Another issue not taken into account is that Rodríguez read Rousseau in Caracas in the eighteenth century, under the peculiar conditions of "cultural translation," a reinvention of meaning and cultural codes or, rather, a transculturation. Regarding the modification of value that could have occurred between a European text read within the restricting frame of colonial Latin American libraries, see Tomás Eloy Martínez and Susana Rotker, prologue to *Historia de la conquista y la población de la provincia de Venezuela*, by José de Oviedo y Baños, ed. Tomás Eloy Martínez (Caracas: Biblioteca Ayacucho, 1992), 1–48.

words, Rodríguez intends "to discover *differences* where the common man sees only *similarities*, and vice versa" (2:207).

Rodríguez's heterologous writing produces a critical reading that does not allow itself to be unconditionally communicated by the written word alone. It breaks with standard typography in a way so surprising and varied that readers must modify their reading habits. To open a text of Rodríguez is to experience, at first glance, the meaning of fissure, of heterogeneity within the literary system. Working almost a century before Apollinaire, Rodríguez constructed his texts around the size of the words, the spaces on the page, and distinct, varied typographies. There are parentheses, brackets, blank spots, italics, capitals, and bold type, a map of meaning that is surprising even today and that must have shocked the reader of the early nineteenth century. Its havoc, its apparent anarchy, its cries and secrets, its need for order in the middle of such originality become akin to a painting of letters, a fresco in black and white of political upheavals, the presence of *caudillos* and their rival interests. Rodríguez's writing style highlights both the marginalization and the social unrest experienced by South America. In these complex countries Rodríguez attempted to put his ideas into practice, failing over and over again because of his refusal to compromise with the established order.

The emphases and repetitions, in conjunction with the distribution of words, are so egregious in Rodríguez's texts that they distance the reader from the printed word. Besides "painting through writing" (2:223), Rodríguez provides the reader with an obvious opportunity to achieve a metatextual reading:

Examínese, en lo escrito hasta aquí,
si hay conexión   en las Ideas y
        {
                en los Pensamientos
y si todo se reune en una *idea jeneral.* (2:159)

[Examine, in the writing up to now,
if there is a relation among the Ideas and
        {

the Thoughts
and if everything is reunited in a *general idea.*]

He directly appeals to the reader to deliberately slow the process of reading, to be aware of its demands, in order to revise and correct the meaning of what has been read. This appeal of *Luces y virtudes sociales* [Lights and social virtues] (1834) is not, of course, the only one in his work; for example, in *El libertador del Mediodía de América y sus compañeros de armas, defendidos por un amigo de la causa social* [The liberator of South America and his comrades at arms, defended by a friend of social causes], composed in 1828, he dedicates more than five pages to "the right of the reader to be judge" (2:207–12).

Rodríguez strives to give new weight to his words, to make them "feel" (2:161). The graphic arrangements mimic the sounds and movements of the mouth; they reproduce on the page the disposition of thought; above all, they attempt to call attention to the meaning of words. "Printed does not mean good," he warns (2:193). Why not? Because, as he explains in *Sociedades americanas* [American societies] (1828), there is a traffic of language that produces an "intermediate class of subjects" in order to "cut off all communication between the people and their representatives," "to shift meaning," "to exalt the people . . . and to take advantage of them in this state" (1:273).

Rodríguez offers as evidence—makes public—an uncomfortable truth veiled by official writings: two or three decades after the proclamation of independence, nothing had been done to change the basis of the system. The privileges of class had not been suppressed, not even in regard to voting, which continued to be an exclusive right of the educated; the landowners and the church kept their property; and colonial discrimination had scarcely lessened for peasants, Indians, and people of African descent, although slavery had been legally abolished.[4] The

4. See José Luis Romero and Luis Alberto Romero, comps., *Pensamiento conservador, 1815–1898* (Caracas: Biblioteca Ayacucho, 1978); José Luis Romero, *Pensamiento político de la emancipación (1790–1825),* 2 vols. (Caracas: Biblioteca Ayacucho, 1986); Ricaurte Soler, *Idea y cuestión nacional latinoamericanas de la independencia a la emergencia del imperialismo* (Mexico City: Siglo XXI, 1980); Arturo Andrés Roig, "Educación para la integración y utopía en el pensamiento de Simón Rodríguez: Romanticismo y reforma pedagógica en América Latina," *Araisa* (Caracas, 1976–82),

enemy of the emancipation movement was no longer Spanish but the "hypocritical republican," the *godos* who embodied the system of privilege inherited from colonialism.[5] The literati, the liberals and conservatives, the centralists and federalists—all had appropriated the language of emancipation equally, accommodating it to their own needs and principles.[6]

Rodríguez denounces "personal freedom and the right to property" as words used "in order to avoid any sort of collaboration for the public good, in order to demand services without retribution and work without compensation, in order to justify inaction as custom, and procedures as law," "in order to convert FORCEFUL SEIZURE into possession," and in order to allow third parties to enjoy "the title of LEGITIMACY (and this legitimacy is a tolerated abuse)" (2:115). Everything turns out to be a manipulation of language: "Oh, writers! Who consult nothing but the fruition of your desires—consult the interest of the cause that you *pretend to defend*" (2:227). Another example illustrates the biases in textual representations of society: "Popular representation, *in books*, is more a sign than a copy; and if it is THE LATTER, it appears as little or nothing: it has the disgrace of almost all *portraits*— to render the original too favorably in some cases and only a little or none at all in others" (2:241).

Faced with this manipulation, Rodríguez insists on modifying traditional attitudes toward reading. He proposes:

LEER, es RESUCITAR IDEAS, SEPULTADAS en el PAPEL:
Cada Palabra es un EPITAFIO
i que, para hacer esa especie de MILAGRO! es menester
conocer los ESPIRITUS de las difuntas,
o tener ESPIRITUS EQUIVALENTES qué subrogarles. (2:29)

161–87; and Beatriz González Stephan, *La historiografía literaria del liberalismo hispanoamericano del siglo XIX* (Havana: Casa de las Américas, 1987).

5. León Rozitchner, "Defensa de Bolívar," in *Los godos, oh los godos! (Simón Rodríguez, o el triunfo de un fracaso ejemplar)* (Unpublished manuscript, Caracas, 1985), 1.

6. On the rhetorical emptiness of the period see my article "Simón Rodríguez: tradición y revolución," in *Homenaje a Angel Rama*, ed. Beatriz González and Javier Lasarte (Caracas: Monte Avila, forthcoming). For an overview see my prologue to *Ensayistas de Nuestra América: Siglo XIX*, vol. 1, ed. Susana Rotker (Buenos Aires: Losada, 1994), 7–45.

[TO READ, is to REVIVE IDEAS, BURIED in PAPER:
Each Word is an EPITAPH
and, in order to produce this nature of MIRACLE! it is necessary
to know the SPIRITS of the dead (words),
or to have EQUIVALENT SPIRITS to substitute for them.]

Rodríguez's obsession with how one reads and especially with how one speaks differs from that of Andrés Bello, for whom orthography should legitimize what is written, making "writing a faithful and secure repository of the law, the arts, the sciences, and all discourses of the learned and wise of all professions."[7] The mention of Bello is not at all by chance: few Latin American writers demonstrate as clearly the rationalizing function of the "city of letters." Bello's work in this area may be noted through his poetry and essays, his formulation of a civil code and grammar, and his prominent position as the first rector of the University of Chile.

Both Bello and Rodríguez were born and spent their formative years in Caracas. They shared exile in Europe and an interest in orthography and education. The young Bolívar was a disciple of both. But while Bello participated fully in normative and "monotheistic" institutions, Rodríguez developed heterologous or "polytheistic" strategies of discourse in order to make the conceptualization of nationhood less exclusive than it had been.[8]

To promote the correct use of grammar, Bello published "Análisis ideológico de los tiempos de la conjugación castellana" [Ideological analysis of tenses in Castilian conjugation] (1841), and *Gramática de la lengua castellana destinada al uso de los americanos* [Grammar of the Castilian language for American use] (1847), hoping to shift allegiance from Nebrija's Latin grammar, a text of colonial education. Bello's idea, shared by the Mexican Fray Servando Teresa de Mier, the Argentine Domingo F. Sarmiento, and Rodríguez himself, was to simplify the alphabet by reducing the number of letters to equal the num-

7. Bello, *Obra literaria*, ed. Pedro Grases (Caracas: Biblioteca Ayacucho, 1979), 460.
8. Michel de Certeau, *The Practice of Everyday Life*, trans. Steven Rendall (Berkeley: University of California Press, 1988), 48.

ber of sounds in the spoken language.[9] The object was to avoid "incoherent babbling" (1:266) or "babelization" in order to preserve "the language of our fathers in its purity, as a providential means of communication and a fraternal link among the various nations of Spanish origin strewn across two continents" (Bello, 390–1, 557).

Bello's assertions regarding orthography, law, and purity are quite distinct from Rodríguez's. For instance, Rodríguez states:

> Un signo para cada articulación . . . y siempre el mismo . . . sería preferible á la profusión de caracteres que lucen en la portada de un libro. Letras cuadradas y redondas, con cola, con pelos y con dientes, unas acostadas y otras en pié, son buenas para ejercitar el buril, no los ojos. Si se *limpiase* el alfabeto, podría *fijarse*, y ya fijo, se conservaría invariable: entonces tendría el esplendor de la claridad. (1:266)

> [A sign for each articulation . . . and always the same one . . would be preferable to a profusion of characters that shine on the cover of a book. Letters, squared and round, with tails, with hair and teeth, some lying down, others on foot, these are good for exercising a burin, but not for the eyes. If the alphabet were *cleaned*, it could be *fixed*, and once fixed, it would be preserved without variation: then it would be splendidly clear.]

The gesture of writing is antagonistic. In Bello one reads the voice of institution and authority, a decree from above to those below; in Rodríguez one perceives humor and horizontal irreverence toward his equals. Bello dictates in order to systematize grammar as a foundation for national power;[10] Rodríguez also wants to create a system, but only in order to reformulate the relations of power and to denounce corruption. Bello believes that grammarians were called on to record the language of "the civilized" and therefore to avoid "the scurrilous rant-

9. Bello's efforts to define a distinct grammar failed. In the 1880s the nations of Latin America officially adopted the norms of the Real Academia Española de la Lengua (Spanish-Language Royal Academy).
10. See N. Poulantzas, *Estado, poder y socialismo*, trans. F. Claudin (Mexico City: Siglo XXI, 1979).

ing and idioms of the rabble" (390). Rodríguez suggests, in contrast, that *rabble* is a "word . . . [that] means *insignificant* populace or *insignificant* people . . . *by extension contemptible people*" and that "it is not man that is contemptible but his IGNORANCE." Therefore it is necessary to instruct the rabble (2:290–1).

Bello, a purist, eventually accepted the introduction of neologisms, because "the prodigious advance of the arts and sciences, the diffusion of intellectual culture, and political revolutions *call each day for new signs to express new ideas.*" His only objection was to the adoption of words that either were unnecessary or demonstrated "affectation or poor taste" (Bello, 557; my emphasis). Bello's example reveals very well the mechanics of lettered discourse; it represents only one side of reality. Rodríguez unmasks these strategies of nominalization: "Everywhere one observes political schools teaching how to give other names to the same things and attempting to formulate, in a different style, the commands of days gone by. *The voices are new, in effect, and things seem to have changed as well; but in reality . . . the plan has not varied*" (1:267; my emphasis).

In a noteworthy text, Rodríguez reflects on the relations between language and power in order to disrupt, denounce, and provoke the status quo. In the "Prodrome" of *Sociedades americanas* he forms two parallel columns, one titled "Language" and the other "Government." A national language, Rodíguez affirms, exists so that

all citizens
articulate it, sing it, construct it, and write it
in the same way.

On the side he traces the equivalent concept as it relates to the art of governing and later compares syntax with discipline (1:265). He proposes on the same page:

[La lengua]	[El gobierno]
Parece que la lengua no necesita de letras—que como se forma puede conservarse—por tanto, que la *economía de la palabra* está en la boca.	Parece que gobernar es dar órdenes solamente—que como se forman los Gobiernos pueden conservarse—por tanto, que la ciencia del Gobierno consiste en *tener sumiso al que obedece.*

Piénsese en las funciones de la Escritura, y se conocerá la importancia de la Ortografía.

Todo lo que se confía á la tradición oral, se arriesga.

Piénsese en el verdadero espíritu de las funciones gubernativas, y se verá cuales son los deberes del Gobierno.

Confiar la suerte de los pueblos al parecer de uno ó de muchos Lejisladores, traidos por el acaso á la lejislatura, es arriesgar la felicidad pública.

[Language
It seems that language does not need letters—so that its form can be preserved—therefore, the *economy of the word* resides in the mouth.

Think about the function of Writing, and there you will find the importance of Orthography.

Everything that is entrusted to the oral tradition is risked.]

[Government
It seems that to govern is to give orders only—so that the form of governments can be maintained—therefore, the science of government consists in submission that leads to obedience.

Think about the true spirit of government functions, and you will see what are the obligations of the Government.

To trust that the destiny of the people will be given over to one or many Legislators, brought by chance to the legislature, is to jeopardize public happiness.]

Concerned about the "art of drawing Republics," Rodríguez clearly distinguishes and distances himself from Bello and the learned. "Couldn't they form new laws and govern themselves accordingly?" he asks, and then proposes: "Observing the disposition of the natives, couldn't they succeed in giving them a government that corresponds to them? . . . Pitting them against themselves . . . will not achieve anything" (1:26). His call for change produced an echo half a century later, when José Martí demanded in "Our America" that the government cease imposing foreign political systems and that it learn the needs of its own reality. Rodríguez has no doubts, creating "an *Orthological* orthography, i.e., founded in the mouth" and, at the same time, "An *Ethological* government founded on *customs*," so that all those that speak it may enjoy "social goods" (1:269).

In the notions of "orthology" and "ethology" Rodríguez's divorce from the ideas of Bello becomes clear once again. The idea of founding republics according to the customs of each particular place has little to do with the concrete imposition of neocolonial molds.[11] The Latin American republics called themselves "new" and emancipated, but they adopted schematic molds of modernity and progress that could neither resolve internal conflicts nor construct societies free of a highly oppressive poverty level. Rodríguez repeats over and over again that "America does not have to SUBMISSIVELY imitate; it must be . . . ORIGINAL" (2:16).

The discourse of the nineteenth century literati characterizes itself by dividing reality between civilization and barbarism, which actually copies the European concept of civilization. Juan Bautista Alberdi maintains, in *Bases y puntos de partida para la organización política de la República Argentina* [Basis and points of departure for political organization in the Republic of Argentina] (1852), that immigrants, industrial habits, and the practice of civilization should be brought over from Europe. Sarmiento, like Bello, believed that the "barbarians" were groups of drunkards, savage robbers, and attackers "from whom the world should be liberated," and that the "filthy Indians" were "a submissive prehistoric race."[12] Moreover, the *gauchos* were human only because of their blood.[13] For Sarmiento, as for many educated leaders of the nineteenth century, the health of the republic depended on the ability of the European population to develop a white, urban society, as he explains in *Facundo: Civilización y barbarie* [Facundo: Civilization and barbarism] (1845). In contrast, Rodríguez wants

11. See Partha Chatterjee, *Nationalist Thought and the Colonial World: A Derivative Discourse?* (London: Zed Books for the United Nations University, 1986).
12. David A. Brading, *Orbe indiano: De la monarquía católica a la república criolla, 1492–1867*, trans. J. J. Utrilla (Mexico City: Fondo de Cultura Económica, 1991), 674.
13. Quoted in Enrique Anderson Imbert, *Genio y figura de Sarmiento* (Buenos Aires: Eudeba, 1967), 122.

COLONIZAR el país con . . .
SUS PROPIOS HABITANTES
   y para tener
COLONOS DECENTES
INSTRUIRLOS en la niñez. (2:113)

[TO COLONIZE the country with . . .
its own INHABITANTS
   and, in order to have
DECENT COLONISTS,
INSTRUCT THEM in childhood.]

Who are "its own INHABITANTS"? In *El libertador del Mediodía de América* he elaborates: "Latin American families are composed of indigenous people of *many colors*, due to the mix with Europeans and Africans" (1:256). In *Sociedades americanas* he becomes even more explicit about "who we are":

Huasos, Chinos i Bárbaros
Gauchos, Cholos i Huachinangos
Negros, Prietos i Jentiles
Serranos, Calentanos, Indíjenas
Jente de Color i de Ruana
Morenos, Mulatos i Zambos
Blancos porfiados i Patas amarillas
   i una CHUSMA de Cruzados
Tercerones, Cuarterones, Quinterones
   i Salta-atrás
   que hace, como en botánica,
   una familia de CRIPTOGAMOS. (1:320)[14]

[Rustics, Chinese and Barbarians
Gauchos, Half-breeds and Huachinangos
Negroes, Blackish and Gentiles
Highlanders, Coastals, Indians
People of Color and of Ponchos

14. See Thomas M. Stephen, *Dictionary of Latin American Racial Ethnic Terminology* (Gainesville: University Press of Florida, 1989).

Browns, Mulattoes and Knock-kneeds
Stubborn Whites and Yellow Feet
    and a CREW of Crossbreeds
Terceroons, Quadroons, Quintroons
    and Throwbacks
    that make, like in botany,
    a family of CRYPTOGAMS.]

The possibility of representing society is, then, completely distinct
in Rodríguez's work. Not only does he embrace the diverse Latin
American races, but in his playful pride he delights in enumerating
their diversity. He even refers to himself as "Don Simón the Zambo"
(the offspring of a black and an Indian) (2:534), assuming a condemned identity that was at the bottom of the social hierarchy at the
time.

All of Rodríguez's work points toward heterogeneity in writing.
In addition, he commits the crime of writing without the contextual
and symbolic complicity common in the work of the literati. Even
though his readership was limited and, consequently, easy to reach,
Rodríguez refused to collaborate with other authors who implied that
writing/reading was an act among equals. Brown and Gilman describe
"the solidarity of language": writing reveals like-mindedness or similar
dispositions between author and reader.[15] In the first half of the nineteenth century, writing was for a society of equals, white lettered bourgeoisie or oligarchy of diverse political affinity that recognized their
own reflection in this form and style of writing; Rodríguez broke these
codes and exposed the complicitous winks between the members of
his class.

In a call rarely heard in the literary history of his time, Rodríguez
demands, "GIVE ME YOUR POOR CHILDREN, your abandoned, your
rough, those whom no one can care for, to educate" (1:313).[16] "GIVE
ME" indicates his place of enunciation, which is both inclusive and

15. Brown and Gilman, "The Pronouns and Power and Solidarity," in *Language and
Social Context*, ed. P. P. Giglioli (Harmondsworth: Penguin, 1972), chap. 12.
16. This declaration is similar to the famous poem by Emma Lazarus, "The New
Colossus," inscribed in 1886 inside the base of the Statue of Liberty, in New York
Harbor. "Give me your tired, your poor, your huddled masses . . ." The coincidence
in writing, many miles and years away, was brought to my attention by Margo Persin.

exclusive: he addresses his equals and gives an order, yet he separates himself from the "we" to accuse and condemn an implied "you" for having abandoned their poor.

Rodríguez would never begin by saying, like Bello, "Divine Poetry . . ." He occupies the space in between, associated with neither the elite nor the abandoned masses. He furthers the remapping of social spaces as he traces a representation of the nation's "own inhabitants" in an increasingly irreverent stance. He reworks the divisions that organize and underlie culture by interrupting the social and ethnic boundaries of culture, forming a new space of interaction. Likewise, not only does he request that the schools teach Quechua and Spanish, but he also demands that schools be established for the Indians, because "from the WHITES / little or nothing can be expected" (2:6).

In *Consejos de amigo dados al Colejio de Latacunga,* written in 1845 and published posthumously, Rodríguez carries to an extreme his belief that writing should introduce into the configuration of nationhood another space where the central problem becomes the case of the poor and not the marginalization of racial groups. In the text he constructs a parody of popular language that is, at the same time, a ferocious social satire. In contrast with Bello, who attributes the perfection of spoken language to a specific class, Rodríguez perceives the imperfection of all social classes in this regard. The upper and middle classes are no better than the beggars: ignorance is their common state. Parodic dialogues interrupt the flow of the text: one takes place between the wife of a teacher and girls who are shopping in an extavern (2:6); another, between an old woman and a military man (2:7). Beyond the dialogue, Rodríguez uses a playful onomatopoeic imitation of a chorus of children learning to read, write, and memorize arithmetic by repetition. He writes, for example, that they shout their addition and multiplication tables:

doj vej doj + cuatr.
trej vej sis + disioch
    Si multiplican
        dicen . . .
och po diej + ochent
      si restan

quien de sinc, sin + nás
   si dividen
en nueb siet—unn—i quean doj. [2:28]

[too x too, for
t'ree x sigs, ateteen
   If they multiply
      they cry . . .
ate tims tin, atey
   if you try
fife - fife = ziro
   if they divide
nayne by sevin, there's won and too remain.]

Later Rodríguez pokes fun at those who "babble Latin with their native tongue" (2:37) and derides a female school director because she lacks cultural refinement (2:38). He reflects on the "barbarisms and solecisms" of the young boys and girls, and then he includes a list of 156 popular expressions and their "correct" equivalents (2:38–41). Still not content, he attacks doctors, telling the story of one who used to say:

> DOLDRA. / Le advirtió un Amigo que, el verbo DOLER no es irregular en el futuro, / como lo son PODER, VENIR, SALIR, i otros, / i su respuesta fué = / "He conocido hombres MUI SABIOS! i siempre les he óido decir . . . / DOLDRá." / El Amigo le constestó = "Pues, yo he estado en varios puntos de la España, i ni en la hez / del Pueblo he oído tal palabra."/ "¿Y, qué tenemos nosotros qué ver con la España? para eso somos / INDEPENDIENTES" (fue su descargo)/ El Amigo, encojiendo los hombros, le dijo— . . . "Yo no sabía que la / Lengua Española, en América, hubiese VUELTO CASACA, junto con los / INSURGENTES, i que DOLER fuese uno de los CABECILLAS." (2:43)

> [DOLDRA. / He warned a Friend that the verb DOLER is not irregular in the future, / as are the verbs PODER, VENIR, SALIR, along with others / and his response was = / "I've known VERY WISE men! and I've always heard them say / DOLDRá."/ The Friend

responded = "Well, I have been in various places in Spain, and not even from the scum / of the people have I heard such a word." / "So, what do we have to do with Spain? We are / INDE-PENDENT" (was his counter) / The Friend, shrugging his shoulders, said— . . . "I didn't know that the / Spanish Language, in America, had BECOME A TURNCOAT, together with the INSURGENTS, and that DOLER was one of its RINGLEADERS."]

As the text proceeds, his humor becomes more and more corrosive. When addressing himself to potential critics of his project to have the entire population contribute a *real* a year for education, he uses "correct" language to refer to the clerics, friars, monks, and "GENEROUS RICH" (2:55–6). He anticipates their complaints and describes a scene including a beggar of African descent (which allows him to clarify that "Negroes have a soul in their bodies") and an "exemplary neighbor who is honorable, God-fearing, etc.," nostalgic for the old school, where he learned to recite the prayers of the mass (2:57–8). The satire is biting and very gleeful, but, more important, most sentences are understandable only when read out loud. Thus the reader participates in the orality that the text emulates.

Rodríguez endeavors to do "something for the poor people who have borne the cost of independence through their bodies, their goods . . . or through the meat or the wool of their sheep . . . those who are less free than they were before" (1:226). The failure of his project ought to lead us to consider an even greater issue: the nation's inability to form citizens and produce egalitarian and democratic societies. Regarding its status as a project for Latin America, it is as important today as it was in Rodríguez's time. As Angel Rama states, the project has been preserved "as though it were still waiting for its actualization"(64). What cannot be considered a failure are the works themselves and their heterologous writing, which, to use an allegory from the Enlightenment, throw new light on the lengthy shadows cast by the founding texts of Latin America.

Melodrama, Sex, and Nation in
Latin America's *Fin de Siglo*

FRANCINE MASIELLO

Gossip and public opinion come to play a distinguished role in Latin American narrative of the last *fin de siglo*. The gossip columnist, the reporter, and the intrusive neighbor take a central place in fiction to challenge established truths; they also question the uses of language in relation to the authority of the state. Recall, for example, the canonical novels of the late nineteenth century—*La bolsa*, by Julián Martel; *La charca*, by Manuel Zeno Gandía; *Pot pourri*, by Eugenio Cambaceres; *Oasis en la vida*, by Juana Manuela Gorriti— in which gossip alters the course of events and structures the major aspects of plot. It offers yet another way to classify private life, to name events and feelings, to set society in order. Moreover, it projects the anxieties of the times and allows individuals to speculate on the identities and to publicize the secrets of their neighbors. At the same time, gossip confuses reality and fiction; it disables the registers with which we earlier viewed modern culture and expands categories of analysis to accommodate new information. The voice of the intermediary also announces a tension between chaos and order insofar as it insinuates doubt regarding the identity of citizen subjects. Equally important, it depends for its growth on such topics as sex, crime, and perversion to confront passions and the complexity of social life.

Josefina Ludmer has observed, with respect to *gauchesca* literature, that the delinquent serves to organize the state from beyond.[1] From a post on society's edge, the criminal defines the boundaries of the state

1. Ludmer, *El género gauchesco: Un tratado sobre la patria* (Buenos Aires: Sudamericana, 1988).

and strengthens the metropolitan center. In the same way, urban delinquents of the last decades of the nineteenth century taught by negative example. As wayward subjects, the prostitute, the thief, the pervert, and the dandy formed part of the social imagination of the times. But they also suggested that delinquency was everywhere to be found; even beneath the mask of the good bourgeois lay a delinquent *in potentia*. It was then the task of the gossipmonger and journalist to seek out these social misfits and even to rip off, once and for all, the mask of protection offered to the *gente decente*.

Late-nineteenth-century journalism is densely seeded with such reports, which contribute to the carnavalesque atmosphere of the period. Writers and journalists lamented the absence of public morality, the rise of social crimes, and the suspicious character of any figure who resisted the new state order; stories of double lives fascinated readers and reminded them of nearby transgressions. By the 1870s, coincidentally with general efforts to modernize Latin America, journalists pressed with increasing vigor for data about the behavior of the masses and about their private lives. By doing so, they called attention to the fragility of the social edifice and the failure of the state to control aberrance.

The zones of excess were always articulated as hybrid or marginal areas that confused delinquency and repressed desire. Latin American writers thus began to open their texts to representations of neurosis and hysteria; they studied sex crimes, deviation, and the corruption of home and society. Through rudimentary psychological inquiries, intellectuals tried to make sense of divergent human experience, while criminology was legitimated as a field on which to support the modern state.

In Argentina, for example, Krafft-Ebing's studies of crimes of passion were eagerly received in Spanish translation. Even José Ramos Mejía, in *Las neurosis de los hombres célebres* (1878), attempted to describe Latin American history in terms of the interior lives of important figures.[2] Rosas, Aldao, Monteagudo, Dr. Francia, Admiral Brown entered Ramos Mejía's book as hysterics driven to seek power by their deliria. In other words, the politics of the South were explained by psycho-

2. Ramos Mejía, *Las neurosis de los hombres célebres en la historia argentina*, 2d ed. (Buenos Aires: L. J. Rosso, 1932).

biography. Equally important, social events were correlated to the unchartable nature of desire. José Asunción Silva's hero of *De sobremesa* (1896) constantly posed the question "¿Qué es la vida real?" [What is real life?], while Clorinda Matto de Turner, in her novel *Herencia* (1895), insisted that public life and desire were hopelessly intertwined. Angel Rama rightly observes that "desire contaminated the totality of operations that shaped the social milieu" of the late nineteenth century.[3] Explosions, excess, irrepressibility, crossovers of social identities: *fin de siglo* literature was a sailor's never-learned lesson about the unfathomable sea.

In these pages I want to underscore the narrative excess that such inquiries produced in literature, in newspapers, and in the gossip columns of the period and then to explore their common bond of melodrama. I focus on melodrama as a way to link the representation of chaos and order in modern life. It plays with appearances and deceptions; it juxtaposes the superficiality of the visible world with the realm of feelings; and it insists on the perversity of gender relations as the sine qua non of fiction and the language of the state. In addition, melodrama links the crisis of modernity with the irrecuperable nature of desire and provokes an inquiry into the very limits of representation. Thus it embraces the conflicts of excess and order in late-nineteenth-century culture.

As such, it is impossible to narrate the *fin de siglo* without the structures of melodrama, whose voice is found in public opinion and gossip. To develop my hypothesis, I want first to review a newspaper account, typical of the interests of the times, and then several *fin de siglo* novels to signal melodrama as the trope that joins periodical and literary discourses and the emerging crisis of individual subjectivities in relation to the modern state.

"Su Monstruosidad Espanta" [His Monstrosity Inspires Fear]

I begin with a story published in 1883 in *Las calamidades de Buenos Aires*, a small Argentine newspaper whose subtitle *Diario viril* [Virile

3. Rama, *Las máscaras democráticas del modernismo* (Montevideo: Fundación Angel Rama, 1985), 86.

daily], brings all its yellow-press efforts together under the sign of gender. On the one hand, the newspaper occupies the space of the masculine, denouncing the effeminate state; on the other hand, it assumes the task of exposing sexual delinquency throughout Buenos Aires. *Las calamidades de Buenos Aires* thus offers some notable stories about urban sex crimes: an assistant police chief rapes a nine-year-old boy with the help of a female go-between; a prostitute steals from hotel guests; a homosexual judge stages a travesty of justice. Omnipresent homophobia and misogyny underlie the melodramatic narrative strategies of the yellow press. Together, they build a paradigm for Latin American fiction of the time.

Melodrama has been described by its linguistic extravagance in the field of realist representation.[4] In nineteenth-century fiction, it inserts a hyperbolic register into discourse. Because of its extreme bipolarity, it discovers the limits of language and marks the very essence of theatricality. As melodrama addresses a mass public, moreover, it shakes the world of feelings, awakens the audience's taste for horror and exploits its passion for violence, and opposes criminal and victim. Melodramatic inflections of the yellow press also link state corruption to horror.

One serialized tale covered for many months is about Zenon Lista, the assistant chief of police accused of raping the nine-year-old son of Italian immigrants. From the start the reporter assumes a hyperbolic tone. Exoticism, delinquency, and the revelatory power of the journalist frame the story, and an important theme runs its length: what name fits the crime? How might we classify it within the ordinary limits of language? From the start, then, a gap detected between reason and classification, on the one hand, and our immediate perceptions, on the other, leads us to speculate on ways to *feel* or experience the crime while giving it a name. Analytic and sensory reactions are drawn together; the nature of the crime demands both an intellectual and a physical response from the reader. Indeed, the story's novelty may well lie in its insistence on the physiological; through a visceral

4. See especially Peter Brooks, *The Melodramatic Imagination: Balzac, Henry James, Melodrama, and the Mode of Excess* (New Haven, Conn.: Yale University Press, 1976); and Christopher Prendergast, *Balzac: Fiction and Melodrama* (London: Edward Arnold, 1978).

response to horror, readers might come to comprehend evil.[5] Of
course, within the positivist package of late-nineteenth-century Argentina, all moral affirmations were defended through concrete, experiential responses. Hence a game of surface operations prevails; first,
the immediacy of response is privileged in narration, and only later
are readers expected to supply a proper interpretation of what has
been seen.

Time and again, the journalist asks how the crime can be understood. Which categories of analysis can be used to inscribe its events?
The writer even invokes Edgar Allan Poe to organize our conceptual
framework:

> Edgardo Poe, el sublime borracho Edgardo Poe pudo haber apu-
> rado su fantasía para describir escenas tenebrosas y amalgamadas
> de horror, cuando hechos inverosímiles cuya misma inverosimil-
> itud manifestaba la potencia extraordinaria de su embotada intel-
> igencia.
>
> Pero Edgardo Poe no pudo encontrarse jamás con un Zenon
> Lista y con un Luis de Mare, porque entonces hubiera escrito la
> novela inmortal del más grande de los crímenes. Y no ha encon-
> trado la personificación de estas dos individualidades, horrorosa
> la una y angelical la otra, porque los crímenes de la magnitud de
> que nuestros lectores conocen son un verdadero aborto entre los
> que han conmovido a las sociedades por medio de las mas fuerte
> sacudidas.[6]

[Edgar Poe, that sublime drunk Edgar Poe, was able to accelerate
his fantasy of darkness and horror with improbable events whose
very unlikelihood reveals the extraordinary powers of his average
intelligence.

But Edgar Poe never met up with a Zenon Lista or a Luis de
Mare, because if he had he would have written the immortal

5. For an excellent discussion of sensationalist literature and the centrality of physiological reader response see D. A. Miller, *The Novel and the Police* (Berkeley: University of California Press, 1988), esp. *"Cage aux Folles*: Sensation and Gender in Wilkie
Collins's *The Woman in White"* (146–91).
6. "Luis de Mare: La víctima del asesino Zenon Lista: Horror y lágrimas," in *Las
calamidades de Buenos Aires: Diario viril,* 15 March 1883, 3. My translations.

novel of the greatest of crimes. He never met these personalities
—one awful, the other angelic—because crimes of the magni-
tude that our readers know are freakish even among those societies that have known great cataclysms.]

The comparison of terror between cultures suggests that this crime
could not be repeated beyond the Latin American circuit. In effect, as
Sylvia Molloy and Oscar Montero have noted, crimes of sexuality are
valued as a way to confirm the originality of Latin America.[7]

Once private experience is beheld by a third party, it generates a
political tension of its own. After all, who is the witness here? Not simply the reporter but also the prostitute, Cristina Almeyda; the two com-
pete for the narrative space to produce their own stories and for the
power of representation before the reading public. Journalist and
prostitute take over the sentimental realm; in place of the republican
mother, so frequently evoked in nineteenth-century fiction, we are left
with the evil woman, an accomplice.[8] Later, however, even Almeyda is
exiled from the discourse and denounced for her lies by the reporter.
In effect, he, the carrier of public opinion, intervenes as the protective, good mother, while the child's father tells the story with "tears
and a voice filled with horror" (3). Both home and state are sites
where traditional representations of gender are inverted: the father
fulfills domestic obligations, the reporter provides a supportive voice,
yet the assistant police chief, as a representative of the state, violates
the child. As a unit, they expel all women from the discursive network.
The politics of domesticity are usurped by the state and by public
opinion.

Through its titillating effect, the story brings us remarkably close to
pornography; at the same time, it demands the response of the reader

7. Molloy, "Too Wilde for Comfort: Desire and Ideology in Fin-de-Siècle Spanish
America," *Social Text*, nos. 31–2 (1992): 187–201; Montero, "Before the Parade
Passes By: Latino Queers and National Identity," *Radical America* 24 (1990): 15–26.
8. In *Between Civilization and Barbarism: Women, Nation, and Literary Culture in Modern
Argentina* (Lincoln: University of Nebraska Press, 1992), I elaborate on the importance of republican motherhood in early-nineteenth-century Argentina and argue
that 1880 (the moment of state consolidation, the rise of consumer culture, and
increased attention to units of public exchange) marks a crucial transition in the discourse on gender and the representation of women. After 1880 the prostitute and
the female criminal emerge as protagonistic figures in Argentine literature.

to bring about social justice. The dramatic force of the tale, owing to its revelatory tone and emphasis on sensationalism, ushers us into the realm of melodrama. Thus we learn the tragedy of the victim, the poor child, the son of immigrants, who will never reach adulthood. A pen-and-ink portrait helps us visualize his innocence and pain. Finally, although the text tracks Lista's aggressions, his crime still refuses definition; neither reporter nor father and son can tell what happened.

Toward the end, the narration contrasts private and public lives to condemn the corruption of the state:

> En la vida privada del hombre hay cosas que no pueden descubrirse sin que la hediodez que despiden asfixie al imprudente que pretendiera hacerlo; pero cuando esas cosas o esos hechos ultrajasen los caracteres de la vida privada para ir a afectar al hombre público y a las instituciones, no hay más remedio que levantar el velo, volver la cabeza, y sacudir el latigazo que ha de convertirse en freno más tarde para la reproducción de esos y otros hechos escándalos y deprimentes.

> [In the private life of man, there are things that cannot be revealed without exposing the observer to an asphyxiating stench; but when these events surpass the limits of private life to affect public figures and institutions, there is no solution but to lift the veil, turn one's head toward the crime, and crack the whip that will later stop the reproduction of these and other depressing scandals.][9]

"Lift the veil"; expose the most scandalous details of domesticity; invade private lives to denounce what is seen in them; exercise social justice on the sexualized body: such projects inform the melodramatic text produced during Latin America's *fin de siglo*.

"Levantar el Velo" [Lifting the Veil]

I have cited this newspaper account to suggest the importance to turn-of-the-century society of melodrama, which organizes all inquiries

9. "Asuntos asquerosos: Otros grandes escándalos," in *Las calamidades de Buenos Aires: Diario viril*, 11 February 1883, 3.

about the conflict of public and private lives while bringing order to
the emergent social body. But melodrama also dominates the so-
called high culture of the late nineteenth century. Literary texts often
refer to sex crimes to underscore the corruption of national values.
Passions disturb progress; decadence undermines public order. Moreover, melodrama projects an obsession, among elites, for the emergence of mass culture; by always minding the presence of new populations, the writer finally resorts to the literary form destined for
them. *Amistad funesta*, by José Martí; the corpus of fiction by Eugenio Cambaceres; the detective series by Luis Varela; the naturalist
fiction of Clorinda Matto de Turner; the novels of Mercedes Cabello
de Carbonera: all take on the topic of private transgressions set
against the rise of the modern state. They tell of social climbers, of
the attempted founding of a new social order, and explicitly link
sexual desire to the failings of Latin America. Their authors call on
the uses of gossip, the power of social reporters, or the friendly *causerie
et débat* that sets the stage for public morality and condemnation.

I would venture to say that the corpus of late-nineteenth-century
fiction is based on "horror and tears." In *Amistad funesta* (1885), his
only novel, Martí describes how jealousy and passion among the traditional social classes challenge progress in Latin America.[10] Before
the retrograde vision of a provincial Central American oligarchy, the
noble plan of Juan Jérez to found righteous nations ultimately stalls.
The excess of passion—the very basis of melodrama—is generated
by the women of the novel: Lucía Jérez, promised in marriage to
Juan, her cousin, and her friend Ana, are both seen as inimical to
Juan's liberal project. Hypersensitive, devoted to art and gossip, Lucía
and Ana are joined in what Martí suggests is an unholy, erotic alliance. In the end Juan's plan fails because of Lucía's jealousy. Fearful
that he will devote his attentions to another woman, she enlists an
Indian to provide a weapon to murder her rival. Then Juan disappears, possibly murdered, and Lucía falls into Ana's arms.

Thus Martí announces the inability of family romance to structure a narrative of progress and also exposes a range of sentiments
and gestures inadmissible in a future republic: "Aquí todo es pecado;
contra la naturaleza" [Here sin abounds, against nature] (49). Like

10. Martí, *Amistad funesta* (Mexico City: Novaro-México, 1958).

the chronicles of *Las calamidades de Buenos Aires*, Martí observes that America indulges a preference for perversion. The women in his novel insert a register of expression beyond liberal control; not only do they reveal their passion for each other, but they also rely on the complicity of subaltern groups to get their way. In this double schema, domesticity confronts progress, and to shape the conflict, Martí turns to melodrama.

It has been said that the fundamental condition of the novel is its defense of privacy. One could argue also that the reader's private space and the private lives of characters are constantly interchanged in the reading systems proposed by fiction. Nevertheless, in late-nineteenth-century Latin American literature the private life is feared; characters set out to spy on its workings and to revile uncommon behavior. Accordingly, different registers meet violently; they force an encounter between liberty and spectacle, private life and public denunciation.

Not all literary texts, however, defend the voyeur's mission. Against Martí's project, in which passion must be controlled, other writers use melodrama to expose the malfeasance of meddlers. In Cabello de Carbonera's *Blanca sol* (1889), for example, the subversive nature of gossip is condemned.[11] The vox populi generates its own kind of horror, fragmenting the social whole that dominates the *fin de siglo*. Rumor and gossip, insofar as they give name to the manifestations of desire, inaugurate fantasies of adultery and crime.

In *Blanca sol* the eponymous heroine, untutored in ethical matters, yields to evil suggestions and falls into sin. The author sympathetically describes her as the helpless victim of slander. Yet at the close of the novel, in line with the principles of melodrama that always mark the overlapping of formerly separate lives, Blanca Sol indulges public speculation about her morality by turning to prostitution as a means of survival.

Cabello de Carbonera shows that the language of the gossip-monger or the newspaper reporters in her novel is simply incommensurate with daily experience. By equating public perception and language with deformations of reality, she opens an investigation into the cataloging of knowledge. She criticizes dictionary labels assigned to

11. Cabello de Carbonera, *Blanca sol* (Lima: Carlos Prince, 1889).

events, decries the bourgeois desire to define privilege with titles of nobility, and exposes lineages and identities founded on confected documentation or accumulated possessions and wealth. Most important, she explains that categories of knowledge cannot circumscribe desire.

What conclusions can be drawn from these observations? How might the cultural forms of *fin de siglo* Latin America be rethought? First, sexuality as a metaphor is necessary for shaping the ideological systems of both the novel and the state. Nevertheless, the Freudian family romance does not provide a paradigm for action, nor are gendered exchanges to be read as allegories of nation; instead, the state metaphorical system depends on images of perversion and takes definition (by analogy or opposition) before scandal. Second, the *fin de siglo* demands classification of all human knowledge; the catalog prevails as a hallmark of the times. Indeed, in Latin America's late-nineteenth-century literature, in which naturalism and *modernista* movements are represented as antithetical, intellectuals in both camps express the anxiety to name and shape new experiences and to discuss the details of private life in terms of excessive, unrepressed passions. In literature and the press, the struggle to open the registers of language is assumed by the reporter and the intrusive neighbor as shapers of public opinion and observers of progress. Third, to construct a narrative of late-nineteenth-century experience, intellectuals rely on an aesthetic juxtaposition of forcefully opposed visions; hyberbolic views of good and evil, of surface details and sentiments, clash on public and private agendas. Melodramatic form is invoked to describe bipolar worlds and, finally, to delineate the contradictory forces that result when individuals and public opinion face off. The texts examined above suggest different ways to consider the formation of a Latin American social community in the late nineteenth century. Using the tropes of confused identities, deception, and multiple lies, the authors of the *fin de siglo* investigate excess and try to lift the veil from citizens and their unnamed desires.

Italian Opera in Early National Mexico

NANCY VOGELEY

Twelve years after Gioacchino Rossini's opera *Mahometto II* had its pre-
miere in Naples, it was performed in full company in Mexico City. The
event, on 15 June 1832, saw the same tenor entertaining in the former
Spanish colony who had sung in Europe; the production was part of a
series, begun the year before at the invitation of the Mexican government, to introduce Italian grand opera into the new nation.[1]

Cultural importation seems to have been a calculated plan on the
part of the regime in power at the moment. Vicente Guerrero, a popular general in the independence war and former president, had
just been assassinated (through plotting by the new leaders, who had
resented being governed by the mixed-blood son of a peasant); it
appears that the arrival of opera was intended to divert attention from
the deed. The government's "civilizing mission," its enlightened concern for peacetime activities after the war with Spain had ended in
1821, was thereby publicized. Music suggested cultivated taste and the
movement of the heart of free people. But its business signaled a
return to law and order as citizens were reassured that they could venture out at night to attend the theater; supposedly, factional warfare
was over.

Most important, this variety of drama, sung in Italian by real Ital-

---

1. See Ramón Pulido Granata, *La tradición operística en la Ciudad de México (siglo XIX)*
(Mexico City: Secretaría de Educación Pública, 1970); José Octavio and Mónica
Escobedo, *Dos siglos de ópera en México*, 2 vols. (Mexico City: Secretaría de Educación
Pública, 1988); Enrique de Olavarría y Ferrari, *Reseña histórica del teatro en México,
1538–1911*, 3d ed. (Mexico City: Editorial Porrúa, 1961); and Luis Reyes de la Maza,
comp., *El teatro en México durante la Independencia (1810–1839)* (Mexico City: Universidad Nacional Autónoma de México, 1969).

ians, was intended to be an improvement over Spanish theater, which Mexico had received during the colonial years. That theater, dating from Spain's Golden Age, was now regarded as too marvelous, too religious; more recent theater, following French neoclassical aesthetics, was thought tediously moralistic. But Italian theater seemed worldly and political—just the entertainment form to teach good lessons for success in international exchange.

Opera, which had replaced courtly pageants and masques in European capitals, communicated openness and cosmopolitanism. The frivolity and sexual play of the opera buffa and the unrestrained passion and often violent criminality of the tragedies would never have been tolerated by the Spanish censors; now that that cultural monopoly was ended, however, Mexicans were free to experience the cultures of other European nations. By patronizing the company of a famous Roman (Filippo Galli), the Mexican government attracted the attention of the civilized world; the relocation of a group of primarily Italian singers and musicians to Mexico was widely commented on as the first such happening in the New World.

From 1831 to 1835, when the Italian company remained in Mexico, a new class of traders and merchants, whose power was tied to England and the United States, attempted to gain control of the state. Although in the ascendancy since the 1820s, they were at odds with the old elite, who had intermarried with the Spanish aristocracy and, after the order of 1828–29 had expelled all Spaniards born in Spain, stayed on in Mexico as Spanish loyalists. Still powerful, they drew their wealth from mining and agriculture, and their conservative politics contrasted with the liberalism and republicanism that the mercantile class professed.

The new elite had the task of consolidating its own power and extending the state's limits. Pursuing pacification and colonization in the northern borderlands, in the belief that the Indian race and its way of life were "barbaric," they appropriated Indian lands and sold them to white colonists from the United States, England, Italy, Germany, and elsewhere.[2] In the Yucatán, the state fought to take over Indian holdings and to force the indigenous peoples into peonage.

2. Generally I use the term *Indian* to refer to the indigenous peoples, so as not to change the vocabulary with which Mexicans generally referred to them.

(In 1824 Mexico's Constitutional Congress had officially ended the traffic in black slaves, so that landowners had sought another source of cheap labor.) The ruling faction's anticlericalists also tried to cut the power of the church, which they identified with Mexico's Spanish past. Catholicism was thought to inspire fanaticism and blind obedience in the populace; moreover, it was understood to paralyze the Mexican economy as the church's valuable lands remained unused and its priests (judged unproductive because of their celibacy and the immateriality of their work) failed to contribute to the formation of new wealth. Accordingly, the government taxed church properties and sought to develop a secular culture in its project of nation building and modernization.

Italian opera provided the new interests with the vocabulary they needed to state their difference from Spanish culture and to legitimate their control. Opera's physical appearance, by itself, was a decolonizing sign of cultural newness. But its plots, which often relied on conflict between Christian and Moor, also helped Mexicans reflect on their own history, during which they had been judged idolatrous and racially inferior by their European conquerors. Operatic language, which highlighted the categories of "civilized" and "barbaric," permitted liberals and conservatives alike, whether *criollos* or *mestizos* of the Mexican elite classes, to rethink Spanish uses of the terms; they could shift onto Indian peoples in the peripheral areas and an uneducated populace in the capital the label of "barbaric," thereby cleansing themselves of inferior colonial status.

To demonstrate the use that Mexicans made of a borrowed cultural form, I will focus on *Mahometto II*, a representative work whose protagonist is based on a historical character, the Muslim leader who conquered Constantinople in the fifteenth century, consolidated the Ottoman Empire, and threatened Venice and the rest of Christian Europe. In this *melodramma serio*, the infidel emperor attacks the Venetian colony of Negroponto, and angry choruses of Moorish and Christian soldiers convey what the battle must have been. The military struggle is complicated, however, by the fact that the Christian governor's daughter, Ana, has fallen in love with the Moor, who has appeared on the island, incognito, to reconnoiter it in preparation for the attack. When Ana discovers that her lover is her father's hated enemy, her loyalty is divided between them, between desire and religious faith. Mahometto is called "inhuman" by the father and "beloved" by the daughter; thus labels of hatred and love, applied to the same person, are called into question. The Moor and his soldiers are repeatedly characterized as "barbaric" (seven times in the thirty-one-page libretto); "barbaric" is also used three times to describe the moment in which the girl confronts her dilemma, her deception, and her fate.

It may be theorized that *Mahometto II* was a success in Mexico because of Ana's story, in which love and hatred meet. Her character has many variations in the Mediterranean world. In *Galerias de mugeres fuertes* (Madrid, 1794), for example, P. Pedro Lamoyne describes a "victorious captive" who, desirous of escaping the seraglio in which she is held prisoner, blows up the Muslim fleet preparing to sack Nicosia. In the Mexican context, however, Ana's destiny reproduced that of La Malinche, Hernán Cortés's Indian interpreter and mistress, whose betrayal of her people for love of an invading Spaniard was a frequent topic of discussion in postindependence Mexico. Ana's father and her lover both describe her as their "prize." When she is carried off to the Moor's tent and the other women there sing of their multiple loves, she agonizingly recognizes that her understanding of love is different and that she is in an alien world. When the Moor protests that he is not barbarous but "a refined lover," the opera appears to say that men's relationship to women, often named "love," is frequently a point of confused interracial and intercultural contact, in which ownership conflicts arise. The Moor's courtly language and powerful manner are ambiguously attractive; his refinement might have suggested chivalric ideals associated with Spain's oriental past, which many Mexicans admired yet also resented. For them, Ana's suicide on her mother's grave may have signified their women's complicity and victimization in the territorial takeover and sexual conquest of Mexico.

The message Mexican audiences received from *Mahometto II*, when they saw it for the first time, is unclear. One review records an awareness of the opera's historical significance: "Without a doubt, when Rossini composed it he had previously read the pages of history that characterized the first sultan who established his seat in Constantinople as a mixture of monstrousness and heroism."[3] If Mexicans seem to have had difficulty in understanding who was the hero and who was the villain, since Venice and Turkey had both been imperial powers, it is because independence had posed the same dilemma to them. Should they sympathize with the Christian or with the Moor, since, in their recent war with Spain, they had fought a Christian nation and now, in its aftermath, continued to be suspicious of the church's power? Should they identify with the opera's male ideological struggle or with the female emotional one? No mention of race is found in the review, perhaps because the opera contains no reference to skin color; yet it seems probable that the Italian company used black and white to stage difference.

The confusion in the opera as to what "civilized" meant suggests the ongoing debate among Mexicans as to their American nature. After repudiating their identity in the Spanish Empire as "American Spaniards," Mexicans were forced to seek "civilized" status elsewhere. Some political thinkers cited the glorious pre-Columbian ruins that were just being unearthed as a source of Mexican pride; they also found in Mexico's racial hybridity a symbol of nationhood. Yet others, remembering how Spanish rhetoric had stigmatized the Indians, and mindful of the primitiveness of the Indian masses, persisted in their belief that the race was "barbaric"; they could see no benefit in basing Mexicanness on this image and so denied their Indian nature.

Mahometto II was performed on 11 September 1834 in honor of Antonio López de Santa Anna's victory over the Spanish at Tampico (9–11 September 1829), and Santa Anna was in the audience. The opera was appropriate for the occasion: the repulse of Spanish forces, which had tried to retake the former colony, can be read into its story of republican resistance, and the message of triumphalism also extended to the successes of the Mexican central government in its Indian campaigns, as well as to its control over rival factions.

The libretto for the 1832 production at the Teatro Nacional proves that the work had a greater influence than the attendance might suggest. My copy of *Mahometto II* has the Italian text and the Spanish translation on facing pages. The newspapers report that many Mexicans felt excluded from opera because it was sung in a foreign

3. *El sol,* 26 June 1832. My translation.

language, and the translation may have been a response to their complaint. Printed in Mexico City, with facts about the opera's performance on its cover, the libretto testifies to opera's role as a reading as well as a theatrical experience.

Other Rossini operas with oriental motifs were performed in Mexico City and reinforced Italian cultural categories in the Mexican imagination: *L'italiana in Algeri*, *Il barbiere di Siviglia* (an earlier version of which was *Il turco in Italia*), *Torvaldo e Dorliska*, *Semiramide*, *Tancredi*, *Mosè in Egitto*, *Ricciardo e Zoraide*, *Zelmira*, and *La gazza ladra*. Rossini's *Otello* had been seen earlier, in 1827, when a traveling Spanish company performed it; the publication of its text in 1835 helped spread the tragic story of Moorish male and Christian female.[4]

Some European music of the period also drew on American Indian and Spanish stories. For example, Frederick the Great wrote the libretto for an opera called *Montezuma* (1755), which his court composer, Karl Heinrich Graun, set to music. Gaspare Luigi Pacifico Spontini's opera *Fernand Cortez ou La conquête du Mexique* (1808, 1817) was produced for the king of Naples by Rossini at about the same time that he wrote *Mahometto II*. Significantly, however, these operas of self-representation were not brought to Mexico.

The introduction of Italian opera into postindependence Mexico poses an important lesson for students of the postcolonial condition. The faction hiding behind a liberal ideology seems to have thought of decolonization only in terms of ending Spanish influence on the former colony. By borrowing the new vogue, the faction may have set itself off culturally from retrograde Spanishness and "barbaric" Indianness. By sponsoring stories of political intrigue, this elite made believe that it was learning the realpolitik of post–Congress of Vienna Europe; *Turk* and *Christian*, formerly religious terms, now suggested only political differences, which could be refreshingly negotiated. By looking to representations of another European other (one thinks of colonial allegories in which America, Asia, and Africa opposed Europe), Mexicans seemed to find another equivalent self; the Ottoman Empire,

4. *L'italiana in Algeri* was performed by a traveling company as early as 1823–24, as were two other orientalist operas, Manuel García's *Abúfar* and *Le calife de Bagdad* (variously attributed to García, Esteban Cristiani, and "a French composer").

which was attempting to modernize, to separate government from religious influence, and to introduce commerce, was a useful example of a parallel world, racially and culturally non-European, whose experiences Mexicans read about in the newspapers and whose exoticism they were increasingly familiar with in opera. In many ways, then, opera was liberating in its mirroring of Mexican concerns. It even gave Mexicans the language to express new hatreds; the despotic Spanish king, Fernando VII, for example, was called a "sultan" in one contemporary newspaper.[5]

In the plans for a national agenda, opera had a certain logic. It afforded the possibility of spectacle and therefore controlled the release of deep emotion. Liberalism, which sought to replace religious and monarchical displays of power with new public forms, had found a different way of engaging the populace. For example, *Semiramide*, the hit of the Italian company's repertoire, apparently used the exoticism of worship at the altar of Baal to suggest that the Mexican government now had more power than the church, which would have prohibited the performance as pagan ritual at an earlier time. In 1836, after Galli's company had left and other impresarios had taken over, the closing down of Bellini's *I Montecchi e Capuleti* revealed the fear that this spectacle of civil strife might be imitated in the streets. The exhibiting of an elephant from India and balloon ascents by a Mr. Robertson, which newspapers enthusiastically record, were other ways in which a still shaky government employed spectacle to create the illusion of power and to take credit for the public's edification.

Mexicans continued to talk of opera as theater and seem to have expected of it the benefits that neoclassical aesthetics insisted derived from this "school of customs." Yet the literature of the period does not specify what lessons it might have taught, or to whom, apart from the training in civility that attendance at a secular event might have given. It had been easy once to refer to uneducated Indians as the recipients of culture. Now, perhaps, liberals could not openly identify their fellows in the elite class who persisted in their traditional monarchical and religious sympathies and required an education in modernization. The discussion justifying opera in Mexico, according to an earlier

5. *El sol,* 15 June 1830.

rationale, seems to have been an instance of the nation-state papering over its indoctrination with the "friendly" vocabulary of the Spanish imperial culture.

Nevertheless, in many ways Italian opera contained the seeds of further colonization and retarded decolonization in Mexico. It hindered early attempts at cultural independence by adding to a colonialist attitude that the Mexican self needed foreign help to create a worthy culture. For years afterward the Mexican elite relied on British, French, and North American cultural sources to satisfy its artistic needs. Performances that called for sitting through hours of incomprehensible Italian singing, for tolerance and appreciation of such oddities as a woman dressed as a man, and for a voyeuristic interest in the intimacies of others helped make the Mexican elite class more like audiences in non-Spanish Europe; yet cultivated taste, which ignored Mexican realities, deepened the split between this class and the rest of the nation. Indeed, in a celebrated poem, the Argentine midcentury writer Estanislao del Campo makes fun of the gaucho who naively thinks that he sees the devil onstage during a performance of *Fausto*. The poem is an early example of a developing Argentine literary style, but the humor also ridicules the rustic in his first contact with European civilization.

"Civilization," which in the colonial period meant membership in a Christian community, was now being redefined in certain European republican circles to indicate an international political consciousness as new coalitions of republican nations contested the power of old, reactionary monarchies. Yet these European circles also produced cultural artifacts that continued to validate the colonizing force of "civilization" and "barbarism" as they circulated in remote areas. For example, it is not clear that the resonances of the two terms for the Italian production of *Mahometto II*, when it opened in revolutionary Naples, carried over to Mexico. Cesare della Valle's libretto, based on a story by Voltaire, seems to have pleased Neapolitan audiences more than the music; perhaps they saw in the conflict between two Mediterranean powers an indictment of ideological struggle, which historically had tragic consequences for innocent individuals caught in the middle. Naples, at that time part of the Kingdom of the Two Sicilies, was ruled by the Bourbon Ferdinand. Son of Carlos III (ruler of Naples and then Spain, from 1759 to 1788) and husband of the Austrian empress Maria Theresa, he thus involved Naples in the politics of European imperialism.

Race and religion continued to mark differences in Italian opera; and if *Turk* was losing its dark connotations in Europe as diplomacy made coexistence possible there, it continued to validate the cutting power of the old colonial terms in a prestigious setting a world away. The self-hatred that the colonial experience had bred in Mexicans and the hatred for Spain that the independence war had wrought in many were transmuted into hatred for the "barbaric" underclasses, which were culturally, linguistically, and racially removed from the new metropolitan center, the Mexican capital. Thus, "internal colonialism" was psychologically expedited; republican dreams of equality and national unity were thwarted.

That Mexico borrowed a foreign mode intact, contributing nothing to its production and not altering it to fit Mexican circumstances, may have caused Mexicans to preserve their colonial fetish for performance. When one reads in review after review that "the soprano sang beautifully" or "the costumes were lavish," one concludes either that the reviewers were bound to use such descriptions or that Mexicans continued to measure their "civilization" according to how closely it imitated European standards.

Finally, what I think has not been explored in nineteenth-century studies is the way the Mexican elite—but also the new ruling classes in other Spanish American countries—used various cultural forms for different purposes at this time of national formation. I am intrigued by the relationship between opera and the emerging national literatures. Under Porfirio Díaz in the last decades of the century, Mexico City became a cultural mecca for European entertainment; the Palacio de Bellas Artes was built then, and opera apparently flourished. In 1877 a Mexican printing house produced a huge number of libretti, presumably spreading word of the operatic form. However, I find no other evidence that opera shaped the Mexican imagination, for example, by influencing other art forms.[6]

The preference for foreign styles of music, dance, architecture, dress, and so on was therefore at odds with the interest that the elite

6. I do not know how opera may have affected Mexican music.

also showed in an emerging indigenous literature. Mexican novelists such as Ignacio Altamirano increasingly set their stories locally, with recognizable personages often drawn from the lower classes. National writers like Victoriano Salado Alvarez turned to the Mexican past to create "episodios nacionales mexicanos" (Mexican national tales). Historians set to work to retrieve Mexico's Indian history and to analyze events of the independence war and ensuing developments. Why, then, was the "performance" of opera appropriate for stating international membership, while the practice of literature was somehow suitable for expressing nationalism? Why did Mexicans choose public art to accomplish one political goal and private art to accomplish another? Discussion of the communication value of the various art forms, of the necessity of reaching all members of a multilingual society, is to be found in Mexican newspapers from the last years of colonial rule. I find it suggestive that, in the postcolonial period, national leaders imported an art form that was so exclusive. It is possible that opera's orientalist stories of gender and racial encounter hinted at Mexico's internal divisions yet also permitted fanciful escapes from the excruciating problems Indians posed. Opera's very foreignness, I believe, reproduced the denial of the Indian self that Mexican governmental policies, which attempted to eliminate Indians and their culture, increasingly pursued in the nineteenth century.

The Real Thing (Our Rigoberta)

JOHN BEVERLEY

This essay is about Rigoberta Menchú and what she means, or does, for us.[1] The title alludes to the advertising slogan "Coke is the real thing" and to the Lacanian notion of the Real as that which resists symbolization absolutely—the unrepresentable, in other words. What may be less familiar, however, is the peculiar sense Lacan (in his seminar on the ethics of psychoanalysis) gives the capitalized form of the word *Thing*, following on the Freudian term *das Ding*. For Lacan, *das Ding* designates a traumatic Otherness that cannot be represented or incorporated by the subject—just the opposite of the reassuring image of the ego that the mirror or specular other (the face of the parent or careperson) gives back to confirm "orthopedically," in his own phrase, the subject's either yet unformed or perpetually fading sense of self in the mirror stage.

In an essay on *The Crying Game*, Slavoj Žižek elaborates the concept apropos the representation of the Lady in the discourse of courtly love as a tyrant "submitting her subjects to senseless, outrageous, impossible, arbitrary, capricious ordeals." "The Lady is thus as far as possible from any kind of purified spirituality"; rather,

> she functions as an inhuman partner in the precise sense of a radical Otherness which is wholly incommensurable with our needs and desires; as such she is simultaneously a kind of automaton, a

1. This is an abridged version of a paper I presented at a 1994 conference on Rigoberta Menchú at the University of Wisconsin—Milwaukee, organized by Julio Rodríguez Luís. The full text is forthcoming in a collection on testimonial narratives that Georg Gugelberger is editing for Duke University Press.

machine which randomly utters meaningless demands. This coincidence of radical, inscrutable Otherness and pure machine is
what confers on the Lady her uncanny, monstrous character—
the Lady is the Other which is not our "fellow-creature," i.e. with
whom no relation of empathy is possible. . . . The idealization of
the Lady, her elevation to a spiritual, ethereal Ideal, is therefore
to be conceived as a strictly secondary phenomenon, a narcissistic
projection whose function is to render invisible her traumatic,
intolerable dimension. . . . Deprived of every real substance, the
Lady functions as a mirror onto which the subject projects his narcissistic ideal.[2]

Our Rigoberta, then? The Lady in question. Why does it seem so
natural to refer to Rigoberta Menchú as Rigoberta? The use of the
first name is appropriate to address a friend or children, servants,
women, animals, that is, the subaltern. But we are not exactly addressing Rigoberta Menchú as a friend in the work we do on her *testimonio*.
We would not say with such ease, for example, Paul, for Paul de Man,
or Fred, for Fredric Jameson. In a recent interview with Alice Britten
and Kenya Dworkin, Menchú herself insists on claiming her rights as
author, which involve among other things the right to the use of her
full name. She is referring to the appearance of her book as the work
of Elisabeth Burgos-Debray, the Venezuelan anthropologist who
served as her interlocutor.[3]

I make it a point to say or write Rigoberta Menchú or Menchú,
but I have to keep reminding myself on this score; my inclination is to
say Rigoberta, too, and I must constantly censor myself in the name of
what I at least perceive to be political correctness, not to say polite-
ness or respect for a person I have met only formally. But of course, in
another sense, I would like to address her as a friend, a *compañera*, in

2. Žižek, "From Courtly Love to *The Crying Game*," *New Left Review*, no. 202 (1993):
96.
3. "Lo que sí efectivamente es un vacío en el libro es el derecho de autor. . . . Porque
la autora del libro, efectivamente, debió ser más precisa, compartida, ¿verdad?"
[What is really a gap in the book is the rights of the author. . . . Because the authorship of the book really should have been more correctly indicated, shared, no?]
(Britten and Dworkin, "Rigoberta Menchú: Los indígenas no nos quedamos como
bichos aislados," *Nuevo Texto Crítico* [1993]: 214).

156   John Beverley

the way we used to say Fidel or Che—someone in the same party or movement.

Does Rigoberta Menchú have a psyche? It is possible to read *I, Rigoberta Menchú* as an oedipal bildungsroman whose narrative core describes the working through of an Electra complex in something like the following sequence: an initial rejection of the Mother and motherhood in favor of an Athena-like identification with the Father (an Indian activist); an authority struggle with the Father, who does not want his daughter to become literate, as it will mean her divorce from the community; the death of the Father at the hands of the army, which leads to the possibility of reidentification with the Mother, now seen anew as someone who controls the subversive arts of subaltern speech and rumor; the death of the Mother, also at the hands of the state; and finally the emergence of Menchú as a full speaking subject, an organizer in her own right, represented by the production of the *testimonio* itself.[4] The text not only narrativizes but also embodies in its own aporias the tensions involved in this sequence, which marks the transition from the Imaginary to the Symbolic in the Lacanian schema, from gemeinschaft to gesellschaft, from the local to the global, and from oral to print culture.

What such a reading would do is to foreground the "complexity" of *I, Rigoberta Menchú*, the fact that its analysis is interminable, that it resists simply being the mirror that reflects back our narcissistic assumptions about it.[5] Despite the misunderstandings her essay has provoked, a similar recognition is surely Gayatri Spivak's point in answering the question "Can the subaltern speak?" in the negative.[6] She is trying to show, behind the good faith of the "committed" ethnographer or solidarity activist in allowing or enabling the subaltern to speak, the trace of the colonial construction of an Other who is available to speak to us—with whom we *can* speak or feel comfortable

4. *I, Rigoberta Menchú: An Indian Woman in Guatemala*, ed. Elisabeth Burgos-Debray, trans. Ann Wright (London: Verso, 1984).
5. Doris Sommer, in "Rigoberta's Secrets," *Latin American Perspectives* 18, no. 3 (1991): 32–50, was the first to theorize and analyze in detail the forms of agency of the testimonial narrator as opposed to those of the interlocutor or reader of the text.
6. Spivak, "Can the Subaltern Speak?" in *Marxism and the Interpretation of Culture*, ed. Cary Nelson and Lawrence Grossberg (Urbana: University of Illinois Press, 1988), 271–313.

speaking with—neutralizing the force of the reality of the difference and antagonism our relatively privileged position in the global system might give rise to.

Elzbieta Sklodowska has something similar in mind when she criticizes what she feels is the appeal in accounts of *testimonio*, including my own, to the authenticity of a subaltern voice. Such an appeal stops the semiotic play of the text, she implies, fixing both it and the testimonial subject in a unidirectional gaze that deprives them of their reality.[7]

However, the appeal to the "many-leveled, unfixable intricacy and openness of a work of literature" against the illusion of the transparency of a subaltern voice—the phrase is Spivak's, but I think it captures Sklodowska's position[8]—also has to be suspect, given that this openness happens in literature only in a structural relation in which literature itself is one of the key social practices that generate the difference registered as subalternity in a text like Menchú's. Thus, Dinesh D'Souza's claim, in the debate over the Stanford humanities requirement, that *I, Rigoberta Menchú* is not good or great literature should not bother us too much.[9] I happen to think that it is one of the most interesting works of *literature* produced in Latin America in recent years. But I would rather have it be a provocation in the academy, a radical otherness, in the way D'Souza feels it to be, than something easily integrated into an elite university's curriculum for "multicultural" citizenship. I would like my students to understand that almost

7. *Testimonio* "no representa una reacción genuina y espontánea del 'sujeto-pueblo multiforme' frente a la condición postcolonial," Sklodowska concludes, "sino que sigue siendo un discurso de las élites comprometidas a la causa de la democratización" [does not represent a genuine and spontaneous reaction of a "multiform popular subject" in conditions of postcoloniality, but rather continues to be a discourse of elites committed to the cause of democratization] ("Hacia una tipología del testimonio hispanoamericano," *Siglo XX* 8, nos. 1–2 [1990–91]: 113). The concept of the multiform popular subject is from the Chilean critic Jorge Narváez.
8. Spivak, *In Other Worlds: Essays in Cultural Politics* (New York: Methuen, 1987), 95.
9. To be precise, D'Souza writes: "To celebrate the works of the oppressed, apart from the standard of merit by which other art and history and literature is judged, is to romanticize their suffering, to pretend that it is naturally creative, and to give it an esthetic status that is not shared or appreciated by those who actually endure the oppression" (*Illiberal Education: The Politics of Race and Sex on Campus* [New York: Free Press, 1991], 87).

by definition the subaltern, which will in some cases be a component of their own class or group identity, is not, and cannot be, adequately represented in literature or in the university; that literature and the university are among the institutional practices that *create* and sustain subalternity.

There is an important political and cultural point to be made by answering Saul Bellow's infamous question (which I paraphrase) "Who is the Tolstoy of the Zulus? The Proust of the Papuans?" with the names of Ousmane Sembene and Ngugi wa Thiong'o (who are entitled to ask in return what Bellow has written lately, anyway). This is in part what Edward Said intends in *Culture and Imperialism* when he sees the Great Tradition of the European novel as detached from its complicity with colonialism and appropriated and transformed by non-European writers in the process of decolonization. But the inadequacy of European languages and of the novel itself for the representation of postcoloniality led Sembene to become a film director and Ngugi to abandon the novel altogether in favor of theater pieces composed in Kikuyu. Where Said envisions an intellectual capable of producing "new narratives of equality and human community" as the protagonist of decolonization, part of the force of *testimonio* is to displace the centrality of intellectuals, at least as they are usually thought of, in social history.[10] Rigoberta Menchú is of course an intellectual, but clearly in a different sense than Said intends. Said has in mind more a "traditional intellectual," in Gramsci's sense of the term—someone like Toni Morrison, for example, who meets the standards and carries the authority of literary high culture at the same time that he or she "represents" the subaltern. The concern with *testimonio* depends, by contrast, on the suspicion that intellectuals and writing practices themselves actively establish and maintain relations of subalternity and domination.[11]

Sklodowska misunderstands the nature of the claim I make vis-à-vis *testimonio* by treating it as if it were an appeal to the transparency of a subaltern voice. She is right to point out that the voice in *testimonio* is a textual construct, a *différend* in Lyotard's sense of the word, and that

10. Said, *Culture and Imperialism* (New York: Knopf, 1993), xiii.
11. See Ranajit Guha, *Elementary Aspects of Peasant Insurgency in Colonial India* (Delhi: Oxford University Press, 1983).

we should beware of a metaphysics of presence. But I would pose against her warning René Jara's observation that "more than an interpretation of reality, testimonio is *a trace of the Real,* of that history which, as such, is unrepresentable."[12] Since the Real resists symbolization, it also collapses the pretense of any particular form of cultural expression to representational adequacy and value. It is, like the monstrous Lady in Žižek's account of the discourse of courtly love, a semiotic black hole or vanishing point. As such, it is, like the subaltern itself (with which it is connected both conceptually and really, i.e., in the Real), not an ontological category but a relational one, historically, socially, and psychically specific. Just as there are different strokes for different folks, we might say that there are different Reals for different Symbolics.

On the other hand, the Real is not the same thing as the idea of a "reality effect," which we may be more used to. The picaresque novel of Cervantes aimed to dismantle the idealistic genre conventions of pastoral and chivalric narrative in the Spanish Renaissance. But when Lazarillo is beaten or the blind man crashes against the stone post or Don Quixote is knocked off his horse, they experience the Real, not a "reality effect." The experience of the Real—here perhaps Sklodowska and I find common ground—is not too different from what the Russian formalists called *ostranenie* or "defamiliarization." Intending the pun with the French *touché,* Lacan uses the Aristotelian category of *tuché,* "fortune," to describe the (sudden, fortuitous) encounter with the Real: the telephone ringing that interrupts our dream, for example, or the piece of gum or dog shit that sticks to the sole of our shoe, resisting all attempts to dislodge it.[13]

Something of the experience of the body in pain or hunger or deprivation inheres in *testimonio.* That is certainly the sense of the extraordinary passage in *I, Rigoberta Menchú* in which Menchú narrates the torture and execution of her brother in the town plaza of Chajul in the Guatemalan highlands. At the climax of the massacre, she describes the witnesses' involuntary shudder of revulsion and anger,

12. Jara, "Prólogo," in *Testimonio y literatura,* ed. René Jara and Hernán Vidal (Minneapolis, Minn.: Institute for the Study of Ideologies and Literature, 1986), 3.
13. Lacan, "Tuché and Automaton," in *The Four Fundamental Concepts of Psychoanalysis,* trans. Alan Sheridan (New York: Norton, 1978), 53–66.

which puts the soldiers on their guard. The reader experiences the same reaction through identification, just as the viewer does at the most intense moments of *Schindler's List,* for example, when the women in the Cracow concentration camp who are relaxing after an interrogation suddenly realize that in the meantime their children have been rounded up and are being trucked to Auschwitz. During such instances the experience of the Real breaks through the repetitious passivity of witnessing imposed by repression itself. By contrast, romanticizing victimization (as *Schindler's List* does in other ways) would confirm the Christian narrative of redemption that underlies colonial and imperialist domination in the first place and leads in practice more to a moralistic posture of liberal guilt than to effective solidarity.

The narration of the death of Menchú's brother is of course precisely the passage whose literal veracity the anthropologist David Stoll (among others) contests, claiming on the basis of his own interviews in the area, where he spent several years doing field research, that the massacre happened differently and that Menchú remembers some of the details wrongly. The implication is that she is less than representative of the needs and desires of the Mayan communities in the Guatemalan highlands. Menchú denies the charge, and what is not contested by Stoll or anyone else is the torture and murder of her brother by the Guatemalan army or the genocidal counterinsurgency it waged against communities like Chajul in the early eighties. The question is, who has the authority to construct the narrative, and on what basis? Appealing to the objectivity of social science, Stoll is suspicious of a "postmodernist" ethnography that depends on "the text, the narrative, or the voice instead of the society, culture, or political economy."[14] But his own challenge to Menchú's account depends on . . . other *testimonios*: other narratives, other voices, other texts. The problem is that there is not, outside of human discourse, a level of social facticity that guarantees the truth of this or that representation, given that what we call "society, culture, or political economy" is not an

14. I quote from a manuscript copy that Professor Stoll kindly made available to me of "*I, Rigoberta Menchú* and Human Rights Reporting in Guatemala" (Paper presented at the conference "'Political Correctness' and Cultural Studies," University of California, Berkeley, 20 October 1990), 11.

essence prior to representation but rather the consequence of struggles over representation.[15]

The question of the relation of Menchú to Mayan traditionalism comes up in this regard. In my opinion, there is nothing more "postmodern," nothing more traversed by the economic and cultural forces of transnational capitalism, nothing we can claim, anyway, than the social geography that Menchú and her family live and die in. Even the mountain *ejido* that forms the backdrop of the story is far from the remnant of a millenarian Mayan gemeinschaft it is often taken for; it is rather a shantytown thrown up hastily on unoccupied lands high in the mountains in the wake of its inhabitants' dispossession by landowners from previous places of residence, much as squatters from the countryside have created the great slums that encircle Latin American cities. I do not mean to diminish the force of Menchú's insistent appeal to the authority of her ancestors or of tradition, but simply to indicate that her appeal is being activated *in the present*, as a response to the proletarianization and semiproletarianization that subjects like her and her family experience in the context of the same processes of globalization that affect our own lives. There is a question of agency here, and as Menchú puts it in the interview with Britten and Dworkin, "Los indígenas no nos quedamos como bichos aislados, inmunes, desde hace 500 años. No, nosotros hemos sido protagonistas de la historia" [We indigenous peoples have not remained like strange, isolated beasts for five hundred years. No, we have also been protagonists of history] (212).

The Real is supplementary in the Derridean sense, in that it indicates something that is always in excess of the closure of representation. Menchú sees her own text in this way, too: something undone by what is not included in it; the imperfect metonym of a different, all-embracing text open to the contingencies of history. Except for the issue of authorship, she does not complain about Burgos-Dubray's editing of the original transcript. Rather,

15. "Any statement of authority has no other guarantees than its very enunciation, and it is pointless for it to seek another signifier, which could not appear outside this locus in any way. Which is what I mean when I say that no metalanguage can be spoken, or, more aphoristically, that there is no Other of the Other. And when the Legislator (he who claims to lay down the Law) presents himself to fill the gap, he does so as an imposter" (Jacques Lacan, *Ecrits: A Selection*, trans. Alan Sheridan [New York: Norton, 1977]: 310–1).

ahora, al leerlo, me da la impresión que es una parte, que son fragmentos de la historia misma, ¿verdad? Tantas anécdotas que uno tiene en la vida, especialmente la convivencia con los abuelos, con la familia, con la tierra, con muchas cosas. Son fragmentos los que tiene el libro y ojalá que algún día pudiéramos redocumentarlo para publicarlo, tal vez para nuestros nietos, posiblemente después de poner una serie de otras leyendas, testimonios, vivencias, creencias, oraciones, que aprendimos de chiquitos, porque el libro tiene una serie de limitaciones. (217)

[Reading it now, I have the impression that it's a part, that they are fragments of history, no? So many stories one comes across in life, in our experiences with the grandparents, with the family, with the land, with so many things. What the book has are fragments, and I hope one day we could republish it with new material, maybe for our grandchildren, adding perhaps a series of other stories, testimonies, experiences, beliefs, prayers that we learned as children, because the book has a lot of limitations.]

Note that Menchú distinguishes her narrative as a *testimonio*—the printed text we read and discuss in our classrooms: "el libro"—from *testimonios*, in the plural, as heterogeneous, primarily oral practices of witnessing and recounting in her own society, as in "una serie de otras leyendas, testimonios, vivencias, creencias, oraciones." In other words, *testimonio* in the singular—books generically like *I, Rigoberta Menchú*— is only one form of a much larger testimonial practice, which includes the arts of gossip, rumor, graffiti, narrative ballads, and skits. *Testimonio* is the form that *we* get to see (hence its essentially metonymic character), but this is not to say that it is not also connected to the larger practice, that it simply manifests our desire to have a "native informant."

What *I, Rigoberta Menchú* forces us to confront is the subaltern not only as a represented subject but also as the agent of a transformative project that aspires to become hegemonic in its own right. In terms of this project, which is not immediately our own but in fact involves structurally a contradiction with our relative privilege and authority in the global system, the testimonial text is a means rather than an end in itself. I have no doubt that the humanization of college students in the United States (or in Guatemala, for that matter) through a reading of *I, Rigoberta Menchú* has reciprocal effects on the extreme repression and deprivation the text describes; as an organizer and activist, Menchú must be aware that *testimonios* are an important tool in human rights and solidarity work. But her primary purpose in making the text is not to humanize college students, or to give literary theorists something to argue over, but to act tactically through the text as a way of advancing the interests of the group or class represented in the *testimonio*.

The idea of a larger process of subaltern cultural production that we do not have access to and that in a sense does not concern us may be the best way to confront the fact that the moment of *testimonio*, or (in Lacan's phrase) the "state of emergency" it carried that drove our fascination and critical engagement with it, has undoubtedly passed, if only by the logic of aesthetic familiarization. *Testimonio* began as an adjunct to armed liberation struggle in Latin America and elsewhere in the third world in the sixties. But its canonization was tied even more, perhaps, to the military, political, and economic force of counterrevolution and the resulting domination of the Right after 1973. *Testimonio* was the Real, the voice of the body in pain, of the disappeared, of the losers in the rush to marketize, that demystified the claims of neoliberalism to have finally reconciled history and society and that at the same time relativized the more liberal, even progressive, claims of the high-culture writers and artists of the boom to speak for the majority of Latin Americans. *Testimonio* was intimately linked to international solidarity networks in support of revolutionary movements or struggles around human rights, apartheid, democratization; but it was also a way of testing the contradictions and limits of revolutionary and reformist projects still structured in part around elite assumptions about the role of cultural and political vanguards. In the context of redemocratization and cultural and media globalization, *testimonio* loses its special aesthetic and ideological power and runs the risk of becoming a new form of *costumbrismo*, the Spanish term for "local-color" writing.

The definitive epitaph for *testimonio* is Javier Sanjinés's essay on the shift in Bolivia from the working-class culture represented by Domitila Barrios de Chungara and her well-known *testimonio, Let Me*

Speak! which dates from 1976, to new forms of popular and subaltern culture.[16] Barrios de Chungara ends her story with the question of how to return testimonial narratives like her own to the mining communities that give rise to them.[17] But the Bolivian tin mines, like the gigantic steelworks of my own city, Pittsburgh, have all but ceased to exist in the last decade as transnational capitalism has rearranged the country's social patterns. Sanjinés's point is that *testimonio* is no longer an adequate representation of the Bolivian subaltern under domination, that it has become a nostalgia, that proletarianization is taking on new and sometimes virulent forms, that, as in everything else in life, we have to move on. While she speaks in her interview of redoing *I, Rigoberta Menchú*, Menchú also senses that returning to *testimonio* is now beside the point; there are other things she has, or wants, to do. That is as it should be, because it is not only *our* purposes and desires that count in relation to *testimonio.*

16. Sanjinés, "Testimonial Discourse and New Popular Trends in Bolivia," *Mediations* 17 (1992): 50–9.
17. Barrios de Chungara, with Moema Viezzer, *Let Me Speak! Testimony of Domitila, a Woman of the Bolivian Mines*, trans. Victoria Ortiz (New York: Monthly Review Press, 1978), 234–5.

Reading Loose Women Reading

DEBRA A. CASTILLO

Who reads novels in Latin America these days? In view of the post-boom disillusion with the role of the writer in society, what is the use value of fiction? According to Mexican sociocritic Sara Sefchovich (her extensive body of work includes important critical studies like *México: País de ideas, país de novelas* [Mexico: Country of ideas, country of novels (1987)] and the two-volume anthology *Mujeres en espejo* [Women mirrored (1983–85)], as well as two best-selling novels: *Demasiado amor* [Too much love (1990)] and *La señora de los sueños* [The lady who dreamed (1993)]), her success and that of other women writers like Angeles Mastretta and Laura Esquivel point to a very clear answer to the first question: women, especially leisured middle-class women, read, and they overwhelmingly read works by other middle-class women in which women have positive protagonistic roles (pers. com., June 1994). Even more interestingly, works like hers and those of her colleagues who make it to Mexican best-sellerdom tend to highlight women who freely express their sexuality and are not castigated for their adventurous love lives. Unsurprisingly, perhaps, this interest in fictional loose women has spilled over into a parallel publishing boom-let in the *testimonios* of actual loose women. While the phenomenon has been noted with increasing frequency in critical discussions of con-temporary Mexican literature, its implications have remained largely unexplored. What is needed, and is only intermittently beginning to make its appearance in studies like those of Jean Franco, Doris Sommer, and Sefchovich herself, is a theory of the reading woman.

My purpose in this essay is to make a modest contribution to this theory by exploring a specific instance of the use of both fictional texts and critical studies about loose women by other loose women and to ask what these marginalized women find of value in such works and what use we academic readers make of them.[1] One hint comes to me from recent Europeanist studies. In *Women for Hire* Alain Corbin writes that the nineteenth-century ethnographic study of Parisian prostitutes by Alexandre Parent-Duchatelet was so influential that it not only affected later studies of prostitution in France and other countries but also, indirectly, became a force shaping women's lives: "Parent-Duchatelet's portrait of the prostitute was repeated so often in the literature on prostitution and inspired so many novelists that, in addition to distorting the vision of later researchers . . . it determined to some extent the behavior of the prostitutes themselves."[2] What I find fascinating is Corbin's contention that a specific academic exercise had a major effect on fictional practice and that fictional versions of this produced knowledge in turn influenced certain social practices (those of real prostitutes), which were then reencoded in Corbin's own anthropological construct of them.

A similar process of life influencing fiction influencing life underlies Xorge del Campo's "sociological" study of prostitution in Mexico: "Fenómeno curioso en las prostitutas: son numerosas las que aman la lectura. ¿Pero qué leen? Fotonovelas, revistillas románticas, por supuesto, en las cuales espigan ideas y lugares comunes que luego expanden a su contorno" [There is a curious phenomenon among prostitutes; many of them love reading. But what do they read? Comic books, romance magazines, of course, in which they spot the ideas and commonplaces that they later expand to their surroundings.][3] In both del Campo and Corbin, the construction of an informative, even scientific, study of loose women is hinged upon and tightly implicated in the relation between lives and fictions. In each study, the loose women

1. This essay is part of a book in progress on loose women in modern Mexican fiction. I thank Doris Sommer for the invitation to participate in this special issue and would like to acknowledge as well Doris's enormous contribution in shaping the terms of this discussion.
2. Corbin, *Women for Hire: Prostitution and Sexuality in France after 1850*, trans. Alan Sheridan (Cambridge, Mass.: Harvard University Press, 1990), 7.
3. Del Campo, *La prostitución en México (dossier)* (Mexico City: Editores Asociados, 1974), 124. My translations.

are seen not only as fictionalizers but as fictional subjects and as fictional objects. The women tell fictions that writers turn into novels; the women read the novels and turn the fictions back into their daily lives and their work as part of a storied experience tailored to the tastes of the client. Consequently, the sociologist can never be sure if the stories he hears are lived or read or imagined, since the essence of the life is already an artifice. Furthermore, as Corbin recognizes, the knowledge structures that guide the researcher are also artificial; they too are stories that shape the researcher's vision.

A parallel, equally convoluted process occurs on another level with Federico Gamboa's best-selling turn-of-the-century novel *Santa*, about the rise and fall of a Mexican prostitute. Like the nineteenth-century French and English narratives it superficially resembles, Gamboa's novel turns contemporary sociological and anthropological truisms about fallen women into an aesthetic product, self-identified as artifice and served up as such to an eager reading public. Despite its contrived frame, however, the novel, taken as a faithful biography, spawns a veritable cult of fans, who organize trips to the heroine's "birthplace" and "tomb." Santa, like the Velveteen Rabbit, like the characters in "fotonovelas" and "revistillas románticas," becomes real and, theoretically, would have real effects on a real society. While I would not attempt to follow Corbin's or del Campo's lead and extend conclusions about the influence of Santa and her fictional and cinematic heirs on the *behavior* of other women or on the social formations instantiated by such fictions—the effort would take me far beyond the scope of this study—I would argue that to some extent Gamboa's novel draws the perimeters for later Mexican intellectual discussions of loose women by critics, chroniclers, and novelists like José Joaquín Blanco, del Campo, Margo Glantz, Sergio González Rodríguez, Carlos Monsiváis, Cristina Pacheco, Marta Lamas, Sefchovich, and Luis Zapata. The trouble with their books, however, is that their ostensible subjects do not usually have the opportunity to read them, much less to respond to the depiction of their lives with their own versions.

Nevertheless, I argue that such works establish the tradition within which or against which later memoirs and testimonials by women are published, including works like the one I use as an example here, Antonia Mora's *Del oficio* [The life]. Mora's story of her life as a ghetto-bred second-generation prostitute and thief, as framed by novelist María Luisa Mendoza's prologue, becomes a tale of sin and redemption. The work enters the marketplace as an artifact: like *Santa*, it offers a construction both moral and artificial, a tissue of pregnant and titillating silences that should or should not be broken, an allegory for an unrecognized or ignored national identity. The book presents itself, or is framed as, terribly serious, highly entertaining, and slightly naughty. The story is familiar yet exotic: the Cinderella myth of the poor girl redeemed by the love of an honest man. The woman whose body confirms the reality of the tale is simultaneously a liar, an able storyteller, a deficient fiction writer, and an honest chronicler. Mendoza reminds her readers and herself of the many options in her description of Mora's relationship to the text, but she carefully does not adjudicate among them. At the same time, Mendoza tacitly acknowledges the reader's expectations and the tradition within which Mora's story will be read:

> Antonia me trae su novela, su cuento, su escrito, su vida pues, convicta y confesa, sin clasificación literaria porque no es un estudio sociológico ni la exaltación del erotismo ni menos de la pornografía ni tampoco de la moraleja que sirva de escarmiento, ni nada de nada. Es simplemente decir lo que vio, lo que supo, lo que es cierto. . . . ¿Es necesario, me dije, que esto se sepa? No lo sé, no lo sabré nunca porque temo que las letras vencidas de su pasado puedan ser ajadas, rayadas, envilecidas por lectores gambusinos de lo caliente sólo y no de lo ardiente que es este libro terrible.[4]

> [Antonia brings me her novel, her story, her writing, her life, her convict's confession, without any literary pigeonhole, because it is not a sociological study or a eulogy of eroticism; even less is it pornography or a moral tale that serves to teach a lesson, or anything else. It is a simple telling of what she saw, what she knew, what is true. . . . Is it necessary, I asked myself, for this to become known? I don't know, I will never know, because I fear that the tale of her defeated past could be crumbled, torn up, and dirtied

4. Mora, *Del oficio*, prologue by María Luisa Mendoza (Mexico City: Editorial Samo, 1972), 10–1. My translations.

by low-minded readers interested only in what is hot and not what burns in this terrible book.]

Mendoza, of course, has promoted the book and prologued it for publication. Her introduction also offers official recognition of the real existence of the woman, Antonia Mora, and the manuscript that purports to tell of her early life. Thus, like the prologue to *Santa*, it provides an aesthetic frame to appreciate the following text. Furthermore, Mendoza acknowledges both the tradition within which it is likely to be read (sociological study, erotic literature, pornography, moral tale) and the readers that it is likely to find (aficionados of those genres), while she tries to have it both ways. The book will sell, she hints, because it is full of hot women and titillating details. It should sell because it endorses good moral values and teaches the middle-class reader about the painful, terrible reality of poverty in the lower classes. Will the readers who buy it for the "wrong" reasons change their minds on reading the work itself? Mendoza does not hazard a guess, leaving the question as open as possible, but suggests a rationalization for those of us who do not want to be identified with low-minded readers. Her gambit is identical to, though less obvious than, that of the blurb writer for del Campo's *La prostitución en México*: "Todas esas mujeres que se enlodan en la disipación y satisfacen la sensualidad tarifada: ¿qué son?, ¿de dónde vienen?, ¿a dónde van? . . . El presente 'dossier' sobre la prostitución en México hará reflexionar a muchos y, desde luego, divertirá y entretendrá a todos" [All those women who muddy themselves with dissipation and satisfy a purchased sensuality: Who are they? Where do they come from? Where do they go? . . . This 'dossier' about prostitution in Mexico will make many people think and, of course, will provide enjoyment and entertainment for all]. In all of these formulations, however, the right reasons (higher knowledge) and the wrong reasons (vile entertainment) belong to the same system, the same theoretical structure. It is a structure that the memoirs retain, but only in a tense, double-voiced relation.

Indeed, the very concept of a *testimonio* by such a woman is theoretically fraught with contradiction. The linchpin of testimonial narrative for Western readers is its absolute reliability; the narrator must be a real witness, who gives evidence about "true" happenings. By definition, the loose woman, particularly the prostitute, cannot testify.

Mendoza's and Gamboa's novels both highlight the invented quality of a loose woman's storytelling. On the one hand, she is relegated to silence as a victim with no personal agency, only a body that she sells on the market. Alternatively, she is silenced as inherently untruthful, reprimanded for an excess of agency and for irresponsibly trafficking in fantasies (and trite, secondhand fantasies at that). Del Campo says bluntly: "Las posibilidades de mixtificación de una prostituta suelen ser extraordinarias. Son capaces de contarse tres veces (o más) la misma historia—la suya, por ejemplo—reinventándola cada vez de cabo a rabo. . . . Esta imaginación desordenada, esta ausencia de dis-cernimiento entre lo verdadero y lo falso, este sentimentalismo novel-esco crea en las prostitutas una verdadera sed de aventuras" [A prosti-tute tends to have extraordinary possibilities for confusion. They are capable of telling someone the same story—their own story, for example —three or more times, reinventing it from beginning to end each time. . . . This disordered imagination, this absence of discrimination between truth and falsehood, this novelistic sentimentalism, creates in prostitutes a true thirst for adventure] (116–7). Curiously, del Campo sees the excessively active and creative imagination of these women as a sign of mental deficiency, subject to early detection in young girls: "De la incapacidad pragmática inicial deriva sistemáticamente un despego intelectual (que se manifiesta, por ejemplo, en una afición desmesurada por la lectura de novelistas sentimentales) y esto origina un descenso cotidiano del coeficiente de inteligencia" [A detachment from intellectual activities derives from an initial practical inability (which is manifested, for example, in an exceptional love of reading sentimental novelists), and from this point originates a daily decrease in the intelligence quotient] (116). I assume that implicitly del Campo is telling his readers that only young men can safely read such tales of famously book-maddened protagonists as *Don Quixote* and *Madame Bovary*, or of such immoral women as *Santa*, since books adversely affect only female IQs and are symptomatic of purely female mental deficiencies. Males may become low-minded readers, but they will retain both their intellectual agency and their sanity.

The loose woman who writes is in the same double bind as the prostitute who speaks of her past. She points toward her life, but with-out license to discuss it, without the reader having to acknowledge her openly or accept her testimony as part of the socially real. She is, by convention, an unacceptable witness to her own reality, since she cannot be counted on to see the difference between truth and falsehood. In more abstract terms, she is, by definition, always already speechless and unreadable. In a highly influential formulation of the relation of women's sexuality to patriarchal discourse, Luce Irigaray notes: "Commodities, as we all know, do not take themselves to market on their own; and if they could talk . . . So women have to remain an 'infrastructure' unrecognized as such by our society and our culture. The use, consumption, and circulation of their sexualized bodies underwrite the organization and the reproduction of the social order, in which they have never taken part as 'subjects.' "[5] There is no place for woman as such in the social contract that Irigaray defines, except as a shifter of men's relationships to each other and as the alien otherness that establishes male selfhood. Sex, specifically the woman's sexuality, is the unspoken, silenced term that shapes the social contract, within which there is no place for a woman's subjectivity. Since there is no possibility of saying "I" except as an othered being, there can be no speech. Judith Butler succinctly frames the paradox: "To speak at all in that context is a performative contradiction, the linguistic assertion of a self that cannot 'be' within the language that asserts it."[6] Specifically, for an admittedly sexually active woman to speak within the Mexican social system, she must silence both her femaleness and her sexuality. Within the system, woman ventriloquizes or performs man, and there are no women except as a convenience of discourse to refer to female persons. Such, at least, is the state of affairs in the traditionally conceived formulation of a male-dominant society.

It all comes down to the fundamental question exercising me in reading these women's personal writings, these memoirs, these *testimonios*, these texts; that is, what theoretical frame can I give the discussion without recourse to unsupportable truth claims or to trite pronouncements about the domination and silencing of women? In his much-acclaimed book *The Signifying Monkey*, Henry Louis Gates Jr.

5. Irigaray, *This Sex Which Is Not One*, trans. Catherine Porter, with Carolyn Burke (Ithaca, N.Y.: Cornell University Press, 1985), 84. Irigaray's ellipsis.
6. Butler, *Gender Trouble: Feminism and the Subversion of Identity* (New York: Routledge, 1990), 116.

describes the African American practice of "signifyin'," which is both a linguistic style of expression and a cultural ritual that always involves a double-voicedness, repetition with formal revision, and a play of ambiguity. Signifyin' is performance talk that calls attention to its performativity and is completely successful only if it convinces the target. As Gates reminds us, signifyin' on us theoretically in his own critical text, the standard English word *signification* "is a homonym of the Afro-American vernacular word. And . . . these two homonyms have everything to do with each other and, then again, absolutely nothing. . . . This confrontation is both political and metaphysical."[7] Gates extends the concept of signifyin' from a definition borrowed from literary critic and anthropologist Roger D. Abrahams: "the language of trickery, that set of words or gestures which arrives at 'direction through indirection'" (125). Elsewhere Abrahams gives examples: "It can mean . . . the propensity to talk around a subject, never quite coming to the point. . . . Also it can denote speaking with the hands and eyes, and in this respect encompasses a whole complex of expressions and gestures. Thus it is signifying to stir up a fight between neighbors by telling stories; it is signifying to make fun of a policeman by parodying his motions behind his back; it is signifying to ask for a piece of cake by saying, 'my brother needs a piece of cake.' "[8]

The effects of signifyin', however, far exceed one-upmanship. Taking as his key notion the concept of "arriv[ing] at direction through indirection," Gates lucidly demonstrates how signifyin' participates in yet subtly undermines dominant discourse. It is, as he says, both a form of troping and a style of political action. In terms of the Mexican social context, it is a kind of *transa* that requires not only a victim but also an appreciative audience.[9] The signifier needs to have his or her style recognized, optimally, by the person signified on. In the interstices of this double-voiced style the loose woman inserts herself as a subject, or as a third term. The women in these books have certainly discovered another method of trading their

7. Gates, *The Signifying Monkey: A Theory of Afro-American Literary Criticism* (New York: Oxford University Press, 1988), 45.

8. Abrahams, *Deep Down in the Jungle: Negro Narrative Folklore from the Streets of Philadelphia* (Chicago: Aldine, 1970), 51–2.

9. *Transa* seems to derive from the Spanish *transacción* (transaction) and can be loosely described as a con game or sting operation.

own use value, in producing a written work that corresponds neither to conventional autobiography nor to *testimonio* but to a third kind of self-writing. On an analogy with Gates's study, we can say that they are testifyin'.

Often, as del Campo complains, the prostitute sells her body by selling her story, or by creating an imagined narrative for the client's pleasure; decoupling the body from the text is the next step, and Gamboa, among others, has already made it part of a common currency linking writing and (metaphorical) prostitution. When the loose woman/ writer brings her textual goods to market, she is only literalizing the established metaphor and eliminating the middleman. At the level of publication and book sales, then, projects overlap as the mechanism of exchange is exploited and reversed to allow a formerly silent nonsubject to speak.

The two terms of this negotiation, this *transa*, remain the loose woman/storyteller and the client/reader. On the one hand, the reader expects the life story to give at least the impression of authenticity. It should speak to and within the growing body of life stories by people marginal to the collective experience of the reading public, books collected by anthropologists, journalists, and historians and marketed as *testimonios*. The text's charm and its charge come partly from its status as a genuine document referring back to a specific female body in which its veracity can be tested. Thus, for example, we can appreciate the value of the prologue by an officially recognized truth bearer like Elisabeth Burgos-Debray (who edited *Me llamo Rigoberta Menchú* [I, Rigoberta Menchú]) or María Luisa Mendoza, who describes the physical characteristics of the narrator and at some level attests to her concrete physical existence in *Del oficio*. Furthermore, the book's use value for the reader is intimately connected to its presumed truth value; the currency that the loose woman exchanges within the textual economy is both her particularity as a human being and her representability as an extension of a collective, if marginal and generally silenced, experience.

On the other hand, unlike canonical *testimonios*, where the very root of the word defining the genre presupposes a juridical truth telling, the loose woman's *testimonio* is presumed less trustworthy. Since the narrator is, again by definition, an unreliable storyteller—

we readers may uneasily suspect that we are victims of a *transa*—and since the life described in the text continually involves *transas* of one sort or another, in bodies and stories and goods, what is finally authenticable is only the staged performance of the *transa* in the referential frame of the narrator/author/testifier. More than other *testimonios*, then, the works that I look at here operate within the borderlands of the genre, in a *transa*-inflected, transitional culture. In telling us the trivia of their lives, invented for us or in conjunction with us, these women are testifyin' to their own storied transactions, both physical and literary.

Open the book *Del oficio*, by Antonia Mora, and flip past the title page to the prologue. Here is the first paragraph:

Antonia es una niña grande con los ojos inusitados de verde y de vida, de estupor. Es menuda y debió de ser frágil. De piel muy blanca, el único maquillaje que luce, el de sus redondos ojos, la adelgaza más aún. Antonia tiene una hija inmensa, triste y adolescente, preocupada como la madre en todos los problemas sociales que urge desentuertar. Antonia tiene un marido joven, elegante. Abogado. Es campeón de las viejas causas difíciles, un loco enamorado de la justicia. Antonia tiene una casa con ventanas a las horas del día que la miran escribir, coser bellos trajes Chanel, hermosísimas capas coloradas de Stendhal, abrigos de Colette, pijamas para ir a bailes o trajes de soiré para dormir; cocinar ricos platillos japoneses o convertir en cristales higos y piñas, naranjas y membrillos. (9)

[Antonia is an overgrown child with unusual, speaking green eyes, full of life and amazement. She is tiny and must be fragile. Her skin is very white, and the only makeup she wears—on her round eyes—makes her look even slimmer. Antonia has an immense, sad, adolescent daughter, as concerned as her mother with social problems that need to be straightened out. Antonia has an elegant young husband. A lawyer. He is a champion of the old, difficult causes, a madman in love with justice. Antonia has a house with windows full of daylight that watch her write; watch her sew beautiful Chanel suits, lovely red Stendhal capes, Colette overcoats, pajamas to go to balls or evening dresses to go to sleep; watch her cook delicious Japanese meals or turn figs and pineapples, oranges and quinces into sweetmeats.]

With her opening sentences Mendoza serves up to the reader a richly seductive banquet of innocence and sensuality, of an unusual and beautiful woman (slim, elegant, with pale skin and green eyes) surrounded by all the markers of an upper-class life. The vision of chaste but sensual, matronly good taste is essential, because it provides the reader with all the codes needed to understand the Cinderella story that follows, to recognize the narrator as a jewel shining in the mud of her surroundings, a pearl among swine, a diamond in the rough.

By beginning the prologue in this manner, Mendoza reminds us of the fluidity of the protagonist's identity. Mora becomes the quintessential madonna, indistinguishable from similarly privileged women. Yet the story she shares with Mendoza, and with us, is of another, altogether different life, dealing in naked truth rather than in glittering costumes and succulent fruits. In the extremes of both poverty and privilege, it offers a glimpse into two lifestyles that are each, on their own terms, exotic. Mendoza's catalog ends on a pious note: "Todo esto no volverá a pasar nunca más. Cuando el lector como usted y como yo entendamos a la mujer de otra manera, a manera de imagen de Dios. Y cuando México sea un país de hombres mejores . . . de hombres, simplemente" [This will never happen again. When the reader like you and I understand woman in another way, as God's image. And when Mexico is a country of better men . . . of men, simply] (12; Mendoza's ellipsis). Simply, facilely, mechanically, Mendoza offers Mora's *testimonio* as an exotic fruit and as a morality play to solve Mexico's gender-related problems.

Mora's own narrative begins, stripped of rhetorical flourish and garnishes, as follows:

Mi madre estaba en la puerta de la accesoria. La oía:
—Ven guapo. Mira que vas a disfrutar.
Y a mí me decía:
—Estoy jugando. Vete para adentro a jugar con los demás niños.
Mis amigos y amigas jugaban a lo mismo. (17)

[My mother was standing in the outbuilding doorway. I heard her: "Come on, handsome. Let me show you a good time." And she told me, "I'm playing. Go inside and play with the other children."

My boy- and girlfriends played the same game.]

The daughter of a prostitute, Mora almost inevitably, from her barely pubescent childhood until her jailing for theft and assault with a deadly weapon, also sells her body. She was born in abject poverty, and when told to "go play," she and her friends choose the adult games familiar to them from their mothers' profession, dressing up in their mothers' clothes and making believe they are prostitutes and clients, or entertaining themselves by inflating and deflating used condoms discovered lying around the area. Unsurprisingly, but still hurtfully, "decent" women do not allow her to play with their children (49). Mora tells us of unintentionally shocking one of her teachers when she answers the stereotypical question "What are you going to do when you grow up?" with a matter-of-fact "Voy a coger, señorita" [I'm going to fuck, miss] (23). At fourteen, she is kidnapped and raped— her first sexual experience. Her mother's reaction is to beat her up for being so stupid as to be tricked into giving her virginity away for free. The lesson is pounded into the girl: "Tengo que coger, y cobrar para que todo esté bien" [I have to fuck, and to charge for it, so that everything is OK] (64). It is not the only time she is raped, but as she becomes integrated into the sites of prostitution, the streets and rent-by-time hotels, rape becomes simply an occupational hazard, a constant threat that adds to her fear and her hatred but does nothing to prevent her from going back onto the streets.

Mora's trajectory is familiar from our reading of nineteenth-century novels and viewing of twentieth-century movies. The young woman runs off with an equally young man. She suffers abandonment and abortion. She learns to drink and to steal. She commits and suffers assault. She pays off corrupt police with kickbacks from her robberies and with sexual favors. She details her dealings with pimps (not so good) and with matrons of houses of prostitution (excellent). She tells of working in strip joints: "Era una sensación rarísima sentirme utilizada y sin coger a nadie"[It was a really strange sensation to feel I was being used but without having to fuck anybody] (90). At each stage Mora's simple, straightforward prose draws back the veil of exoticism from the ugly, sordid details. As Mora becomes more deeply involved in serious crime, she portrays herself more as the victim of circumstance, trapped by acquaintances into acts that horrify her. At the same time, the protagonist of the *testimonio* has vitality and strength no longer present in the pale, sad, beautiful lawyer's wife. She asks pointed questions and stands her ground when challenged. Where the lawyer's wife has dedicated herself to unspecified worthy social causes, the young prostitute takes a more direct approach to women's concerns, and her critique of male-defined customs and sexual practices is transparent:

—Bueno—le dije—, ¿tú nunca le das el mameyoso a tu mujer?
—No, nunca.
—¿Por qué? Si es igual que todas.
—Pues porque se prostituye, se volvería morbosa. Además que no es igual. Es una dama decente.
—Entonces, ¿cómo haces con ella?
—Normalmente, como debe ser.
—¿Qué tal si le da tentación por saber? (92)

["So," I asked him, "don't you ever turn your wife on?"
"No, never."
"Why not? She's the same as any other woman."
"Because it would turn her into a prostitute; she'd catch something. Besides, it's not the same thing. She's a decent woman."
"So, how do you do it with her?"
"Normally, the way it ought to be."
"What if she gets tempted to find out?"]

Good question.
When Mora is required to give legal testimony after her arrest, things become even more interesting. It seems that everyone involved in the courtroom proceedings has a *transa* to complete: everyone is testifyin': "Tanto los agentes como nosotros mentíamos" [Both we and the police lied] (142). To the police psychiatrists, Mora lies again, and she assumes that they are dishonest with her, too. Although she is uncertain what story will best serve her purposes, she cannily avoids

anything that might resemble a confession; a fairy-tale story of an artistic family (or, alternatively, a poor but honest mother) seems safer. On the first day she tries out one story; on the next day, another: "Al día siguiente decidí no contarle nada verdadero. Le narré una infancia que no era mía" [I decided not to tell anything that was true. I narrated a childhood that was not mine]; and on the following day she comes up with a different, equally elaborate narration for the nosy shrink (148–9).

Similarly, Mora learns about tailoring a story to the public when her case piques the interest of the news services. "¿Puedo decir lo que pienso?" [Can I say what I think?] Mora asks a reporter who is advising her on a statement to the press. When he says yes, she begins with a summary of the abuse she has suffered in the prison system, which the reader has already been told in far greater, more horrific detail: "El médico legista no me hizo examen a conciencia y por lo tanto no me reconocieron los golpes ni el aborto que me ocasionaron los agentes de la jefatura y . . ." [The state-appointed doctor did not give me a complete examination and so did not notice the bruises or the miscarriage that the police officers caused and . . .]. The reporter interrupts her: "No, no. Eso no causa simpatías en el público. Mejor di otra cosa" [No, no. That won't gain the audience's sympathy. Better say something else] (163). Essentially, she is to say something innocuous and to look as repentant and as pretty as possible for the cameras. The book ends with Mora's transcription of her brief statement—a very different statement from the exposé she had planned, and one written for her by personnel at the television station: "Estoy arrepentida de haber faltado a las leyes y de haber delinquido, insultando de esta manera a la sociedad, así como a la seguridad y moral de todo ciudadano honesto" [I am sorry for having broken laws and committed crimes, for insulting society and the security and morality of all honest citizens] (163). Her saccharine performance of a rehabilitated criminality leads directly to the work's puzzling final sentence, which hints at complicity between the former prostitute and the television producer (should we extend the analogy to the book publisher?), a completed *transa* of which the television audience (the readers of the book?) are the willing victims, the third term in a slippery game of signifyin' and testifyin': "El hombre me dio las gracias junto con cien pesos" [The man gave me his thanks, along with a hundred pesos] (163). Would it not be naive to ask about the truth status of this *testimonio* that we have just finished reading?

While Mendoza does not act on the performative possibilities of her interaction with the former prostitute, the *testimonio* reveals its constructed quality and its latent storytelling power. Mendoza's prologue to Mora's book creates a piously conventional coda in which the prostitute's core goodness is recognized and everything falls into place—a happy ending of upper-middle-class prosperity. But of course, Mendoza's (and Mora's) *transa* was successful. The book was published, and at least a few of us "lentos" purchased it, read it, and even took the time to write about it. Mora and Mendoza signify on us. The signifyin', testifyin' voice reminds us of the power of story to affect the real, and also of the slippery boundaries of the real when it comes into contact with an able *transa*.

"Damnable Iteration":
The Traps of Political Spectacle
DIANA TAYLOR

On the day of the last Argentine military coup or *golpe*, 24 March 1976, the front page of the daily newspaper *La Razón* featured an imposing photograph of a military helicopter abducting the constitutional president, María Estela Martínez de Perón ("Isabelita"), from the Casa Rosada. Just below the photograph, the headline for another article boldly announced, "No Public Spectacles." The military leaders had temporarily banned everything public, from theater to horse races.[1] They, after all, were the national protagonists, theirs the mission, theirs the drama. The idea was not merely to seize power; they had done that. Now they wanted to usurp the space formerly associated with civil society. Why was controlling spectacle so vital to their political agenda? Was their "process of national reorganization," as they euphemistically called their assault on the civilian population, in itself spectacular? If so, how many spectacles were taking place? Was the coup as act part of a larger, consensus-building spectacle unfolding both before and after 24 March? Or did its status as singular, direct act put it in a different category altogether?

Neil Larsen argues that if "one is able to view the event-form of the 'golpe' as in essence a brief but extremely concentrated civil war ending only in a *military solution*, there then opens up a space for historical interpretation of succeeding events as the struggle to establish a stabilized social *consensus*. It is by means of this consensus that provisional military supremacy (domestic terror) becomes definitive politi-

---

1. The exception to the general ban was the soccer game scheduled for that day. See n. 3. All translations are mine unless otherwise noted.

cal victory."[2] The coup as event, in other words, belongs to a different performative mode than the consensus-producing spectacles needed to make good the coup. The Argentine Dirty War thus seems to have presented two kinds of events. The first, the coup, posed as a unique event, never to be repeated. The second worked to normalize the situation by extending the temporal and spatial reach of the military men into civil society. This second category of event would include various forms of public spectacle—the 1978 World Cup, analyzed in Larsen's essay, as well as other events and images circulating in the public sphere—that the junta used to create a sense of national unity.

I see the spectacles of the Dirty War quite differently. The coup as event and the consensus-building project were intricately related. They created not a consensual society but a militarized zone. As the military's display demonstrated, Argentina was at war. The population, confined to spectatorship, was either seduced or coerced into identifying with the military project. Thus I disagree with Larsen's conclusion that the junta's downfall in 1983 can be attributed to its failure to create a civil society. The disastrous military failure in the Falkland Islands/Malvinas war probably had more to do with it, not to mention the severe economic crisis that resulted from the huge foreign debt incurred to finance the "war on subversion." Although various factors clearly contributed to the military's inability to achieve a "definitive political victory," the immediate causes for its dishonor had more to do with failures of war than with failures to lay the basis for peace.[3]

2. Larsen, "Sport as Civil Society: The Argentinean Junta Plays Championship Soccer," in *The Discourse of Power: Culture, Hegemony, and the Authoritarian State*, ed. Neil Larsen (Minneapolis: Institute for the Study of Ideologies and Literatures, 1983), 113–28.

3. Larsen's example of soccer as a spectacle related to civil society is an interesting one, although, as I argue elsewhere, the 1978 World Cup restaged, in a supposedly nonpolitical space, the same contentious worldview and masculinist values endorsed by the military. The all-male world divided into the "us" versus the enemy "them," the rigorously trained and disciplined male body as the embodiment of national identity and aspirations. The role of the spectators on the sidelines, who could manifest their feelings of national identity only by feminizing and symbolically violating the enemy other, can be seen to have been an extension of the military spectacle (see my book *Disappearing Acts: Spectacles of Gender and Nationalism in Argentina's "Dirty War"* [Durham, N.C.: Duke University Press, in press]).

The coup as event and the consensus-building spectacles converged to feminize the population as it made military violence look necessary, even desirable. Though apparently discrete events, their success and coherence depended on their iterability. The "unique" military coup was, after all, only the most recent of six in Argentina alone since 1930. The showing of the instruments, the total occupation of public space, and the mechanical display of rigid, controlled male bodies against which the leader(s) stood tall illustrated both the mimetic quality of totalitarian performance and the prohibitions built into it; the population was forbidden from mimicking or parodying its gestures. Interestingly, the public exhibition of power was unnecessary from a strictly military perspective, since Isabelita had no one to defend her. The junta leaders were the very men in charge of her armed forces. Rather than whisk her away by helicopter, with a highly visible military backup, they might just as effectively have abducted her by cab. The display of military might was just that, a show, a ritualistic declaration of a "new beginning." The event was not a "brief but extremely concentrated civil war," for that, like all wars, presupposes two sides. In 1976 Argentina, unlike 1973 Chile, for example, no one was fighting back.

The demonstration of strength was necessary for performative rather than military effect. The junta deliberately stressed the ritualistic (and thus quasi-sacred) nature of its endeavor or *proceso* (process). Like the tripartite ritual pattern identified by anthropologists such as Arnold van Gennep and Victor Turner, the process was characterized by a breach (the coup), a moment of crisis or liminality (the Dirty War), and a period of supposed *reorganización* (reintegration).[4] The coup as event inaugurated the new beginning, setting the three junta leaders (who had just hours before served under Isabelita) apart from the old order. The junta nonetheless promised a return to Argentina's original, albeit long-lost, glory. The reintegration or restoration of order associated with the ritual process was declared, though never achieved.

The tripartite staging was, by the logic of ritual, citational. It modeled itself on previous coups that were themselves indebted to earlier displays of heroic military prowess. This all-too-recognizable

4. See Victor Turner, *The Anthropology of Performance* (New York: PAJ, 1986).

show signaled invincibility, virility, superior strength. Part of the efficacy of the coup as event, then, stemmed from its respect for convention. The public immediately saw it as a *golpe* and reacted appropriately, vacating the public spaces. The communication was successful,
though the military show resulted in absenting the addressee (the public). A performance that "disappears" its audience seems to invert
the traditional theatrical dependence on presencing. But there is
nothing nonperformative or antidramatic about a strategy that convinces viewers of the reality and power of what they are not allowed
to see. Pre-Columbian rituals, horror shows, and erotica function on
the same principle. The population got the picture and stayed out of
the way.

Just as the physical staging of this coup mirrored earlier ones, so
did its language sound familiar. Each coup promised the end of the
old order, the dawning of the new, and progress toward Argentina's
glorious future.[5] But the performance's source of power, its iterability,
needed to be kept hidden. Each junta annulled the past by mandating
a new beginning. The joke of so many new beginnings, of course, is
that each junta repeated the slate cleaning of the one before, monot-
onously laying claim to originality.

The consensus-producing spectacles entailed different performative strategies, different modes of presencing, and unfolded in a different temporal and spatial framework. As opposed to the coup, which
both depended on and disclaimed its iterability, the endless parades,
fairs, ceremonies, and celebrations of the military relied openly on
repetition. They affirmed the givenness, even the naturalness, of the
military presence. And unlike the well-produced coup, with its precise
orchestration and strict timing, the national crisis seemed to be everywhere, uncontainable, threatening to undermine all social control.
For months before 24 March, the daily newspapers were filled with
photographs and articles highlighting civil disturbances. The names
and faces of the victims interrupted all broadcasts and intruded even
into the sequestered women's sections of newspapers and magazines.
Nothing was sacred, the reporting suggested. Though the unrest was
real enough, the image of the dangerous, "crazy," "irrational" Left

5. See Graciela Scheines, *Las metáforas del fracaso: Desencuentros y utopías en la cultura
argentina* (Buenos Aires: Editorial Sudamericana, 1995).

responsible for it was, to a great extent, created by the military and its sympathizers.[6]

No doubt of the turmoil. Many well-meaning, committed students and workers organized nonviolent resistance to the harsh economic policies implemented by Isabelita and her adviser, López Rega. Workers went on strike to denounce the escalating cost of living and the drop in wages as Argentina moved into a global market. Students worked in the shantytowns, in community projects, and in universities and high schools to promote social justice and equality. But the military greatly exaggerated the number of armed antigovernment forces to substantiate its assertions that World War III had broken out on Argentine soil. Isabelita's government was shown as hysterical and out of control. "Are We Really Going Crazy?" the headlines asked.[7] The only rational solution, the military-controlled media suggested, was to turn the government over to some good, strong men. Paid political advertisements and "letters to the editor" called for immediate intervention by the armed forces. The coup itself, then, seemed little more than the logical culmination of a mounting crisis, the climax in a drama plotted and staged with all the care and forethought of a Greek tragedy. Everyone expected the coup; most welcomed it. No one, it seems, was caught off guard except Isabelita herself, who is reported to have argued that she couldn't go into political confinement because she didn't have anything to wear.[8]

The spectacles coalesced in staging desire for order and national unity as desire for the military itself. The performance effectively tapped into an *ur*-scenario of nation building that featured a lone male struggling to define himself not only in opposition to other men

6. Aside from the fact that there is no neat Left-Right distinction, there is evidence that oppositional forces had been infiltrated by government agents. Mario Firmenich, leader of the leftist Peronist group, the Montoneros, is said to have been a double agent (see Martin Edwin Anderson, "Dirty Secrets of the 'Dirty War,' " *Nation*, 13 March 1989, 340). The military orchestrated much of the oppositional violence to justify its imposed rule. To complicate matters further, members of the Montoneros and other opposition groups welcomed the social disruption and looked forward to the military coup, not simply because they had little use for "Martínez," as they now called their president, but because they thought that a coup would motivate oppositional groups and the Argentine population to form a united resistance.
7. *Gente*, 22 January 1976, 4–5.
8. "La historia secreta de la caída de Isabel Perón," *Gente*, 1977, 177.

(the enemy) but also in opposition to an empty, hostile, "feminine" environment.[9] To secure power, the dominant male had to feminize and violate the enemy other. This practice was not only symbolic, as attested by the nineteenth-century method of raping one's enemies anally with the *mazorca* (corn cob). Each side watched its back for fear of being overcome and feminized by an antagonist. Though the conflict was cast in gendered binaries, neither side was occupied by real women. Women were backgrounded as historical figures or were "disappeared" symbolically. The same populist rhetoric, as Doris Sommer shows, links this backward-looking tradition to recent bids for modernization and economic autonomy staged by political figures such as Perón.[10] The need to preserve the glorious *patria*, or motherland, justified the national and international battle between men.

This conflictual scenario, with its roots deep in the Argentine imaginary, had compelling explanatory power during the Dirty War. It legitimated the quest for order even as it gendered the enemy and backgrounded the population. Whether they were regaining control from the hysterical Isabelita or fighting the "subversives" (who were feminized as well), or challenging "La Thatcher," whom they portrayed as delusional for clinging to the Falkland Islands/Malvinas, the junta leaders fetishized male virility into a model of authentic Argentineness.[11] But for all its repetition, the deployment of the scenario was anything but static. The image of the soldier took various guises, depending, among other factors, on the political situation. I will explore two uses of the image at two moments in the military's quest

9. In the sixteenth century images began to emerge that portrayed the environment as a "disloyal and fearless" *señora* who hates and kills men. Battles for land and sovereignty were fought over the female body, literally and metaphorically. In 1540, hungry, exhausted, and disillusioned by the lack of gold or silver, Spanish soldiers were encouraged to persevere by their commander, who promised them an abundance of another natural resource: "hot" Guarani women. During the colonial period, indigenous men were accused of stealing white women, an outrage that justified the extermination of the indigenous populations. Aside from the continuing struggles staged on and around the body of real, historical women, the ideal of woman also sublimated into the symbolic *patria* (or motherland).

10. Sommer, *One Master for Another: Populism as Patriarchal Rhetoric in Dominican Novels* (Lanham, Md.: University Press of America, 1983).

11. The cover of the weekly magazine *Tal Cual* lampooned a costumed Thatcher under the headline "Thatcher Is Crazy. She Thinks She's Wonder Woman."

Figure 1

for national support. The first, presented before the military takeover, is tentative, appealing, almost coy: should we or shouldn't we? (fig. 1). The second, occurring after the junta had grabbed political power, was, not surprisingly, bold, declarative, even imperative.

Three days before the coup, a drawing of a lone soldier circulated in the major centrist newspaper, *La Nación*. It was a promilitary political advertisement; the young, innocent-looking soldier was preparing for a just, "clean" war. In a style typical of poster art, the soldier seemed to set out into the dark, unknown terrain to vanquish evil. The medium—a drawing, as opposed to a photograph—presented warfare as no more than a possibility. The viewer was asked to imagine the good fight, to visualize the good soldier. This was not reality, the drawing implied, but an invitation to consider war. It more than foreshadowed upcoming events; it staged what the armed forces presented as their hesitation, almost their reluctance, to take that dramatic step forward. Where would the action lead? the military seemed to ask, even as its financial guru, José Martínez de Hoz, put the final touches on the undemocratic and backbreaking program that the junta unleashed on the workforce a few days later.

The soldier's nervousness emanates from the page. He is truly alone, surrounded by a vast, black emptiness. Should he go forth into the dark? Or, as his glancing over his shoulder suggests, should he watch his back? Where does the enemy lurk, outside in the dark night or within the "pueblo" he hopes will support him? He looks vulnerable, even frightened. He, too, runs the risk of being vanquished and feminized. Which way does heroism lie? Should he fight the good fight? Or should he selfishly, and perhaps with fatal consequences for all, stay out of the fray? His haunted eyes plead for reciprocity and solidarity, pulling the viewer into the frame. The drawing transmits the nervousness of the legitimating project itself. Will the audience respond to the event appropriately?

The emphatic tone and layout of the text counters the soldier's questioning look. "YOU'RE NOT ALONE . . . your nation stands behind you," the caption cries at him. The typesetting attempts to convey the overwhelming clamor of public support. The bold, crowded letters leave no room for contradiction. The speech act aims to create consensus. The Spanish word *pueblo* collapses both the nation and the "masses" that inhabit it, signaling the military's fantasy of a harmonious country united by war, "his" war. "Yes, your fight isn't easy, but knowing that you've got truth on your side makes it easier. Your war is clean." Days before the coup, the ad elevated Argentina's civil conflict to a war. But the armed forces' protestations of a clean war, maintained in the face of all evidence, find an ironic, no doubt unintended counterpoint in the drawing's black, murky background. Insistence continues through the short, choppy clauses: "Because you didn't betray. Because you didn't vow in vain. Because you didn't sell out your Patria. You didn't think of running away." The negative construction of the appeal, beginning with the opening "no," sets the soldier ("you") apart from all the implied "thems." Unlike all the enemies and sissies, the soldier had not (and, of course, could not) "run away." Unlike all the international bankers and financiers (usually associated with Jews), the simple soldier had not "sold out" his country. Unlike the treacherous women like Isabelita who had brought it to the verge of chaos, the soldier stood true and firm. The linguistic juxtaposition of the "Sí, no" inadvertently betrays the mixed message, confirmed by the drawing itself. Though the soldier clutches a rifle, the caption assures us that he holds nothing but the "truth." "You're not alone," repeated again, urges us to suspend our disbelief. Aloneness is transformed into solidarity; a weapon metamorphoses into the objectification of truth. The misrepresentation, more than the darkness, limits our capacity to make out the scenario clearly.

The drawing presents male heroism in opposition to an enemy other lurking somewhere. Danger conflates with femininity, conjured up by all that is dark, threatening, unseen, and inscrutable. This figuration supercedes the gendered mythic scenario in which the male is the doer and creator of cultural difference.[12] The representation recalls a very specific and violent political practice. The soldier must overcome the threatening feminine other or be vanquished and subjected to *mazorca*-esque tortures.

The image of the lone soldier also gendered the viewer. The eyes of the Argentine population (condemned to spectatorship) were fixed on the hero. Viewers were encouraged to identify with him: "You're not alone." Their role was to legitimate, not to participate in, the struggle. Cast in a supporting role, spectators were prompted to feel protective of, even maternal toward, this innocent young man. But the feminization that allowed for maternal support also posed the danger of things feminine. What if the viewers betrayed him? So the unreliable public was simply excluded from the frame. No wonder the soldier watched his back. The image brilliantly enacted military control: it "disappeared" the viewer. A ventriloquist silenced the public by

12. See Teresa de Lauretis, *Alice Doesn't: Feminism, Semiotics, Cinema* (Bloomington: Indiana University Press, 1984).

appropriating its voice. The dialogue staged here takes place between the young man in the drawing and the reassuring (disembodied) words in bold type. The strategy presupposes that the spectators will accept those words as their own. The reluctant soldier calls for louder words, ever more emphatic approval. The end of the caption echoes its beginning: "You're not alone." The circle is closed. What else is there to say? The image of the young warrior male, in a manner typical of fascist iconography, neutralizes its sinister message. Who could imagine, by looking at this young soldier, that thirty thousand people would be abducted, tortured, and "disappeared" by the military during the next few years?

The junta's self-representation, not surprisingly, radically changed immediately after the coup. The decisive step had been taken. The population had not said no to the lone soldier. The photographs included here, taken by photographers who worked for the rigidly censored national and international news services, were reprinted nationally to chronicle the "new" climactic (rather than anticipatory) moment in the performance.

In its first official pronouncement, transmitted nationally as the helicopter lifted off, the junta declared itself the "supreme organ of the Nation," ready to "fill the void of power" embodied by Isabelita.[13] The word *organ* indicates both the fetishistic quality of state power, incarnated in the virile personhood of a few select men, and the explicit link between male sexuality and supreme power. The junta consciously represented itself as the model of leadership: male, measured, mature, and responsible, as opposed to Isabelita, who was female, hysterical, unqualified, and out of control. With a show of muscle, the junta undertook its exercise in national body building, determined to transform the "infirm," inert Argentine masses into an authentic "national being" (Troncoso, 107). The imposition of the *proceso* was portrayed as a "coming of age" for the military males, now free from the corrupting feminine presence.[14] The military heralded its

13. The speech was printed in its entirety in *La Nación* on the day of the coup. It is also reprinted in Oscar Troncoso, comp. *El proceso de reorganización nacional: Cronología y documentación*, vol. 1 (Buenos Aires: Centro Editor de América Latina, 1984), 107–9.
14. "Llegó el momento en que asumimos nuestra mayoría de edad y aplicamos nuestra propia doctrina" (*La Prensa*, 1 April 1981), quoted in Daniel Frontalini and

Figure 2

ascension to power as the "dawning of a fecund epoch," although the
generative process was not, as it recognized, "natural." Isabelita's government was sick; its "productive apparatus" exhausted. "Natural" solutions
were no longer sufficient to insure a full "recuperation" (Troncoso, 107).
As President Videla declared a few months later, the mother *patria* was
"bleeding to death. When it most urgently needs her children, more
and more of them are submerged in her blood" (Troncoso, 59). The
conflict was being fought in her interstices. To save her, the social "body"
would be turned inside out and upside down. "Subversion" (any and
all opposition to the armed forces) was thus hidden, dangerous, dirty.

Opposed to the interiority associated with subversion, the military represented itself as all surface: identifiable by its uniforms,
aggressively visible, on parade for all the world to see (fig. 2). The
moving vehicles simultaneously signaled progress and restoration; the
junta moved forward to reinstate discipline. Staging order, as in ritual,
would make order happen. The iterability of the performance con-

María Cristina Caiati, *El mito de la "guerra sucia"* (Buenos Aires: Centro de Estudios
Legales y Sociales, 1984), 32.

Figure 3

tributed to the dictatorship's legitimacy. The "restored" nature of the
performance suggested that order itself had been restored. The military display acted, enacted, and reenacted the (new—now more
than ever—always) social system: all male, Catholic, and strictly
hierarchical (fig. 3). The display of the military leaders in church
aligned military and sacred power, stabilizing the former through
identification with the latter. The image naturalized the contradiction posed by having armed soldiers positioned around the church.
Wasn't the restoration of a universal and static "good" a sacred mission, after all? In figure 4, the unholy trinity (army, navy, and air
force) appear as one entity, set apart as in religious iconography,
embodying national aspirations of grandeur. The photograph, which
zooms in on the three junta leaders at an air force show, suggests that
their attention is transfixed on transcendent goals. The image distances them from the surrounding figures. Unlike the unruly women
immediately behind them, these leaders focus on the matter at hand.
Unlike the scattered and disorderly men in the background, the leaders stand erect. Isolation augments their aura of power by enlarging
their scale and by projecting a model of visual domination.

Figure 4

The junta leaders' performance fetishized the state into a cohe-
sive whole. By embodying the abstract state, they rendered it visible
and identifiable and endowed it with a "sacred and erotic attraction."[15]
What made the military's version of world order *desirable* stemmed
from the exhibitionistic display of hard bodies and military hardware
(see fig. 2). The feminine ideal, the *patria*, mediated the autoeroticism of the performance. The armed forces obsessively conjured up
the symbolic woman to keep their homosocial society from becoming
a homosexual one. The military men came together in the heterosexual language of love of the *patria* (fig. 5).

The armed forces presented their mission (much as the poster of
the lone soldier had done) as a shared struggle. They urged the population to participate in mimetic desire by desiring that which they
themselves desired: "All the representative sectors of the country
should feel clearly identified with the project. In this new stage there is
a combat role for each citizen. The task is hard and urgent. It is not

15. Michael Taussig, "Maleficium: State Fetishism," in *Fetishism as Cultural Discourse,*
ed. Emily Apter and William Pietz (Ithaca, N.Y.: Cornell University Press, 1993), 218.

Figure 5

without sacrifice but is taken on with the absolute conviction that the example will be set from the top" (Troncoso, 108). The junta leaders explicitly set themselves up as models, urging the population to trust in their power to control events and carry the endeavor forward. They spoke as a central, unified subject; their "we" supposedly included everyone.[16] The combat role that the military envisioned for the pop-

16. For discussions of the representation of the military as a unified subject see Francine Masiello, "La Argentina durante el proceso: Las múltiples resistencias de la

ulation (again) was not an active one. Rather, the appropriate attitude was blind belief in the scenario, empathy for the struggle, and applause for the military effort. In the name of collective well-being (as in classical myths and tragedy), the community was expected to surrender its will to the protagonist. Society as a whole might be in trouble, but, as in all tragedy, only the hero was "born to set it right." The grandiose representation offered a linear progression in which the "climactic moment or goal . . . is an image of perfect immobility."[17] The scenario reaffirmed the universality and inevitability of the hegemonic order. Criminal violence claimed the immutability of art.

The junta's self-representation as a model of "authentic" nationness was both exclusionary and transformative, reenacting an us-them divide. The unitary image denied all other possibilities. But the divide was more complicated than it appeared. Visually, the spectacle affirmed the centrality and supremacy of the leaders in relation to other military males, who were presented as a mass of identical bodies in uniform (fig. 6). While the junta modeled itself on previous ones, composed of men standing just so in identical uniforms, it (like the coup as act) thrived on the appearance of originality. These leaders were singular; they claimed an authenticity that they denied their followers. The soldiers crammed into the photograph were destined to imitate, yet they themselves were unindividuated, unmarked, compressed (as the photograph suggests) into a role that did not quite fit. Their eyes, directed straight at the camera, are hostile and suspicious. Their somewhat disorderly and defiant body language insinuates a threat; they might be subordinates to the junta, but the photographer had better watch his back.

National identity and authenticity, the military staging illustrated, depended on various positions of proximity to the junta leaders themselves. The junta embodied the "national being," the military males

---

cultura," and Beatriz Sarlo, "Política, ideología y figuración literaria," in *Ficción y política,* by Daniel Balderston et al. (Buenos Aires: Alianza; Minneapolis, Minn.: Institute for the Study of Ideologies and Literatures, 1987), 11–29, 30–59. In fact, the three branches of the armed forces were bitter rivals; the "disappeared" were sometimes tortured and killed by one branch as retribution to another.

17. Leo Bersani and Ulysse Dutoit, *The Forms of Violence: Narrative in Assyrian Art and Modern Culture* (New York: Schocken, 1985), 6.

Figure 6

imitated them, spectators identified with them vicariously, and those
who were unsympathetic could no longer claim ties to the social body.
A complicated play of looks marked lines and degrees of inclusion and
exclusion: the junta kept an eye on the military even as the common
soldier looked up at it; members of the population might find themselves more comfortable as an undifferentiated audience than singled
out as objects of the military gaze. Exclusion went in tandem with feminization. While the junta embodied masculinity, the masses were feminized. As before, gender constituted grounds for marginalization;
women and nonassimilable men were pushed to the side.

The junta's political power drew from the unequal visual economy it established with the public. The military male might be on
display, but he did not look back. The leaders' disciplined, virile bodies might seduce, but they were impervious to seduction. Unlike the
lone soldier in the poster, the triumphant soldier denied the reciprocity of the public's gaze. The military's visual self-referentiality
"disappeared" its audience by making it invisible and denying it

legitimacy as spectator. The military's spectacles inflicted percepticide literally on its blindfolded victims and metaphorically on the population at large, which was not allowed to acknowledge the violence taking place around it. People had to participate in their own blinding.

The ahistorical scenarios promoted by the junta obscured the fact that the economic and political crisis that precipitated the military coup of 1976 resulted, in part, from conflicting economic interests specific to the mid– and late twentieth century: international capitalism eroded Argentina's social institutions and programs and clashed with the interests of its labor unions, which had gained power during the post–World War II prosperity under Perón. It is no accident that the junta's dismantling of a constitutional system of collective decision making (such as the dissolution of Parliament and the Supreme Court in the days following the coup) was represented in terms of the lone male, situated in a dark vacuum beyond the boundaries of communal life, with only the stars to guide him. Nor is it surprising that the emphasis on the solitary hero coincided with Argentina's economic drive toward privatization, consumerism, and international capitalism. As the armed forces invaded all public and private spaces, civil society itself "disappeared."

The junta's epic had a beginning and an end; it declared the "dawning of a fecund epoch" and ultimately legislated a *punto final* (full stop) to accusations of human rights violations. The military's efforts to come to closure by erasing all traces of its criminality served as a parody of ritual reintegration. History, as invoked by the junta, was idealized as a founding myth and placed outside, or at the beginning of, what is traditionally called the historical process. All opposing representations or interpretations of Argentina's national drama were prohibited by the military leaders. Theirs, after all, was the ultimate performance. Declaring an end to conflict, they claimed to have put an end to drama. "History," junta leader Eduardo Massera proclaimed, "belongs to me."[18]

Graciela Scheines laments that Argentina "is a country that has not yet been founded," because it lacks "epics, heroes, revolutions, and

18. Quoted in Marguerite Feitlowitz, "Lexicon of Terror" (Unpublished manuscript, 1993), 30.

heroic gestures."[19] It is trapped in "cycles of euphoria and frustration that are typically Argentine. That's what characterizes Argentine failure: everything starts anew and remains frozen in an embryonic state. Nothing comes of it" (ibid.). Here I have suggested the opposite. The brutal paradigm of national individuation has produced, rather than negated, Argentine history. The problem is not that Argentina "has no history," as Scheines states, but that it is founded on myths such as the one staged in the poster of the lone soldier, which positioned the public and curtailed its ability to respond. Predicated on the suppression and even the annihilation of the feminine, it also severely delimited political activism by women. The Madres of the Plaza de Mayo, the only group to confront the military openly, were caught in its spectacle. The Madres deployed the role of "mother" to decry the disappearance of their children, and upright military men who claimed to share Christian and family values could not shoot unarmed mothers. But their role also framed the women in the military's highly coercive definition of the feminine and motherhood. The women's performance reaffirmed stereotypical binaries: the military was armed and powerful, while the aging women were defenseless; the junta's linear movement implied progress, while the circular, repetitive nature of the Madres' demonstrations suggested that they were not getting anywhere. But the scenario of the lone soldier trapped the military itself. In response to Larsen, I submit that the military, entangled in a scenario that had helped legitimate it, could not move on to one predicated on more communal principles, which might have allowed for a civil society. "Damnable iteration," they might have uttered, caught in the citational gesture.

Spectacles, I have posited, function as the locus and mechanism of communal identity, the imaginings that constitute social systems. They reflect and (re)produce spatial configurations and establish both parameters and organizational structures. Hermeneutics thus serves historical analysis. The poster and photographs show a performative continuity: the junta could not simply switch roles and found a consensual civil society. The political denouement of the Dirty War was predetermined by the conflictual performance; no happy ending

19. Scheines, "Interview," by Inés Tenewicki and Eduardo Blanco, *La Maga*, 21 June 1995, 4.

could be scripted into it. The same approach might elucidate cultural contexts far different from the one I explore here. Public spectacles work together, nationally and internationally. They position those who control as well as those who challenge them. But feminist and literary studies have also taught us to be resistant readers. Maybe it is time to take the strategy farther, "reading" but disbelieving some of the spectacular versions of reality that we see with our own eyes.

José Joaquín Fernández de Lizardi and the Emergence of the Spanish American Novel as National Project

ANTONIO BENÍTEZ-ROJO

Repeated efforts to represent as Spanish American novels certain texts written prior to *El periquillo sarniento* (Mexico, 1816), by José Joaquín Fernández de Lizardi (1776–1827), have not achieved a true consensus among critics, not only because of differences in the criteria used to define the novel but also because of the variety in points of view that can be used to judge the Spanish Americanness of a particular text or author. Among the works written before 1816 that have been considered Spanish American novels, Cedomil Goîc, for example, mentions the following: *Claribalte* (Valencia, 1519), a chivalric novel written in America by the historian Gonzalo Fernández de Oviedo (1478–1557); *Siglo de oro* (Madrid, 1607), a poetic narration with a pastoral theme written in America by Bernardo de Balbuena (1568–1627); *Historia tragicómica de don Enrique de Castro* (Paris, 1617), an adventure novel whose principal character is a soldier serving under the conquistador Pedro de Valdivia, published in Spanish by the Gascon Francisco Loubayssin de La Marca; *Los sirgueros de la Virgen sin original pecado* (Mexico, 1620), a religious work with a pastoral theme written by the Mexican Francisco Bramón (?–1654); *El lazarillo de ciegos caminantes* (Lima, 1776), a travel book by the Spaniard Alonso Carrió de la Vandera (1715?–1778?); *Genealogía de Gil Blas de Santillana* (Madrid, 1792), a novel whose second volume narrates the adventures in Mexico of the son of Gil Blas, written by the Spaniard Bernardo María de Calzada; *El evangelio en triunfo* (Valencia, 1797), a long series of epistolary texts with an apologetic theme written by the Peruvian Pablo de Olavide

Translated from the Spanish by Susan Griswold.

(1725–1803); also his "seven exemplary novels" (New York, 1828), among them *El incógnito o El fruto de la ambición*, the only text in the series that has more than one narrative line; and *Sueño de sueños* (1800?), a satiric work that includes imaginary dialogues with Francisco de Quevedo, Miguel de Cervantes, and Diego de Torres Villarroel, published by the Mexican José Mariano Acosta Enríquez (fl. 1779–1816).[1] Other recent studies propose as the first Spanish American novel *El desierto prodigioso y prodigio del desierto*, by Pedro Solís y Valenzuela (1624–1711), born in Bogotá.[2] An interesting baroque work with a religious theme, written in the middle of the seventeenth century, it includes poetry, mystic prose, drama, and fictional pieces, among them a narration that could be classified as a brief novel.

These works and others, however, can all be objected to on the following grounds: (1) they were not written as fictional narratives, or they possess insufficient dialogue or narrativity; (2) or, if they do have these requisites, they were written by foreigners and published in Europe; (3) or, if they were written by American-born authors, their sole theme is the defense and glorification of the Catholic religion; (4) or, in general, they did not propose to refer in any fundamental way to the natural setting, human groups, localities, traditions, or economic, social, political, and ethnological customs and contexts peculiar to Spanish America. In short, none can be read as a *national* novel, that is, as a Mexican or Peruvian or Colombian novel, and even less as a *Spanish American* novel, because, among other reasons, the desire for Nationness had not yet arisen anywhere in Spanish America when they were written.[3]

1. See Goîc, "La novela hispanoamericana colonial," in *Historia de la literatura hispanoamericana*, vol. 1 (Madrid: Cátedra, 1982), 369–406.
2. See Manuel Briceño Jáuregui, *Estudio histórico-crítico de "El desierto prodigioso y prodigio del desierto" de don Pedro de Solís y Valenzuela* (Bogotá: Instituto Caro y Cuervo, 1983); and Héctor H. Orjuela, "El desierto prodigioso y prodigio del desierto, de Pedro de Solís y Valenzuela, primera novela hispanoamericana," *Thesaurus* 38, no. 2 (1983): 261–324.
3. I am indebted to numerous scholars who have written about the relationship between the novel and the national projects of Spanish America. I should clarify, however, that this article is above all the product of the dialogue that Doris Sommer and I carried on for several years at Amherst. In every respect these pages should be seen as a consequence of her initiative, insight, and intellectual curiosity. With regard to the topic, see Sommer, *Foundational Fictions: The National Romances of Latin America* (Berkeley: University of California Press, 1991).

With this lack of consensus in mind, I have decided to follow the majority opinion and consider *El periquillo sarniento* the first Spanish American novel, properly speaking. I think, however, that although earlier works manifest uneven levels of Spanish Americanness and of narrativity, which may render them inadequate as Spanish American novels, a mere inventory of them suffices to suggest a significant body of more or less narrativized texts that ought not be ignored. The apparent anticanonical and dialogic orientation of some of them deserves more than a cursory glance. Rather than attempt to demonstrate that *El lazarillo de ciegos caminantes* or *El desierto prodigioso y prodigio del desierto*, for example, is a Spanish American novel, it is perhaps more interesting to note that the organizing dynamics of fiction had infiltrated, even in the Conquest period, the various genres that were beginning to speak of America.[4] The colonizing enterprise had con-

4. The bibliography on this topic is extensive. I list the following works as a sample: José Juan Arrom, "Becerrillo: Comentarios a un pasaje narrativo del Padre Las Casas," in *Homenaje a Luis Alberto Sánchez* (Lima: Universidad San Marcos, 1968), 41–4; Arrom, "Hombre y mundo en el Inca Garcilaso," in *Certidumbre de América: Estudios de letras, folklore y cultura* (Madrid: Gredos, 1971), 26–35; Arrom, "Precursores coloniales del cuento hispanoamericano: Fray Martín de Murúa y el idilio indianista," in *El cuento hispanoamericano ante la crítica*, ed. Enrique Pupo-Walker (Madrid: Castalia, 1973), 24–36; Arrom, "Prosa novelística del siglo XVII: Un 'caso ejemplar' del Perú virreinal," in *Prosa hispanoamericana virreinal*, ed. Raquel Chang-Rodríguez (Barcelona: Hispamérica, 1978), 77–100; Francisco Javier Cevallos, ed., *Narraciones cortas de la América colonial* (Salamanca: Colegio de España, 1991); David Lagmanovich, "Los *Naufragios* de Alvar Núñez como construcción narrativa," *Kentucky Romance Quarterly* 25 (1978): 27–37; Irving A. Leonard, *Baroque Times in Old Mexico: Seventeenth-Century Persons, Places, and Practices* (Ann Arbor: University of Michigan Press, 1959); Irving A. Leonard, *Books of the Brave: Being an Account of Books and of Men in the Spanish Conquest and Settlement of the Sixteenth-Century New World* (1949; Berkeley: University of California Press, 1992); José Luis Martínez, *Pasajeros de Indias: Viajes transatlánticos en el siglo XVI* (Madrid: Alianza, 1983); Enrique Pupo-Walker, "Sobre la configuración narrativa de los *Comentarios reales*," *Revista Hispánica Moderna: Boletín del Instituto de las Españas* 39, no. 3 (1976–77): 123–35; Pupo-Walker, "La reconstrucción imaginativa del pasado en *El Carnero* de Juan Rodríguez Freyle," *Nueva Revista de Filología Hispánica* 27 (1978): 346–58; Pupo-Walker, "Sobre las mutaciones creativas de la historia en un texto del Inca Garcilaso," in *Homenaje a Luis Leal*, ed. Donald W. Bleznick and J. O. Valencia (Madrid: Insula, 1978); Pupo-Walker, "Sobre el discurso narrativo y sus referentes en los *Comentarios reales* del Inca Garcilaso," in Chang-Rodríguez, *Prosa hispanoamericana virreinal*, 21–41; Pupo-Walker, "La ficción intercalada: Su relevancia y funciones en el curso de la historia," in *Historia, creación y profecía en los textos del Inca Garcilaso de la Vega* (Madrid: Porrúa, 1982), 149–93;

structed a confluent space of languages and intralanguages the density and diversity of which had probably never been seen before. I refer not only to the complex and violent sociocultural encounter between Iberian conquistadors and the numerous indigenous peoples who were colonized. In America, after all, the idea of a Spanish nation took on certain credibility for the first time. In America, Castilians, Catalans, Basques, Galicians, Asturians, Andalusians, Valencians, Aragonese, and Mallorcans coincided shoulder to shoulder as "Spaniards," often scarcely knowing the Romance language their neighbor spoke, as in the case of the Catalan Ramón Pané.[5] Numerous Jews, Moriscos, blacks, and peoples of other kingdoms were also thrown upon New World beaches by the tides of history. From the first notes of Columbus, American contexts lent themselves like those of no other continent to imaginative narrativized representation, in no small measure because the notion that a portentous world existed at the far end of the Atlantic had captured the European imagination for centuries.[6]

Insofar as the Americas are concerned, the publication of *El periquillo sarniento* marks the complex of conditions that preceded the first Spanish American novels and short stories: a narrative tradition that focused on the singularities of the New World; the introduction of the printing press; the founding of educational and cultural institutions; the exercise of letters; the formation of the habit of reading among the middle and upper classes; the impact of Enlightenment ideas on colonial society; the development of a *criollo* consciousness; the practice of a nationalist journalism; the elimination of restrictions on the printing of works of fiction in the Spanish colonies; and finally, although of no less importance, profound institutional crisis. When

---

Pupo-Walker, "Pesquisas para una nueva lectura de los *Naufragios*, de Alvar Núñez Cabeza de Vaca," *Revista Iberoamericana* 140 (1987): 517–40; and Pupo-Walker, "Los *Naufragios* en la tradición narrativa hispanoamericana," in "Sección introductoria," in *Alvar Núñez Cabeza de Vaca: "Los Naufragios"* (Madrid: Castalia, 1992), 141–54.

5. Pané, a monk, reached Hispaniola on the second voyage of Columbus (1493). In his *Relación acerca de las antigüedades de los indios*, included by Bartolomé de Las Casas in *Historia de las Indias*, Pané apologizes for his difficulty in writing in Spanish. See the critical edition by José Juan Arrom, *Relación acerca de las antigüedades de los indios: El primer tratado escrito en América* (Mexico City: Siglo XXI, 1974).

6. See Edmundo O'Gorman, *La invención de América* (Mexico City: Fondo de Cultura Económica, 1958).

Fernández de Lizardi founded his newspaper *El Pensador Mexicano* (a name he would adopt as a pseudonym) in 1812, Mexico City had about 170,000 inhabitants and differed from other colonial capitals not only in its riches but also in its long literary, educational, and journalistic experience. Printing had been introduced in 1539; the university had been founded in 1553; and the city had become the first American center of book publishing. The evangelizing and educational work carried out by Franciscans and Dominicans in the seventeenth century had been followed by the enterprise of the Jesuits, which in Mexico had helped form an early national consciousness among the *criollo* elite. Journalism had been more or less assiduously practiced since the founding of the *Gaceta de México* (1784–1809), and by Fernández de Lizardi's time it was an established profession— *Diario de México* (first era: 1805–12), *Gaceta del Gobierno de México* (1810–21), and so on—that commented on national and foreign affairs and published literary contributions.

These conditions alone, however, do not explain the publication of *El periquillo sarniento* in 1816. One must consider the crisis Mexico was in at the time, as well as Fernández de Lizardi's position in the nationalist debate then taking place. Napoleon Bonaparte's overthrow of the Spanish monarchy had different consequences in Mexico than in the majority of South American colonies, where it prompted the *criollos* to organize provisional government juntas; although at first they swore fidelity to the captive Fernando VII, they soon looked toward independence. In Mexico, however, efforts to create an autonomous government responsive to *criollo* interests ended in resounding failure. The viceroyalty fell into the hands of the conservatives, led by the powerful sector of Spanish merchants. Lacking a transitional form of government to unite them, the Mexican *criollos* were divided between separatism and reformism. The urban group, the most influential, supported reformism, the dominant movement until the promulgation of the Iguala Plan.[7] Thus the majority of *criollos* did not support Hidalgo's insurgence in 1810. The ethnic roots of

7. The Iguala Plan, also called the Trigarante Pact, was proclaimed by Agustín de Iturbide on 24 February 1821. The document gave three guarantees to the people of Mexico: the Catholic religion, brotherhood between Mexicans and Spaniards, and political independence.

the insurgent movement must also be considered. The peasants who followed Hidalgo and José María Morelos were Indians and mestizos whose vengeance drew no sharp distinction between Spaniards and white *criollos*; both had dispossessed them of their lands and held them in oppression under the caste system.

It has sometimes been hinted that Fernández de Lizardi was sympathetic to the independence cause, but nothing in his actions or in his strategies as journalist and writer suggests it. When Agustín de Iturbide ruled Mexico as emperor (1822–23), Fernández de Lizardi did favor a republican form of government, with representatives elected directly by the people, but his opinion of the insurgents was negative: "Muleskinners, farm managers, cowboys, coach drivers, one or another penniless lawyer and a desperate priest or two. Behold our famous generals and our subordinate and beleaguered troops, made up for the most part by poor outlaws and deluded and imprudent men without discipline, order, arms. . . . Here many of those who are called *defenders of the fatherland* have been and will be led by nothing, by no system other than that of pride, ambition, envy, theft, vengeance and fear."[8] Clearly, however, he enthusiastically supported a nationalist reform in keeping with the liberal precepts of the Constitution of Cádiz, particularly the precept of freedom of the press, which would elevate the *criollos* to the heights of political, economic, and social power within the framework of the Spanish Empire.[9] Neither his jour-

8. Fernández de Lizardi, Chamorro y Dominguín, *Diálogo jocoserio sobre la independencia de la América* (Mexico City: J. M. Benavente y socios, 1821), 17–8.

9. Jefferson Rea Spell has extracted from the hundreds of pamphlets Fernández de Lizardi published the following ideas: "He urged a more efficient form of municipal government—one that would provide sanitation, protection and regulation of trade, industry and public amusements. In his religious platform he laid down as fundamental planks complete religious freedom, the ownership of church property by the state, the barring of political offices to ecclesiastics, and the abolition of the Inquisition, ecclesiastical courts, tithing, and the fee system of the priests. He attacked the infallibility of papal power, celibacy, perpetual vows, and infant baptism; and argued for church services in Spanish so that the people might understand them. Above all he stressed the necessity of the submission of the Church to temporal authority.

"Nor was he less radical, for his day, in the social reforms he advocated. The abolition of large estates, grants of land to the poor, and adequate wages for laborers were in his eyes fundamental in a real republic. He exalted the dignity of labor; while he condemned, in no measured terms, the idleness of the beggar. The Pensador stood for compulsory education for all in state schools, free books and clothes

nalistic prose nor his fiction was aimed at the education of the peasant or the lower classes (less than 1 percent of the Mexican population could read and write); his primary purpose was to correct the moral defects he saw among middle-class *criollos*.

Certainly, with regard to its language, its moralizing intentions, and the moderate brand of nationalism it defended, Fernández de Lizardi's narrative work developed out of his conduct as a journalist and editor of *El Pensador Mexicano*. One can also easily discern in his novels the impact of the *costumbrista* verses and the satiric dialogues that appeared in the press in those days, as well as the fashion of mixing Latin and biblical quotations with popular language. In deciding to write *El periquillo sarniento*, he surely understood that prose fiction had more potential to influence the *criollo* mentality than the anonymous satires he was publishing in the newspapers. The last chapter of the novel includes the following commentary: "The mischievous child, the dissipated youth, the young seamstress and even the rogue and insolent rascal handle one of these books with pleasure. . . . They open it with curiosity and read it with pleasure, believing they are simply going to enjoy its sayings and little stories, and such was the only goal its author set himself when he wrote it; but when they least expect it, they have absorbed a portion of moral maxims they would never have read were they written in a serious and sententious style."[10] In a paragraph where he makes it apparent that he understands the power the plot of a novel can exercise over the reader, Fernández de Lizardi adds: "Serious moral books certainly teach, but only by ear, and thus their lessons are easily forgotten. These [the novels] instruct by ear and through the eye. They portray man as he is, and they portray the ravages of vice and the rewards of virtue in everyday events. When we read these events we seem to be seeing them, we retain them in our

---

when needed, the abolition of corporal punishment, higher standards for professional training, especially in medicine, and more attention to ethics in the legal branch. He asked for justice for all—rich and poor alike; for the guilty, he sought a reformed prison system which would uplift those forced to live under it" (*The Life and Works of José Joaquín Fernández de Lizardi* [Philadelphia: University of Pennsylvania Press, 1931], 109–10).

10. Fernández de Lizardi, *El periquillo sarniento*, in *Obras*, ed. Felipe Reyes Palacios, 9 vols. (Mexico City: Universidad Nacional Autónoma de México, 1982), 9.414.

memory. . . . we remember this or that individual from the story when we see another who resembles him, and as a result we can benefit from the instruction provided by the anecdote" (415).

Fernández de Lizardi very likely thought that the novelty of the work, as well as its length and fictional nature, would help fool the censorship apparatus of which he had already been a victim (see also Spell, 31). (In 1812 his articles in *El Pensador Mexicano* on the injustices suffered by the *criollos* under the colonial system earned him a prison term.) In 1816 Mexican nationalism was going through difficult times: Morelos had been shot in December 1815 and Fernando VII—the Constitution of Cádiz having been abolished—was ruling the Spanish Empire in the old absolutist Hapsburg style. The prospects of freedom of the press seemed more remote than ever, and Fernández de Lizardi, always harassed by censors, government officials, and the clergy, must have seen the novel as the most appropriate genre to introduce his nationalist ideas.

Although *El periquillo sarniento* is derived in part from Fernández de Lizardi's own journalistic activity, it is nonetheless clear that its plot owes a great deal to the picaresque novel, specifically to the *Aventuras de Gil Blas de Santillana* (1787), José Francisco de Isla's translation of Alain-René Lesage's work (1715–35). Fernández de Lizardi was attracted to a neoclassical novel, rather than one of the romantic works available in Spanish versions, for an obvious reason: the neoclassical codes, the only ones that spoke of bettering the conditions of life through moral rectitude, provided the most useful means for liberal *criollos* to represent their own economic instability and social marginality with respect to the Spanish. Felipe Reyes Palacios has observed that, besides serving as a suitable formal model, *Gil Blas* portrays the hegemonic desires of the French bourgeoisie, which could be compared to those of the *criollos* in Mexico.[11] After having repented of his bad life, Gil Blas receives a castle with rich lands from a benefactor; similarly, as a reward for reforming, Periquillo inherits his master's tavern and store, symbols of a commercial activity carried on almost exclusively by the Spanish group. In this improbable denouement Fernández de Lizardi reveals with the greatest clarity the aspirations of

11. Palacios, prologue to *El periquillo sarniento*, in Fernández de Lizardi, *Obras*, 8. xvii.

the *criollo*, whose pursuit of economic and social progress was hindered by the obstacles imposed by the colonial system. Fernández de Lizardi's Enlightenment ideas (the influence of Voltaire, Rousseau, Diderot, and other philosophers is evident in his work) are expressed also in the high regard in which Periquillo holds travel, science, and foreign languages, as well as in the chapters in which a black character cites Buffon and speaks against slavery and racial discrimination:

How can I obey properly the precepts of that religion which obliges me to love my neighbor as myself . . . [yet approves my] buying for a pittance a poor black, making him a slave to serve . . . and treating him at times perhaps little better than a beast? . . . If blacks are despised because of their customs, which you call barbarous, and because of their lack of European civilization, you should take note that every nation considered foreign customs to be barbarous and uncivilized. In Senegal, in the Congo, Cape Verde, etc., a fine European would be a barbarian, for he would be ignorant of those religious rites, those civil laws, those provincial customs, and finally those languages. . . . From this one should deduce that to scorn the blacks for their color and for the differences in their religion and customs is an error; to mistreat them on account of this, cruelty; and to persuade oneself that they are not capable of having generous souls that know how to cultivate the moral virtues is too crass a concern. . . . for among you have flourished wise blacks, blacks who were brave, just, dispassionate, sensitive, grateful and even admirable heroes. (217–8).[12]

12. It cannot be said that *El periquillo sarniento* is an abolitionist novel—slavery is touched on in only one of the work's many chapters—but Fernández de Lizardi's antislavery sentiment is clear. The engraving that illustrates this chapter depicts an English officer embracing a black man; the caption reads, "I never believed the blacks were capable of having generous souls." In 1825 Fernández de Lizardi wrote a second part to the drama of the Spaniard Luciano Francisco Comellas, titled *El negro sensible*. Although slavery had already been abolished in Mexico, the work could be considered the first antiracist piece of literature written in America. Nevertheless, without taking anything away from Fernández de Lizardi's democratic attitude, to consider the black within the Mexican nation did not then present a great problem. According to the estimates of Alexander von Humboldt and Gonzalo Aguirre Beltrán, the number of blacks in all of Mexico fluctuated between six and ten thou-

This chapter, as well as the one in which Periquillo makes fun of titles of nobility, provoked the censorship of the fourth volume of the novel, not published in complete form until 1830–31.

El periquillo sarniento, with a probable printing of between three and five hundred copies, must not have had much impact on public opinion in its day. The political turbulence of the country and the revolutionary struggle initiated by Hidalgo and Morelos must have captured the attention of Mexican society. Nevertheless, there are indications that the novel was well received by the few readers who acquired it. Indeed, it was apparently imitated by the *criollo* lawyer Antonio López Matoso (1761–1823?) in his singular *Viaje de perico ligero al país de los moros* (unpublished until 1972).[13] That work, composed with novelistic ambitions, relates the life of its author between the years 1816 and 1820. It presents numerous parallels with *El periquillo sarniento*, among them the protagonist's nickname and varied occupations, a satiric intention, and the influence of the picaresque. Further, López Matoso left Mexico City to go into political exile in Havana—he had been condemned for subversive activities against the viceroy Félix Callejas—on 14 May 1816, by which time Fernández de Lizardi had already published the first two volumes of his novel.

Given its foundational nature, *El periquillo sarniento* was the obligatory point of reference for later Mexican novels, which generally continued to explore its theme of social marginality and combined its journalistic style, its *costumbrismo*, its didacticism, and its melodrama. Indeed, many Mexican novelists imitated Fernández de Lizardi's disdain for artistic concerns and the moralizing intention that characterized his narrative style, for example, Manuel Paynó (1810–94) in *El fistol del diablo* (1845–46), Luis G. Inclán (1816–75) in *Astucia* (1865), and José Tomás de Cuéllar (1830–94) in his long series of short novels, *La linterna mágica* (1871–92). A half century after *El periquillo sarniento* was published, Ignacio Manuel Altamirano (1834–93), the most

———
sand. See Salvador Bueno, "El negro en *El Periquillo Sarniento*: Antirracismo de Lizardi," *Cuadernos Americanos* 183, no. 4 (1972): 124–39.

13. López Matoso, *"Viaje de perico ligero al país de los moros": A Critical Edition of Antonio López Matoso's Unpublished Diary, 1816–1820*, ed. James C. Tatum (New Orleans, La.: Tulane University, Middle American Research Institute, 1972).

widely read Mexican author in his day, wrote: "We desire morality above all, because outside it we see nothing useful, we see nothing that leads to happiness, we see nothing that could truly be called pleasure; and since the sentiments of the heart can so easily be led to individual good and to public happiness when they are formed from adolescence, we desire that there always be a background of virtue in everything that is read at that age."[14] It goes without saying that Fernández de Lizardi, who thought that moral lessons should be long, clear, and abundant, would have recognized as his own Altamirano's ideas about the educational role of the novel.

But the importance of *El periquillo sarniento* goes still further. As Benedict Anderson notes, the illusion of accompanying Periquillo along the roads and through the villages and towns of the viceroyalty helped awaken in the novel's readers the desire for nationness. They could associate Periquillo's universal professions—he was student, monk, physician, barber, scribe, pharmacist, judge, soldier, beggar, thief, sacristan, and merchant—with the particularities of the country, in the sense of imagining what it was like to be a soldier or a thief in Mexico, to be in jail or in a hospital in Mexico, and in no other place.[15] The illustrations Fernández de Lizardi inserted into the work emphasized its Mexicanness also. From the spectrum of customs and stock characters he included, finally, we can clearly appreciate the important nationalist role his narrative has played ever since.

In addition, Fernández de Lizardi invested the nationalist project he desired for Mexico as carefully in the novel, particularly in the chapters in which Periquillo visits the utopian island of Saucheofú, as in his journalism. The project was, in outline, (1) a reformist-style political program to facilitate the rise of the *criollo* to power; (2) a program of public administration to liquidate bureaucratic corruption and to build roads, schools, and hospitals; (3) an economic program of capitalist trend to expand commerce, abolish slavery, and qualify and increase the size of the labor force; and (4)

14. Altamirano, *Revistas literarias de México* (Mexico City: F. Díaz de León y S. White, 1868), 39.

15. Anderson, *Imagined Communities: Reflections on the Origin and Spread of Nationalism* (London: Verso, 1983), 34–5.

a social program based on coordinating the press, the family, the clergy, and the state to perfect educational institutions and eliminate illiteracy, prostitution, theft, alcoholism, gambling, vagrancy, and other vices.

Of Fernández de Lizardi's other three novels, the one that has the most in common with *El periquillo sarniento* is *Vida y hechos del famoso caballero don Catrín de la Fachenda*, a didactic work published posthumously in 1832. In the first chapter the author tells his readers that they will not find "inopportune episodes of wearisome digressions, of worn-out moralities" like those he had written in *El periquillo sarniento*.[16] The warning proved to be reasonably accurate; for many years no novel written in Mexico achieved the balance of its structure and the flow of its urban language. The most notable difference between the principal characters of the two novels is that unlike Periquillo, Catrín remains a reprobate until the very day of his death. The son of a *criollo* family, he aspires to the nobility and imitates the dandies of the viceregal court by not working, by dressing elegantly, by gambling, drinking, and seducing women, and by behaving haughtily. But high living only leads him to poverty, crime, jail, and the hospital, where at thirty-one—in 1820 or 1821, immediately before the independence of Mexico—he dies of diseases contracted through his vices.

Don Catrín de la Fachenda owes much of its literary quality to its brevity and simplicity. It is artistically superior to *El periquillo sarniento*, yet for all its defects the latter, because of its great vitality, is a major work of Mexican literature, as well as a forerunner of *Don Catrín de la Fachenda*. The most influential European source continued to be the picaresque, but given Catrín's refusal to change his life, the model was the old picaresque of *Lazarillo de Tormes* (1554) and Francisco de Quevedo's *Buscón*, some of which was successfully rewritten by Fernández de Lizardi.

El periquillo sarniento and *Don Catrín de la Fachenda* present the alternatives Fernández de Lizardi thought available to the *criollos*: either they could climb the social ladder via civic and professional apprenticeships that would allow them to make Mexico a civilized country, or they could fall, weighted by moral inertia, out of Fernán-

16. Fernández de Lizardi, *Vida y hechos del famoso caballero don Catrín de la Fachenda*, in *Obras*, 7.358.

dez de Lizardi's national utopia. Which ethnic and social strata the paradise of nationness ought to include, in fact, constituted the leitmotiv not only of the Mexican novel but also of the nineteenth-century Spanish American novel.

Fernández de Lizardi's second novel was *Noches tristes* (1818), republished in 1819 with the definitive title *Noches tristes y día alegre* because of the addition of a new chapter. The philosophical tone Fernández de Lizardi sought to achieve in this work led him to adopt a rhetoric that had no room for his *costumbrismo*, his irony, and his popular humor. Furthermore, given the narrowness of its structure and its paralyzing lack of action—five scenes in dialogue—it scarcely offers the narrativity expected of the novel. *Noches tristes y día alegre* takes as its unusual model the preromantic prose of the Spaniard José Cadalso (1741–82), specifically of his *Noches lúgubres* (1798). Fernández de Lizardi must have been attracted to it because its theme, the disinterment of the beloved woman, allowed him to deliver the reader a moral lesson in a fearful setting: a cemetery in the dark of night. But in Fernández de Lizardi's version, the principal character faces not the pestiferous carrion that the adored body has become but an unknown woman's corpse that he has, in his nocturnal fear, confused with his wife. When he leaves the cemetery, he has the joy of finding his beloved at the gravedigger's house, and the couple is reunited with their children on the "happy day" of the last chapter. Borrowing Cadalso's macabre theme, Fernández de Lizardi wrote an edifying reflection on the nature of marriage when the couple is guided by pure sentiments. In the end, the protagonist's wife encounters by chance a rich priest, who turns out to be her uncle. As in the final events of *El periquillo sarniento*, the good priest gives his niece his entire fortune, and she immediately puts it to use in works of charity. One should note that her beneficiaries are neither Indians nor degraded indigents but *criollos* who bear their poverty with stoicism and decency. Fernández de Lizardi often praised such people. Near the end of *El periquillo sarniento*, Periquillo speaks of his last will and testament: his fortune is to be distributed among "decent and married men . . . men of moderate conduct, legitimate poor men, with poor families to maintain, with some profession or ability, neither foolish nor useless men" (397). In summary, Fernández de Lizardi nationalized *Noches lúgubres* because the theme could be manipulated to express his desire to build a solid bourgeois home for the *criollo*.[17]

Noches tristes was followed by *La Quijotita y su prima* (incomplete edition 1818–19; complete edition 1831–32), an exaggeratedly moralizing and tedious novel based on Fénelon's ideas regarding education. Here Fernández de Lizardi compares the lives of two cousins, Pudenciana and Pomposa, both born into middle-class homes. The first receives from her parents an education based on principles of rectitude and prudence and thereafter enjoys the rewards of a solvent marriage and happy offspring. Pomposa, on the contrary, is a victim of the careless indulgence that has surrounded her childhood. Soon she develops delusions of grandeur—hence the epithet "la Quijotita"—and grows accustomed to doing whatever caprice and desire dictate. As an adult, however, she tumbles to the basement of society. Dishonored and robbed of her dowry by an impostor, she is forced to turn to prostitution after her father dies. Then, ravaged by syphilis, she dies in a charity hospital, like the irresponsible Catrín.

Despite the schematicism of Fernández de Lizardi's propositions —the ideal woman is a docile machine for producing virtuous *criollos*—the novel has some interesting chapters. The love story of Carlota and the North American Welster, for example, alludes to Goethe's *Werther*, but plot and characters both shed their tragic nature, and, in the neoclassical manner, the denouement is happy. The story is curious because it reveals the requirements that Fernández de Lizardi's national project placed on foreigners who wished to become citizens. Welster, who already speaks Spanish, has had to renounce Protestantism and liquidate his business affairs in Cuba in order to invest his capital in Mexico. Once he has done so, his prospective in-laws need not hesitate to surrender their daughter to him, since in 1818 marriage to a wealthy North American was useful to the country.

The pages where Fernández de Lizardi sheds light on *criollo* literary tastes are also interesting. La Quijotita's family library contains, besides *Don Quijote* and *Gil Blas*, Francisco de Quevedo's *Obras jocosas*, the *Novelas amorosas y ejemplares* of María de Zayas y Sotomayor, Gaspar

---

17. Fernández de Lizardi did not hide the fact that his novel was an adaptation of Cadalso's work. Indeed, the first edition of *Noches tristes* included, as an appendix, *Noches lúgubres*.

Gil Polo's *Diana enamorada,* Cristóbal Lozano's *Soledades de la vida y desengaños del mundo,* and numerous translations from the English and the French: Samuel Richardson's *Pamela o La virtud recompensada* and *Clarisa o La historia de una señorita,* François-René Chateaubriand's *Atala,* Fénelon's *Tratado de la educación de las jóvenes,* and Beaumont's *Cartas.* This sampling of such dissimilar, anachronistic works gives one an idea of the European books that served Fernández de Lizardi and his followers as models.

After independence, a long period of armed conflict between Federalists and Centralists and, later, between Liberals and Conservatives—provoked in turn by the secession of Texas (1836), the United States invasion that cost Mexico half of its territory (1846–48), the ratification of the Liberal Constitution (1858–61), and the armed intervention of France on behalf of the puppet empire of Maximilian (1861–64)—bled the country and submerged it in political, social, and economic crisis. Not until the 1860s could the nationalist narrative initiated by Fernández de Lizardi be assiduously cultivated in Mexico. As the first self-consciously Mexican work, his fiction inspired Luis G. Inclán, José Tomás de Cuéllar, Vicente Riva Palacio, and Ignacio Manuel Altamirano, among others, to debate the particular form of Mexicanness that he had proposed, advancing the development and diversification both of national discourse and of the novel.

Translation and Revenge: Castilian and the Origins of Nationalism in the Philippines

VICENTE L. RAFAEL

The Fantasy of Communication

In the spring of 1889, the editors of the Filipino nationalist newspaper, *La Solidaridad*, then based in Barcelona, wrote in celebration of the ninth anniversary of the inauguration of a telegraph cable system in the Philippine colony. Running between Manila and Hong Kong, and from there to Europe, the system furnished an "electric language" (*lenguaje electrico*) with which to transmit "patriotic thoughts" directly to the motherland, Spain. Thanks to telegraphy, the Philippines was put in contact with the world in new ways.

This "brave instrument" (*valioso instrumento*) engaged the interest of the editors involved in a campaign for reforms that sought to extend the rights of Spanish citizenship to all those living in the colony. Telegraphy made it seem possible to speak directly and intimately with the metropole and beyond. Its promise of rapid communications at great distances meant bypassing the mediation of the colony's more "retrograde elements" and "enemies of progress," an allusion to the Spanish clerical orders and their bureaucratic allies. Hence, it did not seem to matter that the first transmission, reprinted by the editors, was a profession of fealty and devotion to the Crown sent by the governor-general on behalf of the colony's subjects. It seemed less important that modern technology was used to convey a traditional message of feudal subservience. The editors were drawn instead to the sheer fact of this "sublime discovery" capable of speedy transmissions: a "language of lightning" (*lenguaje del rayo*) that triggered fantasies of immediate communication. Side-stepping the content of the message, they celebrated the capacity of a technology to overcome existing barriers to speech.[1]

The existence of such barriers in large part accounts for the foreign location of *La Solidaridad.* Colonial censorship, fed by the suspicion and hostility of the Spanish friar orders toward any attempt at challenging their authority, along with the threats of imprisonment, exile, and execution, made it dangerous to ask for reforms in the colony. Hounded by colonial authorities, many of those in the first generation of nationalists were forced to leave the Philippines for Spain and other parts of Europe where a more liberal political climate allowed them to speak out.[2]

It is important to underline at the outset the ethnolinguistic heterogeneity of this first generation of nationalists. Though they were all young men of mostly middle-class backgrounds educated at universities in Manila and Europe, they came from the various linguistic regions of the archipelago and differed, at least in the eyes of colonial law, in their ethnic makeup. Most spoke the local vernaculars such as Tagalog, Ilocano, Kapampangan, Ilongo, and so forth as their first language and counted among themselves mestizos (Spanish and Chinese), indios or "natives," creoles (Spaniards born in the Philippines, in contrast to the more privileged *peninsulares,* or Spaniards born in Spain). Collectively they came to be known as *ilustrados,* "enlightened." In Europe during the 1880s and early 1890s they were joined in their campaign for reforms by Spanish liberals and Freemasons, at least one Austrian intellectual, and an older generation of Filipino exiles in England and Hong Kong who had suffered earlier in the hands of colonial authorities. Known in Philippine historiography as the Propaganda Movement, these reformers were based in Barcelona and

---

1. *La Solidaridad,* original texts with English translations by Guadalupe Fores-Guanzon, 2 vols. (Quezon City: University of the Philippines Press, 1967), 1:199. This newspaper began publication in Barcelona in 1889 and later moved to Madrid, ceasing publication in 1895. The translations are mine unless otherwise indicated.

2. See John Schumacher, *The Propaganda Movement: 1880–1895* (Manila: Solidaridad Publishing House, 1973) for a concise overview of this generation. I am indebted to this work for much of the historical background on the formative years of Filipino nationalism.

later in Madrid, with ties to Manila and surrounding towns. *Ilustrados* themselves traveled widely to study at universities in Paris, Berlin, and London, and it was not uncommon for them to be multilingual. Their efforts, largely liberal in character, were focused on seeking the assimilation of the Philippine colony as a province of Spain, restoring Filipino representation in the Spanish parliament, encouraging greater commercial activities, and securing equal treatment of the colony's population regardless of race before the law. That is, Filipino nationalists at this time wanted to be recognized not just as "Filipinos," for this merely meant in the late nineteenth century one who was not quite indio or Chinese, yet not quite Spaniard. They also wanted to be seen as Spanish patriots, as much at home in Spain as they were in the Philippines.

Nationalism in the Philippines thus began as a movement among groups uncertain about their identity and anxious about their place in colonial society. Beneficiaries of the increasing commercialization of agriculture and the penetration of European trade starting the later eighteenth century,[3] they sought not a separate nation—at least not yet—but a claim on the future and a place on the social map. Their initial appeal was not for the abolition of colonial rule but for its reformation in ways that would expand the limits of citizenship and political representation. The first generation of nationalists thus sought not separation but recognition from the motherland. This wish brought with it the imperative to communicate in a language that could be heard and understood by those in authority. Such a language was Castilian.

Traversing ethnolinguistic differences, Castilian served as the lingua franca of the *ilustrados*. Learned haltingly and unevenly first from private tutors and later on for those who could afford it at clerically controlled universities in Manila, Castilian allowed this small group of

3. For details on the economic and political changes of the long nineteenth century in the Philippines, see Jonathan Fast and Jim Richardson, *Roots of Dependency: Political and Economic Revolution in Nineteenth-Century Philippines* (Quezon City: Foundation for Nationalist Studies, 1979); Alfred McCoy and E. J. de Jesus, eds., *Philippine Social History: Global Trade and Local Transformations* (Quezon City: Ateneo de Manila University Press, 1982); and Greg Bankoff, *Crime, Society, and the State in Nineteenth-Century Philippines* (Quezon City: Ateneo de Manila University Press, 1996).

nationalists to speak with one another.[4] Equally important, Castilian provided them with the medium for communicating with others both within and outside colonial society. Thus they could address Spanish officials in Spain as well as in the Philippines; and Europeans and later on Americans who knew the language. With Castilian, they found a second language common to each because it was native to no one.[5] At the same time, they found in Castilian the means with which to translate their interests in terms that were audible and readable within and beyond colonial society. The foreignness of Castilian, the fact that it did not belong to them, was precisely what made it indispensable as a lingua franca for seeking recognition.

There is a sense then that Philippine nationalism did not originate with the discovery of an indigenous identity by the colonized and his/her subsequent assertion of an essential difference from the colonizer. Rather, its genesis lies in the transmission of messages across social and linguistic borders among all sorts of people whose identities and identifications were far from settled. Further, such transmissions had foreign origins and destinations, crossing provinces and continents, emanating from distant cities and strange locales. These transmissions were in Castilian for the most part, a language long heard in the colony but, because of the colonial practice of dissuading natives from learning it, largely misunderstood and barely spoken by the vast majority of those living in the archipelago. Castilian

4. There is no satisfactory history of education in the Philippines, but see John Schumacher, S.J., "Higher Education and the Origins of Nationalism," in *The Making of a Nation: Essays on Nineteenth-Century Filipino Nationalism* (Quezon City: Ateneo de Manila University Press, 1991), 35–43; Encarnaciion Alzona, *A History of Education in the Philippines, 1565–1930* (Manila: University of the Philippines Press, 1932). See also Morton Netzorg, *Backward, Turn Backward: A Study of Books for Children in the Philippines, 1866–1945* (Manila: National Bookstore, 1985) for brief, laconic descriptions of grammar books that were used to teach children Castilian.

5. The exception to this would of course be the creoles, since presumably they would have been speaking Castilian as a first language. However, the number of creoles in the movement was relatively small, and the majority of first-generation nationalists were mestizos and indios. But just as significant is the fact that prior to the 1890s, the creoles were those to whom the term *filipino* with a small "f" was applied by the colonial state. *Filipino* thus began as a term denoting Spaniards born in the Philippines in the same way that *Americanos* first referred to those of Spanish parents born in the New World. That *filipino* was historically associated with the

was in this sense a foreign language to most; and among *ilustrados*, it was a second language with which to represent the interests of the majority of the colonized. Thus we can think of Philippine nationalism as a practice of translation, here understood first as the coming into contact with the foreign and subsequently its reformulation into an element of oneself. From this perspective, nationalism, as I hope to show, entails at least in its formative moments neither the rejection nor the recapitulation of colonialism. Rather, it is about the discovery of an alien aspect residing within colonial society and its translation into a basis for a future history.

The Promise of Castilian

The sense of exhilarating possibilities opened up with one's contact with the foreign comes across in the *La Solidaridad* article on the telegraphy cable system. Reaching outside the Philippines, it was a system that surpassed the communicative limits of colonial society. The "language of electricity" cut across linguistic differences to the extent that it belonged to no particular group or country. That it could send messages to the world was due to the fact that all languages could be translated into its codes. It was thus exterior to all other languages, and this is what gave telegraphic technology the quality of a new kind of lingua franca.

   The nationalist editors did not identify with the inventors of the telegraph or, as we saw, with the contents of its transmission, but with its peculiar power to cross linguistic and geographical boundaries. Such crossings were crucial to their project. We can see this heightened fascination with communication in their reliance on the Castilian language. *La Solidaridad* was not the first Filipino nationalist newspaper, although it proved to be the most influential publication of the movement. An earlier nationalist paper was *Diariong Tagalog*, founded in 1882 by Marcelo H. del Pilar (who would later become the editor of

capacity to speak Castilian as well as a familial link to Spain further underlines the hybrid origins of national consciousness. It was precisely the accomplishment of the first generation of nationalists to convert an ethnolinguistic term into a national one by the beginning of the 1890s.

La Solidaridad). Based in Malolos, a city north of Manila, it was a bilingual publication, featuring articles in the Tagalog vernacular and in Spanish. Though it did not last long, *Diariong Tagalog* was the first in a long line of bilingual nationalist newspapers that would appear in the Philippines through the first half of the twentieth century.[6]

Throughout the history of nationalist publications then, print Castilian always had a significant place. While vernacular languages such as Tagalog or Cebuano were used in specific regions to express political sentiments, Castilian invariably accompanied these expressions, allowing them to circulate beyond their regional confines. We can think of Castilian then as a second language for translating the primary languages of the archipelago. It relayed sentiments and wishes not only across linguistic regions: For those who could use it, it had the power to convey messages up and down the colonial hierarchy, linking those on top with those below. In this capacity, Castilian played a function analogous to that of the telegraph, transmitting messages within and outside the colony.

Given the power of Castilian to expand the possibilities for contact and communication, it comes as no surprise that nationalist *ilustrados* should become invested in its use. Hence in the pages of *La Solidaridad*, we read of the persistent demand among nationalists for the teaching of Castilian to all inhabitants of the colony. Colonial policy from the latter sixteenth through the end of the nineteenth century had installed Castilian as the official language of the state. The Crown had repeatedly mandated the education of natives in Castilian. However, as with many other aspects of colonial policy, such injunctions were honored more in their breach rather than in their observance.[7] By the end of

6. See Schumacher, *Propaganda Movement*, 94–5; Doreen Fernandez, "The Philippine Press System, 1811–1989," *Philippine Studies* 37 (1989): 317–44; Wenceslao Retana, *El periodismo Filipino: Noticias para su Historia, 1801–1894* (Madrid, 1905); and Resil Mojares, *The Origins and Rise of the Filipino Novel: A Generic Study of the Novel until 1940* (Manila: University of the Philippines Press, 1983).

7. For a succinct overview of colonial policy and practice, see John L. Phelan, *The Hispanization of the Philippines: Spanish Aims and Filipino Responses, 1565–1700* (Madison: University of Wisconsin Press, 1959); Eliodoro Robles, *The Philippines in the Nineteenth Century* (Quezon City: Malaya Books, 1969); more recently, see the work of Greg Bankoff, *Crime, Society, and the State in the Nineteenth Century Philippines* (Quezon City: Ateneo de Manila University Press, 1996).

more than three centuries of Spanish rule in 1898, only about 1 percent of the population had any fluency in Castilian.[8]

Several reasons account for the limited spread of Castilian. The Philippine colony was located at the furthest edges of the Spanish empire. Even with the opening of the Suez Canal in 1869, travel to the Philippines from Spain was still a matter of several months. Possessing neither the gold nor the silver of the New World colonies, the Philippines had few attractions for Spanish settlers. Fearful of repeating the large-scale miscegenation between Spaniards, Indians, and Africans in the New World, the Crown had established restrictive residency laws discouraging Spanish settlement outside the walls of Manila. As a result, no sizable population of Spanish-speaking creoles or mestizos ever emerged.[9]

Ilustrado nationalists argued that such limitations could be remedied. Enforcing existing laws, the government, if it chose to, could devote resources to building schools and providing for the more systematic instruction of Castilian. Yet the state seemed not only incapable but unwilling to carry out these measures. It seemed then to be violating its own laws. Such conditions came about, as *ilustrados* saw it, largely because of the workings of the Spanish friars. They had long blocked the teaching of Castilian in the interest of guarding their own authority. It was their steadfast opposition to the teaching of Castilian that kept the colony from progressing. Cast as figures opposed to modernity, the Spanish clergy became the most significant target of *ilustrado* enmity. In their inordinate influence over the state and other local practices, the friars were seen to stand in the way of "enlightenment," imagined to consist of extended contact and sustained exchanges with the rest of the "civilized" world. Thanks to the friars, colonial subjects were deprived of a language

8. See United States, *Census of the Philippines Islands, 1903*, 5 vols. (Washington, D.C.: Government Printing Office, 1905), 2:76–78. The census claims that "less than 10% of the people" could speak Castilian, but that only about "1.6% of the population had superior education." I take the latter figure to be more representative of literacy rates in Castilian than the former, for one can well imagine 10% of the population capable of uttering simple phrases in Castilian in response to the questions of census takers but most likely unable to speak or write fluently in that language.

9. See Nicholas Cushner, *Spain in the Philippines: From Conquest to Revolution* (Quezon City: Ateneo de Manila Press, 1971).

with which to address one another and reach those at the top of the colonial hierarchy.[10]

How did the Spanish clergy assume such considerable influence in the colony?

To answer this question, one needs to keep in mind the immense significance of Catholic conversion in the conquest and colonization of the Philippines. Spanish missionaries were the most important agents for the spread of colonial rule. Colonial officials came and went, owing their positions to the patronage of politicians and the volatile conditions of the home government. They often amassed fortunes during their brief tenure and with rare exceptions remained relatively isolated from the non-Spanish populace. By contrast, the Spanish clergy were stationed in local parishes all over the colony. They retained a corporate identity that superseded the governments of both the colony and the mother country. Indeed, they claimed to be answerable only to their religious superiors and beyond that to a God that transcended all other worldly arrangements. It was their access to an authority beyond colonial hierarchy that proved essential in conserving their identity as indispensable agents of Spanish rule.

Through the clergy, the Crown validated its claims of benevolent conquest. Colonization was legitimized as the extension of the work of evangelization. Acting as the patron of the Catholic Church, a role it had zealously assumed since the Counter-Reformation, the Crown shared in the task of communicating the Word of God to unknowing natives. While the state relied on the Church to consolidate its hold on the islands, the Church in turn depended on the state in carrying out its task of conversion. Missionaries depended on the material and monetary support of the state, drawing on colonial courts to secure its landholdings (especially in the later nineteenth century), on military forces to put down local uprisings and groups of bandits, and on the institution of forced labor for the building of churches and convents.

---

10. For another treatment of the place of the friar in the *ilustrado* imaginary, see Vicente L. Rafael, "Nationalism, Imagery, and the Filipino Intelligentsia of the Nineteenth Century," in *Discrepant Histories: Translocal Essay in Filipino Cultures*, ed. Vicente L. Rafael (Philadelphia: Temple University Press, 1995), 133–58; Schumacher, *Propaganda Movement;* and *Revolutionary Clergy: The Filipino Clergy and the Nationalist Movement, 1850–1903* (Quezon City: Ateneo de Manila University, 1981).

However, the success of the Spanish missionaries in converting the majority of lowland natives to Catholicism rested less on coercion—it could not, given the small number of Spanish military forces in the islands—as it did on translation. As I have elsewhere discussed at length, evangelization relied on the task of translation.[11] God's Word was delivered to the natives in their own tongue. Beginning in the latter sixteenth century, Spanish missionaries, following the practice in the New World, systematically codified native languages. They replaced the local script (*baybayin*) with Roman letters, used Latin categories to reconstruct native grammars, and Castilian definitions in constructing dictionaries of the vernaculars. Catholic teachings were then translated and taught in the local languages. At the same time, the missionary policy insisted on retaining key terms in their original Latin and Castilian forms. Such words as *Dios, Espiritu Santo, Virgen,* along with the language of the mass and the sacraments, remained in their untranslated forms in Latin and Castilian so as not to be confused, or so the missionaries thought, with pre-Christian beliefs and rituals.

Through the translation of God's Word, natives came to see in Spanish missionaries a foreign presence speaking their "own" language. As I have demonstrated elsewhere, this appearance—as sudden as it was unmotivated from the natives' point of view—of the foreign in the familiar and its reverse, the familiar in the foreign— roused native interests and anxieties.[12] For what they apprehended in the friar was the force of communication, that is, the power to cross borders and speak in ways otherwise unanticipated and unheard of, and to do so in a language other than their own. Conversion was thus a matter of responding to this startling—because novel—emergence of alien messages from alien speakers from within one's own speech. It was to identify oneself with this uncanny occurrence and to submit to its attractions, which included access to an unseen yet omnipresent source of all power.

Conversion translated the vernacular into another language, converting it into a medium for reaching beyond one's own world. But the

11. See Vicente L. Rafael, *Contracting Colonialism: Translation and Christian Conversion in Tagalog Society under Early Spanish Rule* (Durham, N.C.: Duke University Press, 1993).

12. Rafael, *Contracting Colonialism,* esp. chaps. 2, 4, 6.

intermediary for addressing what lay beyond was the Spanish missionary. He stood at the crossroads of languages, for he spoke not only the
vernacular but also Castilian and Latin. And because of his insistence
on retaining untranslated words within the local versions of the Word,
he evinced the limits of translation, the points at which words became
wholly absorbed and entirely subservient to their referents. The imperatives of evangelization meant that translation would be at the service
of a higher power. Unlike the telegraph cable, which opened up to a
potentially limitless series of translations and transmissions, evangelization encapsulated all languages and messages within a single, ruling
Word, Jesus Christ, the incarnate speech of the Father.

Through the missionaries, converts could hope to hear the Word
of the Father resonating within their own words. Put differently,
Catholic conversion in this colonial context was predicated on the
transmission of a hierarchy of languages. Submitting to the Word of
the Father, one came to realize that one's first language was subordinate to a second, that a foreign because transcendent presence ruled
over one's thoughts, and that such thoughts came through a chain of
mediations: roman letters, Castilian words, and Latin grammatical categories superimposed on the vernaculars.

We can think of the missionary then as a medium for the communication of a hierarchy of communications that was thought to
frame all social relations. Through him, native societies were reordered
as recipients of a gift they had not expected in the form of a novel
message to which they felt compelled to respond. What made the message compelling was precisely its form. The missionary's power lay in
his ability to predicate languages, that is, to conjoin them into a
speech that issued from above and was meant to be heard by those
below at some predestined time. The power of predication, therefore,
also came with the capacity for prediction, that is, the positing of
events as the utterance of a divine promise destined to be fulfilled in
the future. To experience language hierarchically unfolding, as for
example in prayer or in the sacraments, is to come to believe in the
fatality of speech. All messages inevitably reach their destinations, if
not now, then in the future. Moreover, they will all be answered, if not
in one way then in another. The attractions of conversion thus
included the assurance that one always had the right address.

In tracing the linguistic basis of missionary agency, one can begin to understand how it is they became so crucial in legitimating colonial rule and consolidating its hegemony. The rhetoric of conversion and the practice of translation allowed for the naturalization, as it were, of hierarchy, linguistic as well as social. They made colonization seem both inevitable and desirable. At the same time, one can also appreciate the depth of nationalist fascination with the friars and their obsessive concern with the Spanish fathers' influence over the motherland. As "sons" of the motherland, the *ilustrados* wanted to speak in a language recognizable to colonial authorities. To do so meant assuming the position of the friar, that is, of becoming an agent of translation who could speak up and down the colonial hierarchy, making audible the interests of those at the bottom to those on top. It also implied the ability to speak past colonial divisions: to address the present from the position of the future, and to speak from the perspective of what was yet to arrive. It is with these historical matters in mind that we can return to the nationalist demand for the teaching of Castilian.

The Risk of Misrecognition

Remarking on the royal decrees providing for the teaching of Castilian to the natives, a writer for *La Solidaridad* deplores the failure of authorities to enact these laws. All the more unfortunate since "the people wish to express their concerns without the intervention of intermediary elements (*elementos intermediarios*). Moreover, in the Philippines, the ability to speak and write in Castilian constitutes a distinction. There, it is embarrassing not to possess it, and in whatever gathering it is considered unattractive and up to a point shameful for one to be in a position of being unable to switch to the official language."[13]

To speak Castilian is to be able to address others without having to resort to the help of "intermediary elements," which are of course the Spanish friars. Unlike the Dutch East Indies, for example—where Melayu existed as a common language between colonizer and colo-

13. Anon., "Enseñanza del Castellano en Filipinas," *La Solidaridad*, 1:8–12. The citation appears on p. 8.

nized and would in time become the basis for the national language, Indonesian—in the Philippines, colonial officials almost never learned the local languages, just as most natives were unable to speak Castilian.[14] Both relied on the missionary to translate and therein, as we saw, lay the basis of their influence. Educational reforms that would spread Castilian would eliminate this "shameful" situation. "Direct intercourse between rulers and ruled," would be possible, as the writer would go on to say, as both would come to dwell in a common linguistic milieu.

However, as the writer notes, Spanish friars have refused to give up their position. Instead of recognizing the desire of natives to learn Castilian, friars have come to suspect their motives. He or she who advocates the teaching of Castilian are treated as potential "enemies of the country . . . a *filibustero*, a heretic and depraved (*perverso*)" (11). Not only do Spanish fathers stand in the way of direct contact between the people and those who rule them, they misrecognize natives who speak Castilian as subversives and criminals. While nationalists associate the learning of Castilian with progress and modernity, the Spanish friars see it as a challenge to their authority: a veritable theft of their privileges. For indeed, the word for "subversive," *filibustero*, also refers to a pirate, hence to a thief.

Blocked from disseminating Castilian, nationalists also become suspect. Rather than accept the position laid out for them as "natives," they insist on speaking as if they were other, and thus foreign to colonial society.[15] Responding in Spanish, nationalists claim they have

14. For the history of Melayu, see Henk J. Maier, "From Heteroglossia to Polyglossia: The Creation of Malay and Dutch in the Indies," *Indonesia* 56 (October 1993) 37–65; and James T. Siegel, *Fetish, Recognition, Revolution* (Princeton, N.J.: Princeton University Press, 1997). My understanding of the history of the language of nationalism in the Philippines has been influenced not only by the ways it seems to have differed from the history of the Indonesian language but also by the ways in which such differences have produced at certain moments instructive similarities. Maier and Siegel, along with Benedict Anderson, "The Languages of Indonesian Politics," in *Language and Power: Exploring Political Cultures in Indonesia* (Ithaca, N.Y.: Cornell University Press, 1990) 123–51, have been indispensable guides for thinking through the topics of language and politics in the Philippine case.

15. See "Si Tandang Basiong Macunat," a widely distributed tract written by a Spanish friar Miguel Lucio Bustamante (1885) that lays out these charges. Cited in Schumacher, *Making of a Nation*, 20.

been misrecognized. It is not they who are criminals, but the friars who accuse them. Over and over again, writers for *La Solidaridad* refer to friars as "unpatriotic Spaniards," hence the real *filibusteros.* In an article not atypical in tone and content, one writer asks:

> In fact who is the friar? Somebody egoistic, avaricious, greedy . . .
> vengeful. . . . They have been assassins, poisoners, liars, agitators
> of public peace. . . . They have . . . stirred the fire of the most vio-
> lent passions, aroused in every way the ideas of rebellion against
> the nation . . . converted the people thus into parricides. . . .
> [They] enjoy the sight of fields strewn with cadavers and sing of
> their prowess to the accompaniment of the sad lamentations of
> the helpless mother, the afflicted wife, and the unfortunate
> orphan. Look at the true picture of those great men . . . those
> hypocrites, executioners of mankind, monopolizers of our riches,
> vampires of our humble society.[16]

In the nationalist imaginary, the crimes of the friars begin with covetousness, progress to murder, and culminate in parricide. From their perspective, the friars are subversives who stand in the way of a happier union between the colonial state and its subjects. Yet neither the state nor the Church recognizes this fact. Authorities won't listen, or more precisely, they mishear, mistaking the *ilustrado* desire for Spanish as his or her rejection of Spain. The delirious enumeration of clerical criminality in the passage above reflects something of a hysterical response to repeated miscommunications. Such alarm is understandable, given the grave consequences of being misheard in the way of imprisonment and executions.

What is clear is that having a common language does not guarantee mutual understanding, but the reverse. Castilian in this instance is a shared language between colonizer and colonized. Yet the result is not the closer union that nationalists had hoped for, but mutual misrecognition. Each imagines the other to be saying more than they had intended to. Acting on each other's misconceptions, they come to exchange positions in one another's minds. Questions about language lead to suspicions, conflict, and violence. Rather than reconcile the

---

16. "PADPYVH" (Pio de Pazos), "Los Frailes en Filipinas," *La Solidaridad,* 1:228–30.

self with the other, Castilian has the effect of estranging both precisely by confusing each with the other.

Historically, as we have seen, it was the Spanish friars who had monopolized the ability of the self to speak in the language of the other, controlling the terms of translation by invoking a divinely sanctioned linguistic hierarchy. Conversion occurred to the extent that natives could read into missionary discourse the possibility of being recognized by a third term that resided beyond both the missionary and the native. But by the late nineteenth century, this situation had been *almost* reversed. Nationalists addressed Spaniards in the latter's own language. The friars did not see in Spanish-speaking natives a mirror reflection of themselves. For after all, given the racial logic of colonialism, how could the native be the equivalent of the European? Rather, friars tended to see nationalists as *filibusteros* guilty of stealing what rightfully belongs to them and compromising their position as the privileged media of colonial communication. In their eyes, nationalists were speaking out of turn. Their Castilian had no authority inasmuch as it was uttered outside hierarchy. From the friars' perspective then, nationalist attempts to translate their interests into a second language only placed them outside the linguistic order of colonial society. Thus were nationalists rendered foreign. Speaking Castilian they appeared to be other than mere natives and therefore suspect in the eyes of Spanish fathers.

Speaking Castilian produced strange and disconcerting effects. For nationalists, Castilian was supposed to be the route to modernity. Progress came, so they thought, in gaining access to the means with which to communicate directly with authorities and with others in the world. It followed that Castilian was a means of leaving behind all that was "backward" and "superstitious," that is, all that came under the influence of the friars. To learn Castilian was to exit the existing order of oppression and enter into a new more "civilized" world of equal representation. Castilian in this sense was a key that allowed one to move within and outside colonial hierarchy.

Nonetheless, such movements came with certain risks. Speaking Castilian, one faced the danger of being misrecognized. We saw this possibility in the vexed relationship between nationalists and colonial authorities in the Philippines. The dangers of misrecognition, however, also carried over into Spain. Seeking to escape persecution, nationalists often fled abroad. Most gravitated to Barcelona and Madrid, which became centers of nationalist agitation in the 1880s to the mid-1890s. In these cities, Filipinos found themselves reaching a sympathetic audience among Spanish liberals and other Europeans. Their writings were given space in Spanish liberal newspapers. In Madrid and Paris, Filipino artists such as Juan Luna and Felix Resurrection Hidalgo won a string of prizes painting in the academic style of the period, which one might think of as speaking a kind of Castilian. And in the pages of *La Solidaridad*, one reads of political banquets where nationalists addressed Spanish audiences and were greeted with approval and applause.

Castilian seemed to promise a way out of colonial hierarchy and a way into metropolitan society. However, in other nationalist accounts we also see how this promise fails to materialize. Nationalists find themselves betrayed by Castilian in both senses of the word. Out of this betrayal, other responses arise, including phantasms of revenge and revolution. It is to these successes and failures of translation and recognition and the responses they incur that I now wish to turn.

The Limits of Assimilation

Reading once again the newspaper *La Solidaridad*, we get a sense of the attractions that Castilian and Spain held for Filipino nationalists. An instructive example is the speech delivered in 1889 by Graciano Lopez-Jaena, one of paper's editors, during a political banquet in Barcelona.[17] He begins with a declaration of his own foreignness. He announces to the Spanish audience that he is "of little worth, accompanied by an obscure name, totally unknown and foreign to you, with a face showing a country different from your generous land, a race distinct from yours, a language different than yours, whose accent betrays me" (28). That is, he comes before an audience and tells them in their language that "I am not you." Hence, not only am "I" a foreigner, but one who is in some respects lower than "you." Lopez-Jaena calls attention to the difference of his appearance, aligning it with his accented Spanish, which

17. Graciano Lopez-Jaena, "Filipinas en la Exposicion Universal de Barcelona," *La Solidaridad*, 1:28–46.

"betrays me." Yet he continues, even if "I am a nobody" (*si nada soy*), "I am encouraged by the patriotic interest that my speech might awaken in everyone. . . . Be indulgent toward me." The audience responds with a murmur of approval, "Good, very good" (*bien, muy bien*).

Here, the native addresses the other in the latter's language. He appears as someone acutely conscious of his difference from those he addresses. "I" am not "you," he seems to be saying, yet "I" (*yo*) announce this in your language. The audience hears and responds with approval. In this way, the native not only maps the gap between himself and the other; more important, he succeeds in crossing it. Traversing racial and linguistic differences, his "I" is able to float free from its origins and appear before a different audience. When the audience responds with a murmur of approval, it identifies not with the speaker but with his ability to be otherwise. The audience comes to recognize the native's ability to translate: that is, to transmit his "I" across a cultural divide. The native defers to his audience—"I am nobody"—and that deference, heard in the language of the audience, meets with approval. Recognized in his ability to get across, to keep his audience in mind, and to know his place in relation to theirs, the native can continue to speak, now with the confidence of being able to connect.

The contents of Lopez-Jaena's speech are themselves unremarkable and predictable. The speech contains the usual call for reforms—economic, political, and educational—that would lead to the improvement of the colony. It extols the riches of the archipelago while lamenting the state's inability to make better use of them. And it invariably identifies the friar orders as the source of resistance to change in the colony. Finally, it calls on Spain to rid the colony of friars and devote attention to the development of commercial opportunities in the Philippines and to the needs of its inhabitants.

What is worth noting is the reception he gets. As it appears in the printed version, the speech is punctuated by the sound of applause ranging from "mild and approving" to "prolonged and thunderous," particularly when he lauds Spanish war efforts in repulsing German attempts to seize Spain's Pacific island possessions. By the end of the speech, the audience explodes with "frenzied, prolonged applause, bravos, enthusiastic and noisy ovations, congratulations, and embraces given to the orator" (148).

In the course of his speech, Lopez-Jaena goes through a significant transformation. He starts out an obscure foreigner, but by the latter half of his speech, he begins to refer to himself as a Spaniard. In
criticizing the ineptitude of the colonial state and denouncing the ill
effects of the friars, he says, "There are efforts to hide the truth. But I,
a Spanish patriot above all, for I love Spain, I must raise the veil . . .
that covers the obstacles that prevent the Philippines from forging
ahead" (1:44). From being a mere native, a "nobody," "I" am now a
Spaniard like "you." This transformation is both recognized and produced by the audience's response. Using a language not his own,
Lopez-Jaena is heard. Castilian in this case allows for what appears to
be a successful transmission of messages, of which there are at least
two: the contents of the speech, and the mobility and transferability of
the "I" and "you" into a "we" (*nosotros*). We can understand the frenzied applause at the end of the speech as a way of registering this
event. That a foreigner appears, proclaims his difference from and
deference to his hosts in their own language, thereby crossing those
gaps opened up by his presence; that an audience forms around his
appearance, seeing in him one who bears a message, and recognizes
his ability to become other than what he had originally claimed to be:
this is the dream of assimilation. It is the materialization of the fantasy
of arriving at a common language that has the power to take one
beyond hierarchy. Although it begins with an acknowledgment of
inequality, Castilian as a lingua franca allows one to set hierarchy
aside. To become a "patriot" is thus inseparable from being recognized by others as one who is a carrier of messages and is therefore a
medium of communication. It is to embody the power of translation.

What happens, though, when there is no applause, or when the
applause is deferred? What becomes of the movement from a native
"I" to a Spanish "I" when the sources of recognition are unknown or
uncertain? Outside the banquet, such questions arose to confront
nationalists in the streets of the metropole. We can see this, for example, in the travel writings of Antonio Luna.

La Solidaridad regularly featured the travel accounts of Luna, who
would later become one of the most feared generals of the Philippine
revolutionary army in the war against Spain and would subsequently
be enshrined as part of the pantheon of national heroes by the Repub-

lic. As a student in Paris, he visited the Exposition of 1889 and under the pseudonym "Taga-ilog" (a pun on the word *Tagalog*, which literally means from the river), wrote of his impressions. He was fascinated by the exhibits from other European colonial possessions but felt acutely disappointed that the Philippine exhibit was poorly done. In one article, he praises the exhibits from the French colonies. He is particularly envious of the displays from Tonkin, which show the regime's attempts at assimilating the natives through the teaching of French. Such examples bring to mind Spanish refusal to spread its language in the Philippines. By comparison to those in the French colonies, "We Filipinos (*nosotros filipinos*) are in a fetal and fatal condition."

In the very next paragraph, however, Luna writes,

> The path is shown to us [by the French]. . . . But we, Spaniards (*nosotros españoles*) do not want to follow this path. . . . It behooves this race of ours—this race of famous ancestors, giants, and heroes—to think of greater things. Our Filipinos already know the most intricate declensions of classic Latin; never mind if they do not understand a word of Castilian.

And then in the next paragraph:

> We who had the fortune of receiving in those beautiful regions (of the Philippines) the first kiss of life. . . . learned Castilian . . . without understanding it. Later in that town, isolated from all cultures, we saw among 14,000 inhabitants a teacher without a degree, a priest who alone knew Castilian, a town with one deplorable school without equipment for teaching and without students.[18]

There are at least three references invoked by the pronoun "we" (*nosotros*) in the passages above: *nosotros filipinos, nosotros españoles,* and a *nosotros* that is left unspecified as it sees (*vimos*) the conditions in the colony. What triggers this switch from one referent to another is the embarrassment and disappointment Luna feels in seeing the Philippine exhibit. Its crudeness and inadequacy become suddenly apparent when compared with the French exhibit. Comparison leads

18. "Taga-ilog," "Algo sobre las colonias franceses," *La Solidaridad,* 1:550–4.

him to think of the latter as somehow superior in that it reveals what is lacking in the former. In this sense, we might think of "French" as that which encapsulates "Castilian." Through the perceived modernity of the French, the Spanish comes across as woefully unmodern. The invocation of "French" seems here to have the effect of joining the colonizer to the colonized in the Philippines, implied by the rapid changes of registers in Luna's "we." That "we Filipinos" can also, in the next instance, become "we Spaniards" is precisely because another term, the French, appears as a point of reference.

Here, a different kind of assimilation is at work, one that contrasts with the banquet scene. The audience in Lopez-Jaena's case responded to his speech and took note of his capacity to distinguish, then suture, differences. In Luna's case, the slide from "Filipino" to "Spaniard" and back is provoked by embarrassment, not applause. He sees the Philippine exhibit and imagines others seeing it, then comparing it to the French, as he does. He thus becomes aware of another "we," an unmarked and anonymous presence who wanders into the exhibits and sees him looking. He is of course also part of that anonymous "we," who we could think of as the crowd.

A crowd by definition is something that exists outside oneself. To become part of a crowd is to feel oneself as other. As James T. Siegel writes, "The crowd . . . is a source of self-estrangement within society. One becomes like it and unlike oneself and one does so precisely by responding to it. Becoming alien to oneself and replying . . . are one movement."[19] As part of a crowd of onlookers, Luna's sense of foreignness is intensified. He finds himself not only split between "Filipino" and "Spaniard" but also between one who sees and one who is seen. Castilian addressed to Spaniards allowed Lopez-Jaena to reconceive hierarchy and set it aside, even if only momentarily. In Luna's case, however, Castilian spoken, even to oneself amid a crowd, only produces a redoubling of his alienation. Assimilation occurs without recognition. He finds himself to be where he is not: in Paris, as part of an anonymous crowd, not quite Filipino or Spaniard. Recognition fails him as he shuttles between identifications, unable to consolidate either one.

One can translate, be understood by the other, yet find oneself unrecognized. Luna's dilemma in Paris becomes even more pro-

19. Siegel, *Fetish, Recognition, and Revolution*, 180.

nounced on the streets of Madrid. In one essay, he reports the following exchange with a Spanish woman:

> "But how well you speak Spanish."
> "Castilian, you mean, madam."
> "Yes, señor. I am surprised that you speak it much as I do (*lo posea tanto como yo*).
> "It is our official language and that is why we know it."
> "But, dear God! Spanish is spoken in your country?"
> "Yes, madam."
> "Ahhh!!!"

And in that long "Ahhh," suspicious and expressive, would be wrapped all the opinions formed by that Madrid woman. Perhaps we are thought to be little less than savages or Igorotes; perhaps they ignore the fact that we can communicate in the same language, that we are also Spaniards, that we should have the same privileges since we have the same duties.[20]

In speaking Castilian, Luna is greeted with astonishment, then an "ahhh!!!" He reads into that response a series of possibilities, all of which rest on the suspicion that what he has said has been misplaced. Rather than arrive at its intended address, his message—that yes, "I," too, am a Spaniard; that "I" am not a savage—has been lost. The self that speaks Castilian cannot get across. The native finds himself stranded in that "ahhh!!!" which is neither his first nor his second language, but simply a sign for all that has been left unsaid. On the streets, he discovers that "possessing" Castilian, as the woman put it, renders one an oddity, to which the only appropriate response is suspicion. Her suspicion in turn, triggers his, as he finds himself assimilated into what he thinks is her image of him: a "savage," etc. Castilian as a lingua franca in this context draws him to anticipate misrecognition. That is, he is forced to assume the place of the other where he appears as one who is relentlessly foreign. Rather than embody the power of translation, Luna finds himself the target of insults. In another essay on his impressions of Madrid, he writes:

20. Tag-ilog, "Sangre Torera," *La Solidaridad*, 1:796.

My very pronounced Malay figure which had called extraordinary attention in Barcelona, excited the curiosity of the children of Madrid in the most glaring manner. There is the young girl (*chula*), the young woman, or the fashionably dressed (*modistas*) who turn their heads two or three times to look at me and say in a voice loud enough be heard: "Jesus! How ugly (*¡Que hororoso!*). He's Chinese. He's an Igorot." For them, Chinese, Igorots, or Filipinos are all the same. Small and big boys . . . not content with this proceed to yell out like savages: Chino! Chiiinitoo! Igorot! In the theaters, in the parks, in gatherings everywhere, there was the same second look at me, the mocking smile . . . the half-stupid stare. Often, in thinking about these spontaneous manifestations, I asked myself if I were in Morocco, in the dangerous borders of the Riff, and I come to doubt that I lived in the capital of a European nation.[21]

Subject to racial insults, Luna begins to doubt again. He wonders if he is in Morocco rather than Madrid, that is, whether he is in a civilized society or among those it considers less so. Indeed, he starts to regard his body as if it were not his own, forced to see it as it is seen by others. He thus experiences it as excessively visible, the object of second looks, its difference too pronounced. His mere appearance comes across as a provocation, almost an affront to those who see him and thus an invitation to respond. They do so not by hearing him speak or even by asking about his identity, but by supplying him with others. Called an assortment of names except his own, Luna finds himself assimilated into the category of the "foreign." Yet this foreignness is not that of the crowd. A crowd forms around his appearance, but it is one that sets itself against him. In Paris, he could at least disappear into the crowd and find a place in its anonymity. In Madrid, he is set upon by it.

Being targeted by the crowd—being taken in by being taken apart—drives Luna to speak, but this time to a separate audience. He ends his essay on Madrid with the following warning: "Disenchantment will be terrible. We are told so much about her . . . we think so much of her beauty . . . that when the image melts before the heat of realism, the disappointment is fatal" (686).

21. Taga-ilog, "Impresiones Madrileñas de un Filipino," *La Solidaridad*, 1:682–6.

Assaulted by suspicions and insults in Castilian, Luna talks back. However, his message is no longer directed at Spaniards but to an audience that is absent from the streets of Madrid: Filipinos in the Philippines. It is as if the crowd enables him to find another address. Walking in Madrid, he cannot even recognize Spain, thinking that he might as well be in "Morocco," or at least the Morocco that exists in Spanish minds. The image of Spain, so mystified in the colony, turns out to "melt" on contact with reality. The crowd's speech has the effect of dissipating the colonial aura. It returns Luna back to the very conditions that he had sought to escape: that of being a foreigner under suspicion. Like Lopez-Jaena in the banquet, he, too, transmits messages that he did not originally intend. However, rather than win recognition as one who embodies the power of translation, Luna finds himself made to embody excess.

It is not surprising that amid these scenes of rampant misrecognition, he stops referring to himself as a Spaniard. He turns instead to an absent audience, the "Filipinos in the Philippines," thereby imagining an alternative destination for his words. He thus separates Castilian from Spain, appropriating the other's language not in order to return it to him but to set him aside. In doing so, he assumes the position that had been imputed to him by colonial authorities. He becomes, that is, a *filibustero* who in talking Castilian chooses not to return it to its source. He begins to traffic in stolen goods. In addressing "Filipinos in the Philippines" from Spain in Castilian, he establishes for himself and others in his position a different route for the transmission of messages, one that in circumventing the mediation of colonial authority takes on a new kind of immediacy. By shifting the locus of his address, Luna converts his foreignness into a constitutive element of his message.

Mexicans, Foundational Fictions,
and the United States: *Caballero*,
a Late Border Romance

JOSÉ E. LIMÓN

In the nineteenth century the romance novel became a socially signif-icant literary presence in Latin America.[1] In these "foundational fic-tions" sexualized desire is densely intertextualized with politics, partic-ularly with the task of nation building against the centrifugal forces of faction: "The classical examples in Latin America are almost inevitably stories of star-crossed lovers who represent particular regions, races, parties, economic interests, and the like. Their passion for conjugal and sexual union spills over to a sentimental readership in a move that hopes to win partisan minds along with hearts" (Sommer, 5). In the "erotic of politics" such romances "are all ostensibly grounded in 'natural' heterosexual love and in the marriages that provided a figure for apparently nonviolent consolidation during internecine conflicts at mid-century" (Sommer, 6).

The purpose of my essay is to expand on these vital findings through the interpretive introduction of a newly discovered romance titled *Caballero: A Historical Novel*, by Jovita Gonzalez and Eve Raleigh.[2] The novel takes us to one of Latin America's borders with the United States, specifically to Texas, where for the third time—which is to say, after the conquest and independence—the southern portion of the Americas is redefined, now as modern Latin America, by its proximity

A research grant from the U.S.-Mexico Fund for Culture made this study possible. I gratefully acknowledge the fund's vital support.

1. Doris Sommer, *Foundational Fictions: The National Romances of Latin America* (Berkeley: University of California Press, 1991).
2. Gonzalez and Raleigh, *Caballero: A Historical Novel*, ed. José E. Limón and Maria E. Cotera (College Station: Texas A&M University Press, 1996).

to the United States. All of this is, of course, particularly germane to Mexico.

In this late romance, written in the 1930s and 1940s but set in the Mexico-Texas lower border of the 1840s, we find an erotically charged meditation on the question of Mexican national identity at a "border" where questions of identity are always salient. The meditation concerns those who would in time be known as *los mexicanos de afuera* (the external Mexicans). Former citizens of Mexico, they first confront the United States in 1846–47 during the Mexico–United States war, and after 1848 find themselves nominal citizens of the United States. Yet they continue to live out a strong sense of Mexican cultural citizenship even as they begin to negotiate an uncertain future. But the text has similar implications for the Mexican nation as a whole, which, to paraphrase Porfirio Díaz, begins to move farther from God and closer to the United States in the late nineteenth century and into our own time. For it is a subpremise of my study that since 1848 all Mexicans, *de afuera* or not, have carried on a cultural negotiation at some level with the United States. *Caballero* records the first such intense negotiation.

The representative romance novel of Mexico that Sommer examines barely takes up the "northern" question, if at all. Ignacio Manuel Altamirano's *El Zarco* (1901) is almost wholly concerned with internecine political struggles between liberals and conservatives in the 1850s and 1860s and with the public emergence and resolution of the always racially charged indigenous question. Yet the novel says nothing about the dislocating, intrusive presence, just two decades before the events it reports, of the U.S. army that had captured, sacked, and occupied Mexico City.[3]

On the northern border, however, there was literally another story in the making, but like Altamirano's own late romance, *Caballero* had to wait some time for its events to be narrated. In nineteenth-century Mexico, "the national romance . . . may have seemed imminent to Altamirano, in need only of some galvanizing articulation that would underscore what Juárez's presidency had meant—autochthonous democracy—and that would enflame the country's desire to embrace

3. Altamirano, *El Zarco: Episodios de la vida mexicana en 1861–63* (Mexico City: Ediciones Océana, 1986).

a now corrected and strengthened ideal of a Liberal indigenous republic. *El Zarco* . . . finished in 1888 and published posthumously in 1901, is Altamirano's . . . effort to project that realizable desire. If the effort came late in Mexico, it is probably because, despite Altamirano's optimism, national consolidation kept getting postponed" (Sommer, 224). In similar terms, *Caballero* was not possible until the 1930s because, as we shall see, the national consolidation of Mexicans in Texas also kept getting postponed.

Caballero opens in southern Texas in 1846 at the hacienda of Don Santiago de Mendoza y Soria, patriarch of a large extended family and harsh master of a labor force of mestizo *vaqueros* and Indian peons. Through the prologue we learn with reasonable historical accuracy that Don Santiago's ancestral family came to what is now southern Texas three generations earlier, in 1749, as part of the last major Spanish colonization of holdings in the Americas. It was an implantation situated between San Antonio, Laredo, and Corpus Christi north of the Rio Grande and Monterrey and Matamoros on the southern side. The early chapters focus on the gender roles of the conventional romance characters: Doña María Petronilla, Santiago's meek wife; her not-so-meek widowed sister-in-law, Doña Dolores, the only one to speak her mind to Don Santiago; and two young grown sons, the virile, handsome, hot-tempered, sexually promiscuous Alvaro and his younger brother, the gentle Luis, whom his father thinks effeminate and who longs to be, not a *ranchero* like Alvaro or his father, but an artist. Finally, there are two sisters, both young but marriageable: the dark-haired María de los Angeles, Angela to her family, who is sexually self-effacing in dress and manner and, against her father's wishes, hopes to be a nun helping the poor; and the younger, green-eyed, blond-haired, "beautiful" and "gentle" Susanita, her father's favorite, who returns to him her total love, devotion, and obedience. Supported by their firmly controlled, racially "inferior" laborers, the Mendoza y Soria pass their days in the management of their hacienda and in blissful society with other such families.

But they face an emerging conflict. Made citizens of the new Republic of Mexico in 1821, with little fanfare and few changes to their way of life, they soon identified themselves as Mexicans, albeit of a different breeding and class than their servants. They were suspicious of newly arriving Anglo-Americans, who in 1826, under the leadership of Stephen F. Austin and in agreement with Mexico, settled in the Mexican territory just north of the Nueces River, in and around what is now Austin, Texas. By 1835 these Americans, like other factions, were in open rebellion against centralist, conservative Mexican authority. Following the defeat of Santa Anna in 1836, Texas declared its independence, which it had to defend in numerous battles, including the Alamo, before Santa Anna was finally vanquished. The central problem of the novel is thus established: how are the Mexicans to think and act now vis-à-vis the growing presence of the United States?

At the Mendoza y Soria hacienda and across southern Texas, the conversations are of nothing but political developments. The Republic of Texas seeks annexation by the United States and claims that Texas extends to the Rio Grande. Mexico contests the claim, but the United States supports Texas and, with even larger designs on northern Mexican territory, especially California, dispatches to southern Texas an army that will be in Mexico City soon after war breaks out. Accompanying the army through southern Texas and Mexico are the paramilitary Texas Rangers, many of them veterans of the Texas war for independence, who show neither mercy nor discrimination in the killing of Mexican combatants and noncombatants. Led by Don Santiago, the majority of Mexican males in Texas argue for resistance to all things American, and the younger ones, epitomized by Alvaro, "El Lobo," fight the americanos as guerrillas along the river and in central Mexico.

While the main American army is there, an occupation force stays behind in southern Texas, formerly Mexico and now a relatively peaceful rear military area. Local Mexican cultural life goes on somewhat as before, although everyone feels the presence of the Americans. Mexicans from the outlying haciendas gather at seasonal balls and parties in Matamoros even while dutifully attending special Sunday-morning church services. One Sunday morning Susanita catches the eye of Lieutenant Robert Warrener, a Virginia gentleman in the occupation army. In utter disregard of the ethnic tension and Mexican custom, the handsome, blond, blue-eyed Warrener later appears at a ball, tells Susanita of his feelings, and begins an ardent romance that they carry on covertly, lest they be discovered by Don Santiago.

Two other intriguing love affairs parallel this one. María de los Angeles, the aspiring nun, is courted by a Texas frontiersman, Red McLane, who wants an attractive Mexican wife to aid his commercial and political ambitions in the burgeoning crossroads city of San Antonio. Meanwhile, the sensitive Luis develops a homoerotic relationship with Captain Devlin, a fellow artist serving in the occupation army. Each relationship means a rejection of Don Santiago's patriarchal right to dictate and arrange his children's liaisons. A fourth relationship of desire also appears. On the heels of the occupation army, American civilians settle in southern Texas, acquire land and commercial enterprises, and become economically very attractive to the hacienda peons, who begin to exchange indentured servitude for wages earned from the Americans.

As the novel draws to a close, Don Santiago looks out on a world of changes that signify the end of everything he has cherished. The victory of the U.S. Army over Mexico is complete; his hacienda and those of his compatriots will soon be part of the United States and no longer of his beloved Mexico. His peons have betrayed their traditional obligations; more important, he becomes aware of his children's romantic attachments to his enemies, secretly assisted by the doñas María Petronilla and Dolores; he learns also that Susanita has disgraced herself by riding to Warrener late at night, accompanied only by a male peon, to ask him to help save the life of Alvaro, now a prisoner of the Rangers. Alvaro's death in an altercation with a Ranger is the final blow. Don Santiago dies, in utter despair, at the novel's end.

The romances, however, emerge triumphant. Susanita happily marries Warrener, soon to become a prosperous landowner and merchant in a new, "developing" southern Texas. With Angela by his side, McLane expands his business and political dealings in San Antonio, while she devotes much of her time in service to the poor Mexicans of the city. And Luis? He leaves southern Texas, in the company of Captain Devlin, to go to art school in Baltimore.

Through the idiom of sexualized desire, *Caballero* proposes a symbolic resolution to the social crisis experienced by the Mexicans who first felt the full imperial power of the United States and who, after 1848, were left on the other side of the border to negotiate an uncertain fate. Had it been published immediately after 1848— indeed, anytime during the "long century" ending about 1920— *Caballero* would have been a fiction upon a fiction. The possibility of social marriage between even elite Anglos and Mexicans would have been beyond social relations as we now know them to have been. To be sure, the marriage of Susanita and Warrener is consistent with the very limited elite intermarriages that did occur in certain rural parts of southern Texas.[4] But the narrative foregrounding of these women and their lovers suggests the resolution of ethnic conflict for Mexicans and Anglos as a whole, especially if paired with the peons' fulfilled desire for American lucre in return for their free labor. For the long century of Mexican southern Texas and other parts of the Southwest, this is too much romance. After 1848 social relations between the Anglos and Mexicans there were acrimonious and characterized by intensifying Anglo domination of Mexicans, elites and peons, natives and immigrants fleeing the harsh conditions in Mexico, particularly during the Díaz dictatorship. Anglos saw themselves as racially superior, had an economic stake in acquiring Mexican land by fair or foul means, and blamed all Mexicans for the debacle at the Alamo, for aiding black runaway slaves, and for other offenses.[5] In his autobiography the folklorist J. Frank Dobie, born on a southern Texas ranch in 1888, recalls his mother's injunction "that [her] sons never debase themselves by living with Mexican women."[6]

Had it been published then, *Caballero* would have asked a nineteenth-century reader to view its happy marriages as a plausible projection of the future based on contemporary social relations. I suggest that the long century could no more have imagined such a possibility, even as romance, than it could have imagined a novel of the post-

4. See David Montejano, *Anglos and Mexicans in the Making of Texas, 1836–1986* (Austin: University of Texas Press, 1987).

5. See Arnoldo De León, *They Called Them Greasers: Anglo Attitudes toward Mexicans in Texas, 1821–1900* (Austin: University of Texas Press, 1983).

6. Dobie, *Some Part of Myself*, ed. Bertha McKee Dobie (Austin: University of Texas Press, 1980 [1964]), 89.

bellum Jim Crow South in which a white man and a black woman found true marital bliss. But between 1920 and 1945 *Caballero* could and did occur; indeed, it became viable as a foundational fiction for resolving Anglo-Mexican conflict.

Its authors were as unlikely for the times as the novel itself. Jovita Gonzalez was eleven years old during the ethnic wars of 1915–16, when Mexicans rose up in a last attempt to expel the occupying Anglos from southern Texas but were suppressed, with greater and more indiscriminate violence than ever, by forces again led by the Texas Rangers.[7] By then Gonzalez's family had moved to the San Antonio of María de los Angeles and Red McLane. Like the Mendoza y Soria, the Gonzalezes were in part descended from landed Spanish elites who had come to southern Texas in the eighteenth century. By 1910, however, their fortunes had changed for the worse, and they moved to San Antonio, drawn by better opportunities, including a good education in English, and by the gradual emergence there of a small but stable Mexican middle class, and even a tiny upper class, which helped provide internal supports, among them a Catholic school system probably better than the racially segregated public schools. The Gonzalezes, who continued to struggle, settled into a lower middle class comprising many other migrant families with higher aspirations, as well as newly arriving elites and subelites on the losing side of the Mexican Revolution.[8]

After having graduated from a public high school, Gonzalez obtained a B.A. in Spanish from Our Lady of the Lake College, in San Antonio, in 1927 and an M.A. in history from the University of Texas at Austin in 1930; while in Austin, she met and tutored with J. Frank Dobie. Under his problematic influence, she became, for a time, a professional folklorist, a cultural historian, and a recorder of the customs and traditions of her native community; her master's thesis on the history of Mexican southern Texas was followed by a series of published

7. See Charles H. Harris III and Louis R. Sadler, "The Plan of San Diego and the Mexican–United States War Crisis of 1916: A Reexamination," *Hispanic American Historical Review* 58 (1978): 381–408. This biographical section is based on research of the E. E. Mireles and Jovita Gonzalez de Mireles Papers, Special Collections and Archives, Texas A&M University at Corpus Christi Library.
8. See Richard A. Garcia, *Rise of the Mexican American Middle Class: San Antonio, 1929–1941* (College Station: Texas A&M University Press, 1991).

papers on folklore, all written while she taught high-school Spanish and history in San Antonio.[9] Sometime in the mid-1920s Gonzalez appears to have conceived the idea of writing a book about Mexican southern Texas, and a decade later, supported by a 1934 Rockefeller Foundation grant, she had completed not one but two book-length manuscripts.[10]

In 1935 Gonzalez decided to marry and, like some of the women in *Caballero*, took on what she saw as her wifely obligation to follow her husband in his career choices. Later that year they moved to the very small border town of Del Rio, Texas, where he, also a teacher of Spanish, had accepted a better-paying administrative position in the local school district. Gonzalez continued to teach, now cut off from the thriving Mexican American cultural and intellectual life of San Antonio and from Austin, too. The move limited the time she had for *Caballero* and possibly led to her decision to take on a coauthor, Margaret Eimer, pen name Eve Raleigh, an Anglo-American from Missouri whom Gonzalez probably met in Del Rio.

To judge from their meager correspondence, Raleigh had a considerable hand in the writing of *Caballero*, although the historical material, the plot of ethnic conflict, and the characters must be based on Gonzalez's professional research and cultural background. The novel remained unpublished in their lifetimes. Gonzalez, again following her husband, moved to Corpus Christi in the late 1930s and appears to have stopped writing altogether in the late 1940s; Raleigh moved around Texas and the rest of the country, eventually winding up back in Missouri. The two women lost contact in the 1960s. Raleigh died in 1978, a ward of the state of Missouri. Gonzalez and her husband died in Corpus Christi in the 1980s.

Caballero, an impossibility literally and symbolically in the nineteenth century in Texas, became possible in the 1930s because of Gonzalez's socioeducational base, her ancestral background coincident

9. See my analysis of Gonzalez's work and her relationship to Dobie in *Dancing with the Devil: Society and Cultural Poetics in Mexican-American South Texas* (Madison: University of Wisconsin Press, 1994), 60–75.

10. The second manuscript, also a novel, is titled *Dew on the Thorn* and was solely authored by Gonzalez. I have prepared it for publication, and it is forthcoming from Arte Público Press, in Houston.

244 José E. Limón

with her research interests, and her English-language fluency. And *Caballero* had to be in English, because it is clear from her correspondence with Dobie that Gonzalez meant to reach the new liberal, educated Anglo-American audience with a publication in a major forum. She and Raleigh submitted their manuscript only to the leading New York–based publishing houses of the day, including Houghton Mifflin.[11] Yet Gonzalez must have also counted on the audience forming among her English-literate, relatively well-educated, middle-class Mexican American peers, especially in San Antonio, as Richard Garcia has noted.

Gonzalez and Raleigh envisioned a border romance projecting a national consolidation in *their* time for the future of a significant and growing sector of Latin America: *los mexicanos de afuera*, both the few left behind in the realignment of borders and the many who would join them as they left Altamirano's failed postrevolutionary Mexico. It does not seem at all unreasonable, in fact, that Gonzalez might have read Altamirano's *El Zarco*. She traveled in Mexico extensively and lectured at Mexican institutions of higher education, including the UNAM, during a period of great popularity for Altamirano; conversely, Mexican publications, including a local edition of the novel, were well known in San Antonio.[12]

The most fundamental feature of *Caballero*'s consolidating romance is its setting in the war years of 1846–47. From this position Gonzalez and Raleigh work backward to establish the character of the Spanish Mexicans, who came to Texas before the Anglos, and forward to record the Texas Ranger–led racist oppression and violence that descended on a seemingly tranquil, unified community. Such a strategy might appeal to the guilt and anxiety of Gonzalez's Anglo liberal audience and enlist its sympathy while affirming the

11. This hypothesis is based on archival research in the J. Frank Dobie Collection, Humanities Research Center, University of Texas at Austin. A beleaguered minority in Texas politics and culture, the Anglo liberal community symbolically coalesced around Dobie and vied for power with the conservative and racist Texas establishment during these years and later. See George Norris Green, *The Establishment in Texas Politics: The Primitive Years, 1938–1957* (Westport, Conn.: Greenwood, 1979).
12. The San Antonio edition that Gonzalez could easily have read was published by Libreria de Quiroga. The copy in the Benson Latin American Collection at the University of Texas at Austin is undated, but internal evidence indicates that it appeared after 1916.

historical primacy and moral rightness of the new Mexican middle-class elites in their efforts to lead their community. Yet Gonzalez and Raleigh's representation of the pre-1848 Mexican community is far from idealized. Male patriarchs, such as Don Santiago, and some of their sons, such as Alvaro, wield complete and unrelenting power over their women and their mestizo and peon labor force. But Raleigh and especially Gonzalez seem to reject the patriarchal aspect of her traditional culture as suitable for Mexicans in the twentieth century and in their rapprochement with the Anglo community. In an independent assessment Maria Cotera also notes *Caballero*'s critique of patriarchy and adds that for her, the rejection of it means the rejection of a hitherto sacrosanct trope in Mexican American cultural studies: the "warrior hero," who, in his most famous incarnation, resists the Anglo "with his pistol in his hand."[13] In the novel Alvaro and other warrior heroes are represented in less-than-flattering terms, and patriarchy and armed violence have no place in a symbolic map for the twentieth century. The effect would have been to relieve the Anglo liberals of some of their guilt so that they would join the project of consolidation.

In *Caballero*, as in all such romances, the marriage of initially star-crossed lovers projects the wished-for consolidation of the groups they semiallegorically represent. Certainly Susanita and Warrener project it, and more credibly now in the Texas of the mid–twentieth century. But the narrative, especially toward the end, brackets and defers their relationship as it foregrounds the more complex romance of María de los Angeles and Red McLane. While Susanita and Warrener are represented as blond, green- and blue-eyed, and hopelessly "romantic," Angela and Red are far closer to a certain social reality. Angela is of darker complexion and far less fashionable in dress and makeup than her sister and not at all given to romantic frivolity as she contemplates her life's mission of helping others through God. Unlike the young aristocratic lieutenant from Virginia, Red is rough-hewn. Both he and Angela have a pragmatic outlook; both understand that their marriage

13. Cotera, "Epilogue: Hombres necios," in Gonzalez and Raleigh. Cotera reads *Caballero* as a text that, in its complicated representation of women, fully anticipates much contemporary Chicana writing. See also Américo Paredes, *"With His Pistol in His Hand": A Border Ballad and Its Hero* (Austin: University of Texas Press, 1958).

86 José E. Limón

is to be based not on rapturous love but on what I shall call convenience with consciousness and conscience and on respect and deep mutual admiration. Red intends to be a key player in shaping the new Texas, but in Gonzalez and Raleigh's hands he becomes a liberal who knows that the Mexicans must be included in the new "nation." To this end, but also attracted by Angela's character and determination, Red invites her into his enterprise. She accepts, calculating that through such a marriage she can offer the greatest service to her people, particularly the peons. Consolidation, the narrative suggests, is better carried out by coolheaded, intelligent, resourceful, socially compassionate, "unfeminine" women.

The romance and marriage of María de los Angeles and Red McLane project what was now imaginable for Anglos and *los mexicanos de afuera* in Texas during the interwar years of the twentieth century: recognition of the Mexican community's historical primacy and repression; rejection of racism and violence in favor of pragmatism and mutual respect and admiration; and, notwithstanding the leadership of the emerging elites on both sides, full consideration of the working classes in any meaningful consolidation. For the narrative, in great detail, not only records the oppression of the peons but also takes us into their culture and gives them voice; a late chapter similarly represents the *Anglo* working poor coming to Texas. Angela's marriage continues the norm of patriarchy, albeit less intensely, as she enters Red's home as his helpmate. But in such a romance, the unequal gendered arrangement must be reread in national terms. For as a Mexican wife, Angela seems to represent Gonzalez and Raleigh's perhaps unconscious sense that the new social formation must, for the foreseeable future, admit the Mexican in a still-subordinate position, attenuated by the care and respect that the idiom of romance and marriage makes narratively possible.

That Red and Angela move to San Antonio to consummate their romance makes perfect sense. For in San Antonio, more than anywhere else in the Southwest, the changing social base during the first half of the twentieth century permitted the imagining, though not yet the full reality, of a "marriage" between Anglos and Mexicans. If Red and Angela are taken to exemplify this marriage, then *Caballero*'s projection, based on *some* such reality in San Antonio during the interwar years, may have even greater significance for our own time. We may now also read this large novel of "Anglos and Mexicans in the making of Texas" as a precursor of David Montejano's magisterial history. Montejano relies, in part, on Gonzalez's M.A. thesis, but another relationship may be seen between his sociological history and *Caballero* as a novel of society. In his conclusion Montejano fully affirms in the present (1986), particularly for San Antonio, what *Caballero* projected in the 1930s and 1940s, namely, the pragmatic social marriage of Anglos and Mexicans in Texas—the more or less national consolidation of at least this region of *los mexicanos de afuera.* As a political and cultural child of the marriage, Clinton cabinet member Henry Cisneros, mayor of San Antonio in the 1980s, "himself represents the reconciliation that has taken place between Anglos and Mexicans in Texas. This does not mean that ethnic solidarity has become a matter of the past; it means rather that it has become subordinated to the voices of moderation from both communities. The politics of negotiation and compromise have replaced the politics of conflict and control" (306).[14]

If the romance novel of Latin America was fashioned to speak of the problem of national consolidation for various countries, including Mexico, then who spoke in this genre for the large and growing number of Mexicans becoming part of the United States after 1848? As a cultural nation, Mexico never has ended at the border. In the 1930s Jovita Gonzalez, of border Mexican descent and in frequent contact with Mexico, together with her Anglo-American colleague, Eve Raleigh, fashioned just such a symbolic document, which drew on the past to articulate a romance of Gonzalez's present that imagined a future. Doris Sommer reminds us that the Latin American historical romance invited readers to be "participant observers in the love affairs that generated countries"; an "identification with the frustrated lovers whose union could produce the modern state was precisely the desired

14. For Montejano, the movement toward a working social marriage did not come about without a major "trial separation," namely, the Chicano left-nationalist movement of the 1960s. It is a small but terrible irony that Cisneros's leadership was thwarted by his well-publicized extramarital affair with, as symbolic luck would have it, a blond Anglo woman.

effect on the tenuous citizenry of newly consolidated countries."[15] *Caballero* never had a chance to be tested as an affective document in this manner, and we can only imagine its effect on a distinctive border project of national consolidation. We may not agree with and we may be critical of its proposals, but in Texas, at least, it would seem that this effort in romantic fiction anticipated historical outcome.[16]

15. Sommer, "Textual Conquests: On Readerly Competence and 'Minority' Literature," *Modern Language Quarterly* 54 (1993): 151, rpt. in *The Uses of Literary History*, ed. Marshall Brown (Durham, N.C.: Duke University Press, 1995), 265.

16. *Caballero* itself was anticipated by a romance novel from and about California, *The Squatter and the Don*, also by a Mexican American woman. It offers a far more generalized, ambiguous, and ambivalent resolution of Anglo-Mexican relations, leaving the Mexican elites and working classes alike undelineated and marginalized. If *Caballero* speaks to Texas, *The Squatter and the Don* is the perfect symbolic projection of Pete Wilson's California. See María Amparo Ruiz de Burton, *The Squatter and the Don*, ed. Rosaura Sánchez and Beatrice Pita (Houston: Arte Público, 1992). Yet another novel is deeply implicated in the debate on national consolidation: Américo Paredes, *George Washington Gómez* (Houston: Arte Público, 1990), written during the same period as *Caballero* and also from southern Texas. I am currently at work on such a reading, titled "Cuatro Caminos: Mexicans in the U.S. and Narrative/ National Integration, 1848–1945."

The Repose of Heroes

JULIO RAMOS

What is the gift of poetry to war? The year 1995 marks the centennial of the death of José Martí. He fell in the heat of battle on 19 May at Dos Ríos, in the Oriental province of Cuba, several weeks after the beginning of the war against the Spanish colonial army. According to the testimony of those who accompanied him, Martí rode at the head of his troops on a white horse against an ambuscade.[1] His corpse, captured and mutilated by enemy soldiers, was buried in a potter's field and was not recovered by the liberating army until the end of the war. One hundred years later, around the radical absence of his body, monuments continue to proliferate, speeches multiply. And they dispute the silence.

Martí died for the fatherland. He gave his life for a meaning of justice: the most basic and material condition of his existence for the sake of an idea of a future community. What conditions made such an exchange possible: an exchange between the body of the poet-soldier and the principles of a future fatherland? What discourses intervene to produce an ethic of patriotism, a nexus of identification, the logic that regulates the value of an exchange manifested in the greatest gift of all that a soldier, particularly one who falls in battle, offers his community?[2]

1. Ezequiel Martínez Estrada has collected several accounts of Martí's death in his prologue to *Diario de campaña*, by José Martí (Montevideo: Biblioteca de Marcha, 1971), 19ff.
2. On the ethic of patriotism see the lucid history of the topic *pro patria mori* by Ernst H. Kantorowicz, *The King's Two Bodies: A Study in Medieval Political Theology* (Princeton, N.J.: Princeton University Press, 1957), 232–72. On the economy of the

Almost two decades before his death (while he was living in Guatemala), Martí wrote to General Máximo Gómez, veteran of the Ten Years War (1868–78), a passionate letter of introduction. "Here I live," he laments, "dead with shame because I am not fighting."[3] Initiating an extraordinary exchange between the young writer and the experienced soldier, the letter situates us before the problematic relation between writing and the exigencies of war.

Let us examine the hierarchies that define the subject-positions in the letter, beginning with the distant and peripheral place from which Martí expresses his admiration for the military hero's vitality and vigorous capacity for action. "It has moved me many times to think about the way you fight in battle. I have written about it, I have spoken about it. . . . in the modern history of war I have not encountered anything similar; neither have I seen it in the ancient." Martí petitions Gómez for information, with the objective of writing a book on the war and also a biography of the general. The letter thus acts as a double mirror that at once constitutes the figure of the soldier in Martí's fateful project—to recall from the past a heroism of epic resonance—as it does the intellectual as subject, who is inscribed in the same peripheral site that Martí has marked out for himself. In the double play of who writes and who is written, the writer simultaneously invents the hero and himself.

At first glance Martí places these positions into a hierarchy of unequal and uneven exchange. He recognizes heroism as virile and powerful, while he places himself in the position of what he judges to be the secondariness (*secundariedad*) of words—that mediated and passive space of writing—from which he admires and prioritizes the actions emblematized by the healthy and complete body of the military soldier. "Seriously ill and tightly bound, I think, see, and write," Martí explains, identifying writing with a physical lack, as the contemplative exercise of a subject incapable of military action. "I will be a

---

gift and reciprocity see Marcel Mauss, *The Gift: Forms and Functions of Exchange in Archaic Societies*, trans. I. Cunnison (New York: Norton, 1967); and Jacques Derrida's critical reading of Mauss in *Counterfeit Money*, trans. P. Kamuf, vol. 1 of *Given Time* (Chicago: University of Chicago Press, 1992).

3. *Epistolario de José Martí y Máximo Gómez*, in *Papeles de Martí*, ed. Gonzalo de Quesada y Miranda, vol. 1 (Havana: Imprenta El Siglo XX, 1933), 1.

chronicler, since I cannot be a soldier," he adds, intending one day to publish "the hidden feats of our great men."

And yet it is important that we not overlook the multiple layers (*pliegues*) of the statement, the negotiation at work in the gesture of recognition granted to that powerful other. The chronicler's gaze and act of writing are postulated as the conditions of possibility for any soldier's "greatness" inasmuch as that chronicler makes public, by means of writing, the soldier's "hidden feats." One would also need to explore Martí's critique of violence, which some years later induced him, in a moment of rupture with the military leaders of the revolutionary movement, to remind Gómez that "a people is not founded as a military camp is commanded" (*Epistolario*, 7).[4] From the beginning of the 1880s such a critique would be grounded in the defense of a poetic and spiritual sensibility, which, according to Martí, insured the coherence and meaning of a just war, a revolution inevitably violent yet directed as "a detailed and visionary work of thought" (*Epistolario*, 3).

In contrast, the closure of that first letter is deeply enigmatic, as Martí bids the general farewell by signing himself "the sad mutilated one" (*el mutilado triste*). What mutilation does he refer to? The chronic pain that Martí suffered, in part because of the brutality of his imprisonment in Cuba at the age of seventeen (1870), was certainly not simply metaphorical. However, the dramatic closure of Martí's letter suggests a cut or fragmentation that can also be read, on another register, as the effect of the tense emergence of a subject profoundly divided, split by the incisive opposition between the priority of action and the supplementarity and suspect passivity of representation: a subject split by the "abhorrence that I hold for words that are not accompanied by acts" (*Epistolario*, 2).

The opposition between words and acts—the cut that mutilates, that blocks the possibility and potency of an organic heroic subject— brings to mind the cervantine topos of *armas y letras*, inscribed throughout Latin American history, for example, in the work of El Inca Garcilaso de la Vega and in Ercilla. In the nineteenth century one finds it at work in the writings of Simón Bolívar and in the *Campaña del ejército grande* of D. F. Sarmiento, who emphatically laments the subordinate role of the chronicler on the field of battle. However,

4. This letter is dated 20 October 1884, in New York.

the "shame" that Martí communicates to General Gómez is more radical in the sense that it inaugurates—precisely in the experience of blame, out of an "envy for those who fight"—the constitution of a new kind of intellectual as subject, whose relation to war and the future fatherland will be mediated (up until the very moment of Martí's death at Dos Ríos) by an aesthetic autonomization.

Let us examine this process more closely. From the beginning of the 1880s, when Martí resided in New York, his discourse on war was enmeshed in a complex and intense reflection on the crisis and reconfiguration of modern literature. His 1882 prologue to the "Poema del Niágara," by the Venezuelan poet Juan Antonio Pérez Bonalde, initiated the reflection, by identifying the emergence of "modern poetry" with the "nostalgia of the great deed" and the dissolution of the conditions that had made possible the normative and nomic contents of an epic authority in literature.[5] As Martí suggests, such a process entails the "sufferings of modern man" (213) before the transformations of a "new social state" (207), in which "all images that were once revered are found stripped of their prestige, while the images of the future are yet unknown" (207); it entails an age marked by the "blinding of the sources and the obfuscation of the gods" (210). Martí explicitly relates the new social state—linked to what Max Weber later called the "disenchantment of the world" as an effect of modern rationalization—to the dissolution of a discursive and institutional fabric of belief that until that moment guaranteed the central authority of literary forms in the articulation of the constitutive *nomos* of the social order.[6] Hence the poet with "broken wings": a solitary figure in a landscape of ruins, who "presents himself armed with all of his weapons in an arena where he sees neither combatants nor spectators; nor does he see any prize" (212).

The crisis of heroism that Martí attributes to the dissolution of epic possibilities in modern literature exceeds the simple question of literary genre. It is in fact inscribed in a restructuring of the very con-

5. Martí, "El Poema del Niágara," in *Obra literaria*, ed. Cintio Vitier (Caracas: Biblioteca Ayacucho, 1978), 205–17.
6. Weber, "Religious Rejection of the World," in *From Max Weber: Essays in Sociology*, ed. C. W. Mills and H. H. Gerth (Oxford: Oxford University Press, 1958), 350.

ditions of social communication that, according to Martí, were under-
going an intense fragmentation. In Martí's words this fragmentation is
what brought about the "dismemberment of the human mind" (208)
and the "decentralization of the intellect" (209). An entire symbolic
order that had once insured the articulations of society, the stability of
its nexuses, and the effectiveness of social identification was being
reconfigured.

Such transformations gave a specificity and relative autonomy to
literature. In the process rationalization subjected an emergent class
of intellectuals to a new division of labor, leading to the professionalization of the literary medium and delineating the reassignment of
tasks for writers in the public sphere.[7] Perhaps even more important,
the autonomization of the literary field generated a new kind of subject, distinct and frequently in competition and conflict with other
subjects and discursive practices, all of which in turn demarcated the
fields of their own social authority. This literary subject was constituted
in a new circuit of communicative interaction that led to the differen-
tiation of newly independent yet overlapping spheres of knowledge
comprising the social realm, each of which had its own immanent laws
for the validation and legitimation of its statements. Beyond the simple construction of new objects or themes, we are speaking of an
emerging discursive authority that was crystallized through the inten-
sification of its labor on language as the decisive element in the elaboration of literature's specific strategies of social intervention. Its gaze,
its particular logic—the economy of values with which the literary subject cuts across and hierarchizes social matter—marked out the limits
of that sphere more or less specific to the cultural aesthetic. Perhaps it
is not necessary to go over the contradictions that inflected this
process of autonomization in Latin America, save to mention that it
could not rely primarily on institutional support throughout the nineteenth century.[8] The unevenness of autonomization is what produced
an irreducible hybridity in the literary subject and made possible the
proliferation of mixed forms—the chronicle, the essay—which regis-

7. See the important book by Angel Rama, *La ciudad letrada* (Hanover, N.H.: Ediciones del Norte, 1984). A translation is forthcoming from Duke University Press.
8. These issues are discussed at length in Julio Ramos, *Desencuentros de modernidad en
América Latina* (Mexico City: Fondo de Cultura Económica, 1989).

ter, on the same surface of their heteronomous forms and modes of representation, the contradictory drives (*pulsiones*) that set in motion the hybrid subject constituted on the frontiers, in the zones of contact and passage between literature and the demands of other discursive and social practices.

Autonomization had effects that for Martí were profoundly problematic. Although he welcomed some aspects of the "decentralization of the intellect," which to a degree implied the democratization of media in an epoch when "the beautiful is becoming the dominion of all" (209), autonomization encouraged the folding back of the literary subject upon himself and the demotion of literature's social effects. "Life, intimate and feverish," Martí writes, "neither supported, forceful, nor clamorous enough, has come to be the principal subject and, with nature, the only legitimate subject of modern poetry":

> Out of this the pale and groaning poets; out of this that new tormented and painful poetry; out of this that intimate, confidential, and personal poetry, a necessary consequence of the times, naive and useful, like a song of kinsmen, when it overflows from a healthy and vigorous nature, dismayed and eccentric when it is produced in the strings of the feeble poet. Like women, the men of today would seem to be like weak women, if they are likely to exhaust, crowned with the wreaths of roses, the honey-sweet wine [*falerno meloso*]. (206–7)

Martí responded to the folding back of the lyrical subject with marked ambivalence, even with suspicion that the autonomization of interdependent spheres of knowledge reduced literature to a mere state or position of solipsism, a "weak" form of social intervention. His reflection (as we shall see) inscribes the emergence of modern poetry in a drama of virility that feminizes the marginality of literature with respect to "strong" and effective discourses of instrumental rationality.

Thus one finds in Martí, on the one hand, a "nostalgia for the great deed" (208) and, on the other, the same emphasis with which he, throughout the prologue to the "Poema del Niágara" (along with the better part of his poetry, particularly *Ismaelillo* and *Versos libres*), transposes the functions of a language of war to the "battles" of the solitary poet: Martí offers us a new kind of warrior: "great fighters, who fight with the lyre" (205), as if in some way the metaphor of the poet-soldier insured the vigor and virile will of the subject, thus compensating for the "frailty," the secondariness, and the "feminization" of language, which Martí saw as a special risk of modern poetry. Of course, neither "femininity" nor "frailty" are essential attributes of poetry: we are dealing with a response to autonomization, a reaction that ambivalently associates the new lyrical subject with malleable, weak forms of thought. Such a reaction was motivated by the suspicion that the interiorization of literary language into its own sphere had at least two effects: on the one hand, it reduced the capacity of literature to intervene in public affairs and, on the other, in the most radical and nocturnal instances of the lyrical subject's folding back and over itself, it problematized the relation between an aesthetic drive and ethicopolitical imperatives, since the radicalization of the aesthetic drive tended to collapse the economy of truth that formed the very basis of social communicability.

Hence Martí's reticence in publishing two books of verse, *Ismaelillo* (1882) and *Versos sencillos* (1891), and in deciding to leave unpublished his most extensive work, *Versos libres* (written in New York during the 1880s and early 1890s).[9] "Before I make a collection of my verse, I would like to make a collection of my actions."[10] However, he never stopped writing poetry. It proliferated, motivated by the same tensions generated by the autonomization of the literary, by the struggles of an intensified writing set in motion precisely by the double movement of the interstitial subject positioned between *dos patrias* (two fatherlands) —Cuba and the night—in the memorable poem from *Versos libres*.[11]

Dos patrias

Two fatherlands do I have: Cuba and the night.
Or are the two one? Just as his majesty

9. On Martí's ambivalence regarding the moral value of poetic practice in *Ismaelillo* see Enrico Mario Santí, "Ismaelillo, Martí y el modernismo," *Revista Iberoamericana*, no. 137 (1986): 811–40.
10. Martí, *Cuadernos de apuntes*, selection in Vitier, 403.
11. "Dos patrias" used to be included in Martí's posthumous collection of poetry, *Flores del destierro*, edited by Gonzalo de Quesada y Miranda in 1933. In their critical edition of Martí's *Poesía completa* (Havana: Editorial Letras Cubanas, 1985), E. de Armas, F. García Marruz, and C. Vitier identify "Dos patrias" as part of *Versos libres* (127).

the sun retires, with long veils
and a carnation in hand, silent
Cuba, as a sad widow, appears to me.
I know well that bloody carnation
that trembles in her hand! Empty
my breast, destroyed and empty
that place where my heart used to be. Now is the time
to begin dying. It is a good night
for saying farewell. Light disturbs
as does the human word. The universe
speaks better than man.

                                    As a flag
that calls us to arms, the red flame
of the candle flickers. The windows
I open, too tight in me. Mute, breaking off
the petals of the carnation, like a cloud
that darkens the sky, Cuba, a widow, goes by . . .

The first verse places the subject, initially emphatic, marked by the
sign of possession, between two *patrias*. But how can one have two
fatherlands? It would seem that the concept of *patria* refers to the
native country, to the place of origin, so longed for by Martí in the
course of his exile. But if so, neither the duality to which the title
refers nor the allusion to the night in the first verse is explained. The
origin, by definition, is the only source of identification for a subject;
hence the constitutive paradox of the poem in its assertion of irreducible duality at the very foundation. The paradox is intensified by
the unstable division between Cuba—the *patria civil*, the proper
name of an emerging nation—and the night.

How can a fatherland be the night, or a night the fatherland?
Certainly, night can be a fatherland only in a metaphorical sense,
which may lead us to think that the shift between Cuba and the night
registers the problematic passage between the proper, univocal name
of the political fatherland and a metaphorical designation. Of course,
the metaphor of a nocturnal fatherland runs through the wider context of *Versos libres*. We read in "La noche es la propicia," for example,

"For creation is darkness most suitable . . . the fecund darkness of the night." In "Aguila blanca," we read:

> And dark
> afternoons attract me as if my fatherland were
> the ever-widening shadow. O verse [my] friend:
> I die of solitude, of love am I dying!

In the second verse of "Dos patrias," the brightness of the sun, "his majesty," is opposed to the darkness of the night, which is associated with the practice of poetry, the second fatherland, of the subject. Thus the subject is placed on the borders that separate two radically distinct modes of naming: he is situated between two fatherlands, two modes of producing sense and meaning, two spheres of legitimacy. Between two laws: on the one hand, the demand for an ethicopolitical denomination—the *patria civil*, Cuba—and on the other, the metaphorical fatherland of the night: that dark, rebellious practice and nocturnal intensity of the aesthetic drive. The subject emerges precisely there, between the opposed spheres of legitimacy, to enable the passage, the nexus between both laws, attempting to overcome the scission or fragmentation brought about by autonomization. The interstitial subject will be the one to turn the trajectory of poetry around and back, to the center of combat, and from there bring forth the gift of poetry to war.

"Or are the two one?" The synthesis, we should perhaps emphasize, appears immediately interrogated. The poem certainly suggests that a synthesis can be employed to overcome the paradox between a political designation and metaphor. The assumption of a synthesis, of binding, of connections, between Cuba and the night may well be the principle that overdetermines the tropological trajectory of the poem, whose configuration deploys, from the third and fourth verses, the metaphorical conjunction of two laws via the condensation of the dark widowed Cuba that appears before the poet at the precise moment when the brightness of the sun, the other law, withdraws. The metaphorical proceeding redistributes the field of oppositions in a double movement: first, it separates Cuba, the political *patria*, from the brightness of the sun (the king), in order to transpose it immediately into the dark reign of the night, the domain of the aesthetic drive—as if the subject asserted, by means of a metaphorical rearticulation, an alternative mode of thinking politics in accordance with the nocturnal drive of an aesthetic legitimacy, opposed to the solar luminosity of the *patria civil*. Such an assertion can certainly be seen in "Aguila blanca":

> O night, sun of the sad one, dear breast
> From whence revives the heart its force,
> Perpetual, (as) the sun goes out,
> Free me, eternal night, of the executioner,
> Or give, that might be given to me, with the first
> dawn, a clean and redeeming sword.
> With what must it be made? With the light of stars!

Nocturnal luminosity guarantees the return, the passage of the poet toward combat and the political itself. It is indeed a luminosity designated by the gendered darkness surrounding it, the breast of the night that appears in "Dos patrias" as eroticized in that revealing reinscription of the femme fatale who breaks off the petals of a carnation, beneath the window of the solitary subject observing her. Eroticization is crucial: the heart is transposed, with the figurative passage of the metaphorical object (the carnation), from the breast of the subject into the hands of the *patria*:

> I know well that bloody carnation
> that trembles in her hand! Empty
> my breast, destroyed and empty
> that place where my heart used to be.

More than just a metaphor, then, the bloody carnation is a commentary on the metaphorical procedure, the passage from one *patria* to another, the night; a reflection on the transformative process of metaphor, designated as a mechanism of articulation, of an amorous exchange between the poetic subject and the patriotic ethic.[12] The metaphor transports the blood of the heart to the emblem of the patriotic flower. Metaphor guarantees a passage not only between two

12. On love and country see Doris Sommer, *Foundational Fictions: The National Romances of Latin America* (Berkeley: University of California Press, 1991); and Pierre Legendre, *L'Amour du censeur: Essai sur l'ordre dogmatique* (Paris: Seuil, 1974).

spheres of legitimacy separated in the first verse but also between the body of the subject and the principles of the *patria*. Metaphor acts here fundamentally as an oblational figure of exchange: it is the bearer of a gift on which a patriotic and amorous interpellation is based. And the gift is tied inexorably to death, to the emptiness of the body's destroyed chest, which nevertheless marks the sublime encounter with the All in which "the universe / speaks better than man."

The final verses, in contrast, take up the scene of writing. The red flame of the candle—another instance of nocturnal light, which condenses within it the color of blood and of the flag as it burns brightly—is set forth as the condition that makes writing as a form of combat possible. However, these final verses come to situate the subject in the interiorized and solitary space from which he sees Cuba "go by." That is, this interior refers us once again to the space demarcated by the aesthetic autonomization that Martí ties to the solitude of the modern poet. "And I, poor me! prisoner in my cell / The grand battle of men I see," we read in "Midnight," from *Versos libres*. "The windows / I open, too tight in me," the poet adds in "Dos patrias." But outside the Cuba that goes by is a bold line that crosses and darkens the transparent sky: an object in motion, elusive, lost. Far from any synthesis, the movement of the dark line cancels the gift, the epiphany of the encounter. And yet, one must not underestimate the weight, the exasperation, of the attempt, which nevertheless motivates the becoming (*devenir*), the movement of desire in Martí's poetry, even, perhaps, as this desire brought Martí to a fate that he heroically confronted at Dos Ríos, *between two rivers*, in that moment of death for the *patria*.

Although the lyrical subject observes the loss of the object, the evanescence of Cuba as it passes by, this subject cannot account for the multiplicity of positions intertwined within Martí's discourse. The solitude of the folded subject in *Versos libres*, along with his exile from the *patria civil*, evidently finds itself counteracted by the reinsertion of the political into Martí's life, particularly after his return to active politics in the late 1880s, culminating partly in the interventions centered on the founding of the Cuban Revolutionary Party (Partido Revolucionario Cubano) in 1892; and later, in his discourse on the revolution as a just

war. Indeed, Martí's engagement in the Cuban emancipatory movement would seem to have definitively overcome the isolation and inaction of the subject divided by the paradox of *dos patrias*, just as his
heroic militancy would seem to have overcome the principal opposition between the prioritization of acts and the demotion of the word
and representation as secondary, only to place the word in an even
more radical silence, in the definitive repose that death concedes to
the poet-soldier on the field of battle.[13] While he lived, however, his
discursive practices were grounded in more than one field of opposition, in more than a resting place of a synthesis capable of overcoming
radical gaps and differences; his discourse traverses the borders, the
thresholds that separate and with the same movement create zones of
contact, points of intersection and passage.

Perhaps it would be fitting to recall the passage of the poet in his
return to the native land. Martí began to write the *War Journal* (*Diario
de campaña*), his lucid account of the formation of the soldier-subject,
in the Dominican Republic, where he arrived from the United States
en route to Cuba in 1895.[14] The narrative continues on his journey
through Haiti and closes only hours before his death at Dos Ríos. Like
no other text written by Martí about war, the *War Journal* mounts a
sharp critique of violence that asserts the necessity of aesthetic mediation, the only kind of mediation capable of containing and granting
meaning to the ineluctably aggressive energy of the revolutionary
forces:

> The spirit I have sown is that which has spread, across the island;
> with it, and guided in accordance with it, we will soon triumph,
> and with the greatest victory, and for the greatest peace. I foresee
> that, for a little while at least, the force and will of the revolution
> will be divorced from this spirit—it will be deprived of its

13. On Martí's fascination with death see Calvert Casey, "Diálogos de vida y muerte,"
in *Memorias de una isla* (Havana: Editorial Letras Cubanas, 1964), 19–24.
14. In spite of its conjunctural nature, the *War Journals* has been extremely influential in twentieth-century Cuban literature, particularly since José Lezama Lima and
the Orígenes group celebrated the text's fragmentary, intense poetic prose. The *War
Journals* is a pivotal point of reference in Lezama's crucial Latin Americanist essay, *La
expresión americana* (1957; Madrid: Alianza Editorial, 1969). Lezama celebrates
Martí's will to create an event—a political event, we may add—through the poetic
image (117). On Lezama's readings of Martí see Arnaldo Cruz Malavé.

enchantment and taste [*encanto y gusto*], and of its ability to prevail from this natural consortium; [it] will be robbed of the benefit of this conjunction between the activity of the revolutionary forces and the spirit that animates them.[15]

Martí finds the revolution also to be divided by a double drive: on the one hand, by the deployment of an uncontainable and violent activity; on the other, by the "enchantment and taste" of a spirit that needs to be called on to direct action. Is this not the call of the aesthetic ("enchantment and taste") in the midst of war? Martí's insistence on it at various times in the *War Journal* is only partially explained by his recorded disagreements with General Antonio Maceo, another military leader of the patriotic army, who at one point accused him of being "a city-bred defender of the obstacles and hindrances hostile to the military movement" (89). More important, the opposition splits the revolutionary subject; it unleashes the dispute among differentiated positions, all of which need to intervene in the multiple movement toward emancipation. For war, in Martí, is what is outside discourse, both feared and desired: the violent energy to shatter the order of forms.[16] Hence, the revolutionary movement required the intervention of another subject, perhaps "weak" and "malleable," but capable of conjoining and mediating the tendency constitutive of war toward dispersion and destruction; a subject capable of guaranteeing the meaning of justice behind every act of violence. In the vicissitudes of that subject would be inscribed the gift of poetry to war.

15. Martí, *Diario de campaña* (Montevideo: Biblioteca de Marcha, 1971), 100.
16. On war as a problematic of meaning and justice see Kantorowicz (n. 2) and also Walter Benjamin, "Para una crítica de la violencia," in *Para una crítica de la violencia y otros ensayos*, trans. R. Blatt Weinstein (Madrid: Taurus, 1991), 23–45.

His America, Our America:
José Martí Reads Whitman

SYLVIA MOLLOY

I want to contextualize this piece within the framework of the project on which I am working, as part of a more general reflection on turn-of-the-century Latin American literatures and most especially on the anxiety-ridden construction of gender and sexual norm, and of gender and sexual difference, in Latin American cultures during the construction of the budding nation-states. My reflection assumes that the definition of norm does not precede but is arrived at, and indeed derives from, the gender and sexual differences that purportedly deviate from it—in the same way that the definition of health, in psycholegal studies of the period, follows that of disease, and decadence gives birth retrospectively to notions of maturity and fullness. This assumption measures, of course, the apprehension informing those constructions and definitions. By focusing my reflection on Latin America at the turn of the century, that is, at the moment of its complex entrance into modernity, I must take into account two related issues: first, the ideological implications of these issues in debates on national identity and national, even continental, health; and second, the double pressure of continued cultural dependence vis-à-vis Europe and of United States political expansionism that informs these debates on national identity, as it does all forms of cultural production of the period.

In my larger project I devote particular attention to manifestations of uneasiness concerning gender constructions (or manifestations of panic, in the sense given the term by Eve Sedgwick) in what I would like to call scenes of translation, in which Latin America encounters its influential cultural others and, depending on the sense attributed to the encounter, reads itself into, or reads itself away from, those others, for specific ideological reasons. Rubén Darío's reading of Oscar Wilde, or rather Rubén Darío's reading away from Oscar Wilde, is one scene of translation; his reading of D'Annunzio's *Le Martyre de Saint Sébastien*, another. José Martí's reading of Oscar Wilde's *figure*, during his North American tour of 1882, is a third example of anxious translation. Rodó's reading of Rubén Darío, and maybe of all *modernismo* in its more patently decadent mode, is a fourth. In this piece I consider yet another scene of translation, Martí's very complex reading, erasure, translation, and re-creation of Whitman and the part he assigns Whitman in the national, or rather continental, program he proposes.

> It is good to love a woman; but it may be better to love a man.
> —Martí to Manuel Mercado, 14 September 1882

An obsessive meditation on progeniture and filiation runs through the pages of José Martí. Of his first book of poetry, *Ismaelillo*, celebrating his three-year-old son, he writes (in French) to his friend Charles Dana, editor of the *New York Sun*: "I have just published a little book, not for profit but as a present for those I love, a present in the name of my son who is my master. The book is the story of my love affair with my son [*mes amours avec mon fils*]: one tires of reading so many stories of love affairs with women."[1] Even in its homier aspects, the love affair appears to be an intensely pedagogical venture. In a notebook fragment striking for its fatherly fetishism, Martí observes that "when I decide to store the little straw hat and the booties that my son wore a year ago, I check to see if what is written in the newspaper in which I am about to wrap them is the work of men's passions or if it defends just causes. I go ahead and wrap them in the latter case. I believe in these contaminations" (21:186). Since I too believe in these contaminations, though probably not in the way envisioned by Martí, I shall

---

1. Martí, *Obras completas*, 28 vols. (Havana: Editorial Nacional de Cuba, 1963–73), 21:253. Translations, unless otherwise indicated, are my own.

proceed to explore the very fertile conjunction of fathers, sons, and just causes—without forgoing men's passions, the adhesiveness (to borrow from Whitman) that holds them together.

Intensity of fatherly emotion reverberates throughout *Ismaelillo*. Martí writes about his son and for his son, and, in another example of contamination between written page and child, he refers to the book itself, with an intensity that goes beyond trite comparison, *as* his son:

> What different shapes this son of mine takes when warmed up by my love! . . . That is why I love this book, because the little one running loose within its pages, now sad, now cheerful, now mischievous, the simple creature whom I, with the potency of my love, turn into my king, my sorcerer, my knight, has really passed before my eyes, airy, shining, bubbling, just as I depict him. I have seen a beautiful little boy, barely clothed in the lightest of shirts, sitting on a very high mound, waving his little pink feet in the air, and I have said to myself: "As this child looks down on those below him, so does he govern my soul. And I have called him my magician." And I have imagined him on a throne, humid and fluid as a throne that would shine for Galatea, and myself, coming before him, like a hunter surrounded by his dogs, bringing him, my king and master, my passions for tribute. (21:221)

Fatherly rapture over the "airy, shining, bubbling" little one, in whom it is easy to see a prefiguration of another lithe spirit and male muse, Rodó's Ariel, is matched, in Martí, by intensity of filial feeling. As the figure of the son structures affection and desire in Martí's writing, so does the figure of the father. It functions as an allegorical construct ensuring historical continuance:

> The Father
> Must not die till richly armed
> Into the fray he thrusts the son!
> (16:148)

It functions too as a thematic prop, or as a transhistorical principle: "Everything moves toward unity, towards synthesis; essences move to one being; . . . a father is father to many sons; a tree trunk supports many boughs; a sun emits innumerable rays. In every case, unity proceeds to multiplicity, and multiplicity merges and resolves itself back into unity" (21:52).

Martí's obsession has been diversely commented on first by Angel Rama and then, most convincingly, by Julio Ramos, who reads Martí's insistence on filiation as a way of setting up a new model of *affiliation*, in Said's sense of the term, as the replacement of one family model by another.[2] That women are excluded from Martí's new family model— this "rigid and self-sufficient male couple," as Rama calls it—is, of course, obvious.[3]

The notion of a new family model allows me an entrance into Whitman, or into Whitman as read by Martí. Two observations qualify and complete Rama's statement. The first is the place of the subject in the new family model—family romance, really. Between opposing but reversible male foci of love, the son and the father, the I operates as a shifter, brokering the relation and effectively subverting its rigidity, playing father to the son and son to the father, making the son his father and the father his son. Another fragment from the notebooks, a charming little scene of pedagogy that, in spite of its mocking stance, should be taken at face value, stresses their reversibility: "I see myself playing with you. And in order to make you learn joyfully, I make you a little teacher's hat, and I place my spectacles on your nose, and I sit you down on the highest chair, so that you get used to being big in every way." (21:167). The playful give-and-take, which should be taken most seriously, assures not so much the presence of a "rigid . . . couple" (the expression might be best applied to Sarmiento's scene of instruction with *his* son, in *Vida de Dominguito*) as the polymorphous, nonhierarchical exchange of all-male feeling. My second observation is the undubitable *political* import attributed by Martí to this intense male bonding:

2. Ramos, *Desencuentros de la modernidad en América Latina: Literatura y política en el siglo XIX* (Mexico City: Fondo de Cultura Económica, 1989), 184.
3. "Martí is the only writer capable of that double outburst of love, successfully uniting father and son in an emotional bond from which all feminine presence, be it maternal or marital, is elided" (Rama, "La dialéctica de la modernidad en José Martí," in *Estudios martianos: Memoria del Seminario José Martí*, by Manuel Pedro González, Iván A. Schulman, et al. [San Juan: Editorial Universitaria, Universidad de Puerto Rico, 1974], 150).

This generous preoccupation [*miedo generoso*], this care for son and father *at the same time*, this love that encompasses all those who are needy for it, both those who lack it and those who are not even aware of it, this dogged vigilance, this labor of preparation, this attention to the substance of things and not to their mere form, this politics that founds instead of fragmenting, this politics of elaboration is the revolutionary. (22:47–8; emphasis added)

It is in light of these characteristics—the *fluidity* of male/male feeling, the reciprocal learning experience afforded by that exchange, and the *revolutionary* value ascribed to that feeling by Martí—that I wish to read his essay on Whitman. Surely one of Martí's most famous pieces, written during his exile in the United States, it is routinely read and celebrated for its programmatic value as are, unfortunately only too often, most of Martí's works. In celebrating Whitman, such a reading goes, Martí is really celebrating democracy and is considering Whitman an exemplary influence on the Latin American project for which Martí is justly famous. This reading deals less with Whitman himself than with what Enrico Mario Santí has called the *idea* of Whitman, that is, with what Whitman has come to signify, many years after Martí's piece and in part as a result of it, in the Latin American cultural imaginary.[4] As such, the reading is anachronistic; yet the greater of its ills is that it is repressive. Inattentive to detail and to the essay's dynamics, it replaces process with the end product.

I wish to look instead at how Martí, in a complex series of moves, deals with his personal reactions to the Whitman text and, through them, packages Whitman for Latin American consumption. The essay is dated 19 April 1887, four days after Whitman delivered his annual lecture on the death of Lincoln during his last visit to New York. Resorting to the didactic model he uses successfully in other essays written for a Latin American public, Martí adopts the role of go-between: Here is the poet (or the event), and here am I, the witness, to interpret him (or it) for you. The Whitman he presents to Latin America is, at first glance, conventionally simple, one more version of

4. Santí, "The Accidental Tourist: Walt Whitman in Latin America," in *Do the Americas Have a Common Literature?* ed. Gustavo Pérez Firmat (Durham, N.C.: Duke University Press, 1990), 160–1.

the good gray poet: grandiose, prophetic, robust, and, above all, *natural.* Martí's elaboration of the natural is worthy of comment. How could this astonishing book (*Leaves of Grass*) not be prohibited by the shortsighted, Martí asks, rhetorically, "since it is a natural book?" He continues:

> Universities and academic knowledge have separated men so that they no longer know one another. Instead of falling into each other's arms [*echarse unos en brazos de los otros*], attracted by all that is essential and eternal, they draw apart, competing with each other like fishwives [*placeras*], for purely trivial differences. . . . Philosophical, religious and literary trends restrain men's thinking the way a lackey's body is restrained by his livery. . . . Thus, when they stand before the man who is naked, virginal, amorous, sincere, potent—the man who walks, loves, fights, rows his boat—the man who does not fall prey to unhappiness but recognizes the promise of final joy in the grace and balance of the world; when they stand before Walt Whitman's sinewy and angelic man-father [*hombre padre*], they flee as if from their own consciences, refusing to recognize in that fragrant and superior humanness the true type of their own discolored, cassocked, doll-like [*amuñecada*] species.[5]

The concept of the natural, to be more precise, of an American natural is represented by an ever-embracing masculinity ("men . . . falling into each other's arms"), while the fall from the natural—into isolation, into a culture of imitation—is signified by a particularly degraded notion of the feminine, *amuñecada,* diminished by connotations of passivity, triviality, and artifice. Repository of fragrant and superior male humanness, Whitman the "man-father" leads his "sons" back to their lost unity.

This notion of the natural, a cultural construct if ever there was one, has illustrious classical antecedents. The virtues that Martí saw as

5. Martí, *On Art and Literature: Critical Writings,* ed. Philip S. Foner, trans. Elinor Randall, with additional translations by Luis A. Baralt, Juan de Onís, and Roslyn Held Foner (New York: Monthly Review Press, 1982), 168–9. References are to this edition, which I have modified considerably at times for the sake of accuracy. The original Spanish text, "El poeta Walt Whitman," is in *Obras completas* 13: 131–46.

embodiments of an American natural from which men had deviated had already been ascribed by John Addington Symonds, and in strikingly similar terms, to a different "national" tradition: "Hopeful and fearless, accepting the world as he finds it, recognizing the value of each human impulse, shirking no obligation, self-regulated by a law of perfect health, he, in the midst of a chaotic age, emerges clear and distinct, at one with nature, and therefore Greek."[6]

What follows in Martí's essay is a fairly extensive web of Whitman quotations and near quotations, woven with remarkable textual familiarity and rhetorical ease into the commentary. Also notable is the choice of particular texts by Whitman. Martí plunges immediately into *Song of Myself*, then goes on directly and unerringly to the *Calamus* poems:

> Since [Whitman's] books and lectures earn him barely enough money for bread, some "loving friends" see to his needs in a cottage tucked away in a pleasant country lane from which he rides out in an ancient carriage drawn by his beloved horses to watch the "athletic young men" busy with their virile diversions, to see the comrades who are not afraid of rubbing elbows with this iconoclast who wants to establish the institution of "the manly love of comrades," to see the fields they cultivate, the friends who pass by arm in arm and singing, the pairs of lovers, gay and vivacious like quail. This he relates in his *Calamus*, the extremely strange book in which he sings of the love of friends: "Not the orgies . . . Not the pageants of you, not the shifting tableaus, your spectacles, repay me . . . / Nor the processions in the streets, nor the bright windows with goods in them, / Nor to converse with learn'd persons . . ./ Not those, but as I pass O Manhattan, your frequent and swift flash of eyes offering me love, . . . Lovers, continual lovers, only repay me."(171–2)

That Martí gravitates to the adhesiveness celebrated in *Calamus*, where, indeed, men fall "into each other's arms," that he even works his way from the poems back to the man who wrote them, turning the old "man-father" into a son to his "loving friends" and his life into a

---

6. Quoted in Phyllis Grosskurth, *John Addington Symonds: A Biography* (London: Longmans, 1964), 152n.

pastoral, is to be expected. Yet even as he openly exalts male bonding in the spirit in which Whitman ostensively wished it to be read—that is, for its political significance, as posited in the 1876 preface to *Leaves of Grass* and in *Democratic Vistas*—Martí is not so sure what he is *really* reading. Proof of his insecurity comes in the changes and gaps in the above quotation. The intention of the opening line of Whitman's poem "City of Orgies" is clearly laudatory: "City of orgies, walks and joys." Misquoting, Martí resorts instead to negation, setting limits from the start: "*Not* the orgies." Maybe the modification is automatic for Martí, intent as he is on reading the *Calamus* poems "right," that is, on spiritualizing them. Yet if such cleansing, conscious or not, is at work, the choice of "City of Orgies," so evocative of the male cruising scene, is rather odd. Martí, the inveterate New York flâneur, perceived the danger of speaking of this poem even as he was irresistibly attracted to it; he knew of, or at least intuited, something more than a Benjaminian auratic encounter in the "frequent and swift flash[es] of eyes." After "your frequent and swift flash of eyes offering me love," Martí significantly suppresses the line "Offering response to my own—these repay me," thus removing the first person—Whitman's I and/or Martí's own person—from the circulation of desire and denying it an active role in any fecund transaction of male feelings. In the poem that Martí misquotes, the city acts on the I, but not vice versa.

Martí's highly circumspect, ambiguous reading—gravitating toward dangerously attractive poems while distancing himself from them—is particularly obvious when he attempts to deal, more or less directly, with sexuality:

But who can give an idea of his vast and fiercely burning love? This man loves the world with the fire of Sappho. His world is a gigantic bed, and the bed an altar. . . . One source of his originality is the herculean strength with which he flings ideas to the ground as if to violate them when all he wants to do is kiss them with a saintly passion. Another force is the earthy, brutal, and fleshy way he expresses his most delicate ideals. Only those incapable of understanding its greatness have considered that language lewd. With the affected innocence of dirty-minded schoolboys, fools imagine they see a return to the vile desires of Vergil for Cebes, and of Horace for Gyges and Lyciscus, when Whitman uses the most ardent images of which human language is capable to celebrate love between friends in his *Calamus*. When he sings the divine sin in "Children of Adam," in scenes which make the most feverish images in *The Song of Songs* seem pale, he trembles, shrivels, swells, and overflows, goes mad with pride and satisfied virility, recalls the god of the Amazons who rode through forests and across rivers sowing seeds of life throughout the land, "singing the song of procreation." . . . To find an appropriate resemblance to the satanically forceful enumeration in which he describes, like a hungry hero smacking his bloodthirsty lips, the various parts of the female body, it would be well to have read the patriarchal genealogies of Genesis in Hebrew, and to have followed the naked cannibal bands of primitive men through the virgin jungle. And you say this man is brutal? Listen to his composition "Beautiful Women," which like many of his poems has only two lines: "Women sit or move to and fro, some old, some young / The young are beautiful—but the old are more beautiful than the young." And this one, "Mother and Babe": "I see the sleeping mother and babe—hush'd, I study them long and long." (178–9)

Why, of all things, begin a paragraph whose principal thrust is to set Whitman "straight" (aggressively so, one might add) with, as it were, a weak card—Sappho? It might be argued that the mention of Sappho harks back to notions of a Greek natural similar to the one admired by Symonds. But in all probability the reference is far more complex. By 1887 the mention of Sappho, although susceptible to different interpretations, was surely not innocent. As Joan DeJean has cogently demonstrated, it was put to active ideological use by nineteenth-century philologists following Winckelmann, usually in connection with, and as a corrective to, implications of sexuality in pederastic relations: "Welcker posited an essential bond between male physical beauty, militarism, and patriotism on the one hand and Sappho's chastity on the other."[7] Moreover, "the association forged between Sappho and Greek love leads to a double overreaction that

7. DeJean, *Fictions of Sappho, 1546–1937* (Chicago: University of Chicago Press, 1989), 205.

eventually cuts off both Sapphism and *pederastia* from sensuality" (211). It is indeed to such a use that Martí resorts: if Sappho's passion is chaste or, better yet, sacred (from bed to altar), then so are the *Calamus* poems—ardent, very ardent, but chaste.

Yet one cannot help thinking that this model of Sappho is not the only one for Martí; that Sappho means the spiritual and the chaste yet also hints at the opposite. A reader of Baudelaire, Martí surely has other Sapphos in mind, and a passing reference in one of his letters to someone living "à la Sappho" gives the reader pause. His affirming-while-denying strategy (reminiscent of Symonds's vehement protestations in *A Problem in Modern Ethics*) is reinforced by Martí's other classical allusions, "the vile desires of Vergil for Cebes and of Horace for Gyges and Lyciscus," which merit closer scrutiny. Lyciscus is indeed an object of love in Horace (*Epodes* 11.24–8). But Gyges is not, deserving just a passing mention as the conventional pretty boy whose flowing hair makes him sexually ambiguous (*Odes* 2.5.20). If Martí thinks that "dirty-minded schoolboys" are reading same-sex sex into *Calamus*, guess who is reading it indiscriminately into Horace? A similar overreading may be observed in the reference to Vergil's Cebes, for there is no Cebes in Vergil, at least not in Vergil's *text*. Cebes appears, however, in Vergil's commentators: "Servius proposes that, in Eclogue II, Amaryllis and Menalcas are respectively Leria and Cebes, two slaves belonging to Maecenas whom their master gave to Vergil because he had a fancy for them."[8] So now we have a dirty-minded schoolboy snooping not just into eclogue 2 (a text that, in its explicit consideration of same-sex love, would have been far too obvious) but into Vergil's life, too. It is precisely this interpretive overkill that undoes the efficacity of Martí's disclaimers for *Calamus*, calling attention to them, rendering them suspicious. The overwrought denials betray a preoccupation much more revealing of Martí, and of what Martí represses as he reads Whitman, than, of course, of Whitman himself.

Intimations of homosexuality, more reinforced than disproved by Martí's crossed references, generate in his reading of Whitman a compulsively heterosexual justification whose violence cannot be ignored.

8. H. J. Rose, *The Eclogues of Vergil* (Berkeley: University of California Press, 1942), 70.

If, at the beginning of the essay, the feminine signifies the trivial, the artificial, the devalued—the "doll-like"—it now signifies a force to be destroyed by, and in the name of, heterosexual virility. Whitman's curious roamer of bodies becomes for Martí a priapic fiend, trembling, swelling, overflowing, violating ideas and women; a cannibal in a virgin jungle, "satanically" salivating over female body parts. The only alternative to the bloody celebration, moreover, is admiration for traditionally undesiring and undesirable forms of the feminine: beautiful old women, a mother with child. If, to correct suggestions of deviant male bonding, Martí resorts to woman, the strategy turns on itself. The truculence attending the feminine, in connection with sexual appetites and procreative urges, makes it discordant, literally an obstacle to men.

"It is to the development, identification, and general prevalence of that fervid comradeship (the adhesive love, at least rivaling the amative love hitherto possessing imaginative literature, if not going beyond it,) that I look for the counterbalance and offset of our materialistic and vulgar American democracy," writes Whitman in the 1876 preface to *Leaves of Grass*.[9] In Whitman's communal masculinity Martí recognizes his own all-male affiliative model, the revolutionary family of sons and fathers confounded in a continuum of natural masculine emotion, and also recognizes the continental, political potential of the model, which he elaborates in later essays. (I think, of course, of the discussion on "natural man" in "Our America.") Whitman, for Martí, is the precursor, pointing out "to our astonished times the radiant swarms of men spreading over America's mountains and valleys, brushing their bees' wings against the hem of freedom's robes" (185). That the intensity of this continental masculine adhesiveness not only rivals "amative love," as in Whitman, but precludes it may well account for both the fear and the passion with which Martí reads *Calamus* as a series of poems that need to be translated (and translated away) in order to function as mirror texts.

To his credit, Martí is the only Latin American to have considered, in Whitman, the erotic together with the political and to register his anxiety, even his panic, before that explosive alliance. Only one

9. Whitman, *Leaves of Grass*, ed. Sculley Bradley and Harold W. Blodgett (New York: Norton, 1973), 112.

year later, such a combination was unthinkable: in a mediocre though much-cited poem of *Azul* (1888), Rubén Darío congealed Whitman forever in the Latin American imaginary; totemizing him as the grand old prophet: the "idea of Whitman" was well on its way. While Martí's reading does not necessarily give us a new Whitman, it does give us, provided we read it carefully, a new Martí.

Broken English Memories

JUAN FLORES

Historical memory is an active, creative force, not just a receptacle for the dead weight of times gone by. *Memory* has been associated, since its earliest usages, with the act of inscribing, engraving, or, in a sense that carries over into our own electronic times, "recording" (*grabar*). It is not so much the record itself as the putting-on-record, the gathering and sorting of materials from the past in accordance with the needs and interests of the present. Remembering thus always involves selecting and shaping, constituting out of what was something that never was yet now assuredly is, in the imaginary of the present, and in the memory of the future. And the process of memory is open, without closure or conclusion; the struggle to (re)establish continuities and to tell the "whole" story only uncovers new breaks and new exclusions.

It is in terms of such weighty verities that the well-known critic and Princeton professor Arcadio Díaz-Quiñones ponders the condition of contemporary Puerto Rican culture. In *La memoria rota*, his much-discussed collection of essays from the 1980s and early 1990s, Díaz-Quiñones identifies the most glaring lapses in Puerto Rican historical memory, the ruptures and repressions that have left present-day public discourse devoid of any recognizable field of critical reference.[1] The "broken memory" that he attributes to the current generation is rooted in centuries of imperial mutilation of social consciousness, culminating in his own lived memory in the triumphalist rhetoric of progress and modernization of the midcentury years. His point about the present, end-of-the-century condition is that even though the persuasiveness of

---

1. Díaz-Quiñones, *La memoria rota: Ensayos sobre cultura y política* (Río Piedras, P.R.: Huracán, 1993).

that populist, accommodationist narrative seems to have waned definitively, the historical gaps grounding earlier hegemonies remain largely
unfilled. Despite Díaz-Quiñones's emphatic disclaimer of all "totaliz-
ing" presumptions and of any intention to set forth a "rigorous theory,"
La memoria rota, loosely unified around the suggestive metaphor of the
broken memory, may well turn out to be the book of the decade in
Puerto Rican cultural theory, the 1990s counterpart to José Luis
González's *El país de cuatro pisos* of the 1980s, or René Marqués's *El puer-
torriqueño dócil* of the 1960s, or Antonio S. Pedreira's *Insularismo* of the
1930s.

Díaz-Quiñones's critical eye ranges widely over Puerto Rican political and literary history; his familiarity with the national landscape is
enriched by continual references to congruent and kindred concerns
of other cultural theorists, from Theodor Adorno to Frantz Fanon,
from Edward Said to Angel Rama. Rhetorically, the disjunctures he signals in the official story of the national culture take the form of
euphemisms that have the effect of minimizing the abruptness and
violence of imposed historical change, most notably of European colonization, centuries of slavery, U.S. occupation, ideological decima-
tion of the independence and socialist movements, and mass emigration to the U.S. Díaz-Quiñones shows how the dominant memory
needs to sweeten the pill of colonial power and constantly to construct
and refurbish the illusion of internal harmony, compliance, consensus. Emotionally charged catchwords like *family, symphony of progress,*
and *cultural affirmation* hide the seams and muffle the discord that
make up the real fabric of the society, which without these comforting
mythologies appear as an intricate patchwork of contending claims
and social meanings. In *La memoria rota*, the very concept of "the
national"—what it means to "be" Puerto Rican—has become a battlefield in the struggle for interpretive power.

One exclusion to which Díaz-Quiñones draws repeated attention—perhaps the most pronounced break in collective memory—is
the emigrant Puerto Rican community in the United States. The exo-
dus of Puerto Ricans between the late 1940s and the early 1960s, an
integral and orchestrated part of the island's passage into "modernity,"
is still occluded from the national history; in another new essay,
"Puerto Rico: Cultura, memoria y diáspora" (1994), Díaz-Quiñones

even cites two recent history textbooks, *Historia general de Puerto Rico* (1986), by Fernando Picó, and *Historia de Puerto Rico* (1987), by Blanca Silvestrini and María Dolores Luque de Sánchez, neither of which devotes more than a few pages to the emigrant Puerto Rican community.[2] With all of its revisionist correctives to the colonial, class, gender, and racial biases of the traditional narrative of the nation, the "new historiography," which has gained such prestigious intellectual ground since the 1970s, continues to present the "other half" of the Puerto Rican population as just that, an other lurking in the wings of the main national drama. Puerto Ricans *en el destierro*, or simply *de allá*, persist as a footnote, sympathetic at best but ultimately dismissive and uncomprehending.

To its immense credit, *La memoria rota* places the life of Puerto Ricans in the U.S. squarely on the agenda of contemporary historical analysis. Díaz-Quiñones's insistence no doubt is fueled by his many years of living and working in New Jersey. He points up the long reach of collective experience back to the late nineteenth century and acknowledges the many other writers and thinkers who have recognized its importance, such as Bernardo Vega, César Andreu Iglesias, and José Luis González. More than merely filling in the historical blanks that they have left, though, Díaz-Quiñones asserts the central, constitutive role of Puerto Ricans in the U.S. in the making and breaking of the Puerto Rican nation in the twentieth century. His allusions to other contemporary theorists of diasporic, transnational identity, such as Said, Partha Chatterjee, and Renato Rosaldo, serve him well in contextualizing the dramatic divide in modern-day Puerto Rican history. Far from unique or exceptional, the cultural disjunctures, ambiguities, and reconnections undergone by Puerto Ricans in both localities are paradigmatic of experiences familiar to more and more people, and nations, of the world.

Yet for all his stitching and patching, Díaz-Quiñones still leaves the Puerto Rican broken memory in need of serious repair. It is not enough to point to the break and glue the pieces together by mentioning forgotten names and events. The seams and borders of national experience need to be understood not as absences or vacuums but as

2. Díaz-Quiñones, "Puerto Rico: Cultura, memoria y diáspora," *Tercer Milenio* 1 (1994): 11–9.

sites of new meanings and relations. Here again, as in the exclusionary vision Díaz-Quiñones would transcend, the Puerto Rican community in the U.S. still appears as an extension of discourses based on the island, its history an appendage of "the" national history, with no evident contours or dynamic in its own right. To attend to the break that migration has meant in Puerto Rican history, it is necessary to remember the whole national "project" from the perspectives of the breaking point itself, from aboard the *guagua aérea*.[3]

Remembering in Puerto Rican today inherently involves a dual vision, a communication where languages bifurcate and recombine. Puerto Rican memories are mixed-code memories, lodged at the points where English breaks Spanish and Spanish breaks English. The act of memory defies uniformity; it undermines the privilege typically accorded either of the sundered fragments—Spanish or English, *acá* or *allá*—over the living relation between them, as evidenced in the rupture itself. On this point the metaphor of Puerto Rico's broken memory, and the elegant arguments that sustain it, backs away from its deeper theoretical implications.

A people's memory and sense of collective continuity is broken not only by the abrupt, imposed course of historical events themselves but by the exclusionary discourses that accompany and legitimate them. Thus, while the massive emigration of the Puerto Rican population to the U.S. has involved a geographic and cultural divide unprecedented in the national history, the dismissive rhetoric of "assimilation" and "cultural genocide" has forced the glaring omission of Puerto Rican life in the U.S. from the historical record. In *La memoria rota* Díaz-Quiñones repeatedly takes this ideological agenda to task and reinstates creative agency and continuity in the cultural experience of the emigrant community.

In one of the most moving passages of his lead essay, "La vida inclemente," Díaz-Quiñones argues that "los emigrantes fortalecían— de una manera imprevista por el discurso excluyente de algunos sectores de las élites puertorriqueñas—la necesidad de conservar identi-

3. The title of Luis Rafael Sánchez's story "La guagua aérea" [The air bus], trans. Diana Vélez, *Village Voice*, 24 January 1984, has become proverbial for the commuter status of Puerto Rican culture.

dades, y, de hecho, la necesidad de fijar nuevas descripciones de la identidad" [the emigrants reinforced—in a manner unforeseen by the exclusionary discourse of some sectors of the Puerto Rican elite— the need to maintain identities, and even the need to form new descriptions of identity]. Rather than leave the island behind and forget about their homeland, "había en aquellas comunidades puertorriqueñas la posibilidad de un nuevo futuro que exigía conservar ciertos lugares reales y simbólicos, una nueva valoración de la geografía insular, de sus ríos y lomas, de sus barrios" [in those Puerto Rican communities there existed the possibility of a new future that required the preservation of certain real and symbolic places and that lent a new value to the geography of the island, its rivers and hills, and its barrios] (50–1). Geographic separation and distance, rather than deadening all sense of community and cultural origins, may have the contrary effect of heightening the collective awareness of belonging and affirmation. Referring to Said's accounts of life in present-day Palestinian communities, Díaz-Quiñones contends that "la *pertenencia*, el sentido de 'hogar' y comunidad, se afirma sobre todo en la distancia, con la incertidumbre del lugar. Ello explica, quizás, por qué se puede dar la paradójica situación de que algunos en Guaynabo desprecian su cultura, mientras que otros, en Filadelfia, la defienden con pasión" [the sense of belonging, a feeling for 'home' and community, is affirmed with the strongest emphasis from a distance, when there is an uncertainty as to place. Perhaps this goes to explain the paradoxical situation that people, say in Guyanabo, can take their culture for granted, while others in Philadelphia defend it passionately].

The accuracy of the "paradoxical" inversion of geographic location and cultural belonging resounds in the countless tales of emigrants feeling more Puerto Rican than ever in the New York setting; in the flourishing of *bomba y plena* and *música jíbara* groups in all of the emigrant neighborhoods, from Hartford to Lorraine, Ohio, from Hawaii to Perth Amboy; in the fashioning of island-style *casitas* in the abandoned lots of the South Bronx and Williamsburg, Brooklyn. The contrasting attitudes toward cultural continuity find dramatic expression in much of the literary and artistic work by Puerto Ricans in the United States, most forcefully perhaps in Tato Laviera's memorable poem "nuyorican." The title identifies, in English, the speaker of the poem, a monologue addressed by an irate New York Puerto Rican, in Spanish, to his lost island homeland. "Nuyorican" is an impassioned plea by a son of the migration to his beloved "puerto rico" not to forget why he was born "nativo en otras tierras" and to be aware of the real play of cultural loyalties:

yo peleo por tú puerto rico, ¿sabes?
yo me defiendo por tu nombre, ¿sabes?
entro a tu isla, me siento extraño, ¿sabes?
entro a buscar más y más, ¿sabes?
pero tú con tus calumnias,
me niegas tu sonrisa,
me siento mal, agallao,
yo soy tu hijo,
de una migración,
pecado forzado,
me mandaste a nacer nativo en otras tierras,
por qué, porque éramos pobres, ¿verdad?
porque tú querías vaciarte de tu gente pobre,
ahora regreso, con un corazón boricua, y tú,
me desprecias, me miras mal, me atacas mi hablar,
mientras comes mcdonalds en discotecas americanas,
y no pude bailar la salsa en san juan, la que yo
bailo en mis barrios llenos de todas tus costumbres,
así que, si tú no me quieres, pues yo tengo
un puerto rico sabrosísimo en que buscar refugio
en nueva york, y en muchos otros callejones
que honran tu presencia, preservando todos
tus valores, así que, por favor, no me
hagas sufrir, ¿sabes?[4]

[i fight for you, puerto rico, you know?
i defend myself for your name, you know?
i enter your island, i feel foreign, you know?
i enter searching for more and more, you know?
but you, with your insults
you deny me your smile,

4. Laviera, *AmeRícan* (Houston: Arte Público, 1985), 53.

i feel bad, indignant.
i am your son,
of a migration,
a sin forced on me,
you sent me to be born a native of other lands.
why? because we were poor, right?
because you wanted to empty yourself of your poor people.
now i return, with a boricua heart, and you,
you scorn me, you look askance, you attack the way i speak,
while you're out there eating mcdonalds in american discothe-
ques,
and i couldn't even dance salsa in san juan, which i
can dance in my neighborhoods full of your customs.
so that, if you don't want me, well, i have
a delicious puerto rico where i can seek refuge
in new york, and in lots of other alleyways
that honor your presence, preserving all
of your values, so that, please, don't make
me suffer, you know?]

Such texts, structured for emotional force around the clash between an imaginary and a "real" Puerto Rico, and between jarring identity claims of "here" and "there," abound in "Nuyorican" literature. Works by Sandra María Esteves and Victor Hernández Cruz, Edward Rivera and Esmeralda Santiago, show that "la memoria rota" is the site not merely of exclusion and fragmentation but also of new meanings and identity. They attest to the act of memory at the break itself and thereby move from the pieces of broken memory to the creative practice of "breaking memory." Discontinuity, rather than a threat to cultural survival and inclusion, helps us critically examine prevailing continuities and imagine and create new ones. Homi Bhabha, for whom Díaz-Quiñones expresses great admiration in *La memoria rota*, provides an excellent description of ironically privileged positionality "at the break." Inspired by Said's move from Foucault to the scene of the Palestinian struggle, "from the Left Bank to the West Bank," Bhabha speaks in a recent interview of the possibilities of being, somehow, *in between*, of occupying an interstitial space that was not fully governed by the recognizable traditions from which you came. For the interaction or over-determination often produces another third space. It does not necessarily produce some higher, more inclusive, or representative reality. Instead, it opens up a space that is skeptical of cultural totalization, of notions of identity which depend for their authority on being "originary," or concepts of culture which depend for their value on being pure, or of tradition, which depends for its effectivity on being continuous. A space where, to put it very simply, I saw great political and poetic and conceptual value in forms of cultural identification which subverted authority, not by claiming their total difference from it, but were able to actually use authorized images, and turn them against themselves to reveal a different history. And I saw this little figure of subversion intervening in the interstices, as being very different from the big critical battalions that always wanted to have a dominating authority, opposed by an equally powerful subordinated agency: victim and oppressor, sparsely and starkly blocked out.[5]

The experience of being "in between," so deeply familiar to Puerto Ricans in the United States, thus harbors the possibility of an intricate politics of freedom and resistance. Understood in this way as a kind of phenomenology or philosophy of experiential space, the "break" appears as both a limit and a breaking of the limit. The "third space" and "little figure of subversion" identified by Bhabha summon the notion of transgression and its constant crossing of lines and demarcated limits. In *Language, Counter-Memory, Practice*, Foucault describes this relation between transgression and limit: "Transgression is an action which involves the limit, that narrow zone of a line where it displays the flash of its passage, but perhaps also its entire trajectory, even its origin; it is likely that transgression has its entire space in the line it crosses."[6]

5. Bhabha, "Between Identities: Homi Bhabha Interviewed by Paul Thompson," in *Migration and Identity*, ed. Rina Benmayor and Andor Skotnes (Oxford: Oxford University Press, 1994), 190.
6. Foucault, *Language, Counter-Memory, Practice: Selected Essays and Interviews*, ed. Donald F. Bouchard, trans. Donald F. Bouchard and Sherry Simon (Ithaca, N.Y.: Cornell University Press, 1977), 33–4.

Rather than negate the limit by crossing it, transgression foregrounds and mediates contrasts by illuminating the spaces on either side of the limit. In a striking metaphor, Foucault suggests that the relationship between the limit and its transgression "is like a flash of lightning in the night which . . . gives a dense and black intensity to the night it denies, which lights up the night from the inside, from top to bottom, and yet owes to the dark the stark clarity of its manifestation" (34).

Such insights from contemporary cultural theory point up the need to appreciate the complexity of Puerto Rico's "broken memory" from the vantage point of those living "in between," in the space of the "break" itself. Sandra María Esteves gives voice to this complexity in the opening lines of her poem "Not Neither":

> Being Puertorriqueña
> Americana
> Born in the Bronx, not really jíbara
> Not really hablando bien
> But yet, not Gringa either
> Pero ni portorra, pero sí portorra too
> Pero ni que what am I?[7]

Occupying and transgressing the limit can be baffling, bewildering to the point of existential anguish, yet facing up to the confounding reality can allow for a newfound sense of confidence and identity. Esmerelda Santiago, for one, after years of jostling and juggling between Puerto Rican and U.S. parts of her life, has finally "learned to insist on my peculiar brand of Puerto Rican identity. One not bound by geographical, linguistic or behavioral boundaries, but rather, by a deep identification with a place, a people and a culture which, in spite of appearances, define my behavior and determine the rhythms of my days. An identity in which I've forgiven myself for having to look up a recipe for 'arroz con pollo' in a Puerto Rican cookbook meant for people who don't know a 'sombrero' from a 'sofrito.'"[8]

7. Esteves, *Tropical Rains: A Bilingual Downpour* (New York: African Caribbean Poetry Theater, 1984), 26.
8. Santiago, "The Puerto Rican Stew," *New York Times Magazine*, 18 December 1994, 34, 36.

In what language do we remember? Is it the language we use when we speak with friends and family in our everyday lives? Or does our choice of a language of memory involve a transposition, a translation in the literal sense of moving across: *trasladar*, "de un lado a otro" [from one side to the other]? For Puerto Ricans, half of whom may be on either "side" at any given time, the symbiosis between language and place, and between identity and memory, is especially salient today. Spanish, English, and Spanglish, all in the plural and lowercase, make for an abundant reservoir of expressive codes with which to relate (to) the past. For language is not only the supreme mnemonic medium, the vehicle for the transmission of memory; fifty years of Puerto Rican history has shown that language can be the site and theme of historical action, the locus of contention over issues of identity and community that reach far beyond our preference for, or reliance on, this or that word or grammar. "La memoria rota" makes its most palpable appearance as "la lengua rota" or, as Antonio Martorell puts it in his inspired performance piece, "la lengua mechada" [stuffed tongue].[9]

In his essay "La política del olvido" (1991), Díaz-Quiñones shows that it is not necessary to accept the inaccurate, colonially charged claim that Puerto Rico is a "bilingual nation" in order to stand in equally critical opposition to the officialization of Spanish as the national language. For while the annexationist impulse behind the bilingual-nation idea is evident, Díaz-Quiñones recognizes the

9. Martorell's performance-installation was first presented at the International Colloquium on the Contemporary Social Imaginary, held at the University of Puerto Rico in February 1991. The text, "Imalabra II," appears in *Coloquio internacional sobre el imaginario social contemporáneo*, ed. Nydza Correa de Jesús, Heidi Figueroa Sarriera, and María Milagros López (Río Piedras: Universidad de Puerto Rico, n.d.), 161–4. What Martorell means by "la lengua mechada" (as in "carne mechada," meat that has been larded and stuffed) becomes clear in the following sentence: "Nuestra lengua, querrámoslo o no, está mechada y requetemechada con otras lenguas y con imágenes soñadas, recordadas, olvidadas, combatidas, rendidas, victoriosas y subversivas que versadas o en verso, prosaicas o procaces, silentes o sin lentes, encarnadas o bernejas, berrendas o virulentas dan sabor y grosor a nuestro apetito, extensión a nuestras ansias, caricia a nuestra hambre" [Like it or not, our tongue (language) has been stuffed and stuffed to the gills with other languages and with images which were dreamed up, remembered, forgotten, combated, surrendered, victorious and subversive, well versed or in verse, prosaic or precocious, silenced and no-lensed, incarnate or inchoate, tame or tempestuous, lending flavor and fullness to our appetite, length to our longing, endearment to our hunger].

"Spanish-only" campaign as no more than the chronic recourse of the autonomist leaders (in this case, former governor Rafael Hernández Colón) in their most desperate moments of opportunism. "¿Qué alcance tiene la definición del idioma *único*," he asks, "ante la hibridez y mezcla del español, del inglés y del spanglish que se oye en Bayamón, Puerto Nuevo o en Union City? Las élites puertorriqueñas defienden, con razón, su bilingüismo, que les permite leer a Toni Morrison o a Faulkner, y acceder a la alta cultura del Metropolitan Museum o el New York City Ballet, y, claro, a Wall Street. La diáspora de emigrantes puertorriqueños ha ido mezclando su lengua, una vez más, en sus continuos viajes de ida y vuelta" [What can be gained from defining an *only* language in the face of the hybridity and mixing of Spanish, English, and Spanglish that one hears spoken in Bayamon, Puerto Nuevo, or Union City? The Puerto Rican elites have good reason to defend their bilingualism: it allows them to read Toni Morrison or Faulkner and partake of the high culture of the Metropolitian Museum or the New York City Ballet, and of course of Wall Street. The diaspora of Puerto Rican emigrants has been mixing their languages over and over, in their continual trips back and forth]. New York, Díaz-Quiñones reminds us, has been a Caribbean and Puerto Rican city for over a century now, witness to and deeply influenced by the lives and writings, the songs and struggles, of many illustrious Puerto Ricans, along with Cubans as prominent as José Martí and Celia Cruz. "Yo prefiero la hibridez de las nacionalizaciones" [I prefer the hybridity of nationalities], he continues, and concludes his reflections on the politics of language by challenging Puerto Ricans on both sides of the linguistic divide: "¿Tendremos nosotros la capacidad para descolonizar nuestro imaginario, salir de la niebla colonial de que habló Hostos, sin renunciar a este revolú que nos identifica?" [Will we have the capacity to decolonize our imaginary, to take leave of the colonial fog that Hostos spoke of without relinquishing that special "mess" that identifies us?].

When it comes to language, "este revolú que nos identifica" amounts to a veritable stew, if such a tired and overloaded expression may be pardoned in the interest of differentiating the dynamic of blending and multiple intersection from notions of transition, transfer, interference, or even back and forth movement. It is a *sancocho* whose ingredients include, as Esmeralda Santiago has learned, *sofrito* and not sombreros, because it is not random, much less a sign of confusion and incoherence, as the "English or Español only–ists" would have it. On closer look, bilingualism as practiced by Puerto Ricans on both sides of *el charco*, but especially by the half "over here," constitutes an intricate tactic and strategy of response and assertion, with deep poetic and political implications. "Broken" English, "broken" Spanish, English and Spanish "breaking" (into) each other—who with any contact at all with Puerto Ricans can fail to hear the semantic micropolitics at play in usages like "Cógelo con take it easy!" or "No problema," or in the bent meanings in the use of words like *anyway*, *o.k.*, *foquin*, or *bro-ther* in a Spanish context, or *pero, verdad, este*, or *mira* when speaking English? Whether the primary code is Spanish or English, colloquial Puerto Rican is characterized by its porousness, its undermining and breaking, of the authority of monolingual discourse. Collective memory and identity find their appropriate articulation in a lively, "macaronic" sensibility in which the mixed-code vernacular voice responds in both directions to the imposition of official, standard constructs of "the" national language. Puerto Rican dreams are "broken English dreams," as Pedro Pietri announced in one of his signature poems from the early 1970s.[10] The cultural idiom of many Puerto Ricans and other Latinos in the U.S., their language of expression and fantasy, is captured well by the Cuban American cultural critic Coco Fusco, who calls her new collection of essays on "cultural fusion in the Americas" *English Is Broken Here*.[11]

Yet as fluid as this interlingual practice may be, there is still a here and a there. Its being "translocal" does not erase the efficacy of "locus"; boundaries of difference and distance remain, most obviously in relation to place and location. Geography is the richest metaphorical field for the politics of linguistic and cultural breaking; the contrast between here and there permeates the idiom, from everyday speech to the lingo of popular songs to twists and turns of bilingual poetry. The there not only is imaginary; it is acknowledged and even thematized as imaginary. The imaginary there and then serves as an

10. Pietri, *Puerto Rican Obituary* (New York: Monthly Review Press, 1973), 12–6.
11. Fusco, *English Is Broken Here: Notes on Cultural Fusion in the Americas* (New York: New Press, 1995).

Juan Flores

accessible foil to the intensity of lived presence and often, as in the poetry of Sandra María Esteves and Victor Hernández Cruz, becomes a resource for self-discovery and political insight.

Tato Laviera takes locational counterpoint as the structuring principle of his dramatic poem "migración," in which the lyrics of the proverbially nostalgic ballad "En mi viejo San Juan" share the same lines and stanzas as the words, also in Spanish, of a Puerto Rican on the frozen winter streets of the Lower East Side as he reflects on the death of the song's composer, Noël Estrada.[12] Eventually, the emotionally laden chords of "En mi viejo San Juan," often considered the anthem of the Puerto Rican and Latin American emigrant, bring out the sun and, as they resound in barbershops and nightspots in El Barrio, play their consoling yet challenging role in the familiar here and now. The sharp dramatic interplay between two cultural places, the quoted there of the song lyrics and the unmediated, physical here, allows for a new mode of identity formation freed from the categorical fixity of place. In his essay "Migratorias" the critic Julio Ramos concludes his comments on Laviera's "migración" by speaking of a practical, "portable" identity: "Porque se trata, precisamente, de un modo de concebir la identidad que escabulle las redes topográficas y las categorías duras de la territorialidad y su metaforización telúrica. En Laviera la raíz es si acaso el fundamento citado, reinscrito, por el silbido de una canción. Raíces portátiles, dispuestos al uso de una ética corriente, basada en las prácticas de la identidad, en la identidad como práctica del juicio en el viaje" [It is a way of conceiving of identity that defies the usual topographical connections, along with rigid categories of territoriality and their telluric metaphorization. In Laviera, "roots" may amount to that foundation as a citation, reinscribed as the syllable of a song. Roots that are portable, disposed to use in a "mainstream ethic," based on practices of identity, on identity as practice of judgment in the course of traveling].[13]

The themes of spatial, historical, and linguistic counterpoint are joined by Laviera in his remarkable poem "melao" (27), which enacts

12. Laviera, *La ética corriente/Mainstream Ethics* (Houston: Arte Público, 1988), 37–9.
13. Ramos, "Migratorias," in *Las culturas de fin de siglo en América Latina*, ed. Josefina Ludmer (Buenos Aires: Beatriz Viterbo, 1994), 60.

paradigmatically what I have been calling broken English and Spanish
memories:

> melao was nineteen years old
> when he arrived from santurce
> spanish speaking streets
>
> melao is thirty-nine years old
> in new york still speaking
> santurce spanish streets
>
> melaíto his son now answered
> in black american soul english talk
> with native plena sounds
> and primitive urban salsa beats
>
> somehow melao was not concerned
> at the neighborly criticism
> of his son's disparate sounding
> talk
>
> melao remembered he was criticized
> back in puerto rico for speaking
> arrabal black spanish
> in the required english class
>
> melao knew that if anybody
> called his son american
> they would shout puertorro
> in english and spanish
> meaning i am puerto rican
> coming from yo soy boricua
> i am a jíbaro
> dual mixtures
> of melao and melaíto's
> spanglish speaking son
> así es la cosa papá

Though the narrative voice is in English, Spanish words, sounds and meanings burst through the monolingual seams; every shift in geographic and biographical reference undermines the "official" status of either language standard. Close, repeated reading reveals a vernacular Spanish subtext that explodes at the end but collides and colludes with English semantics in the dead center of the poem. The centrally placed word *disparate*, spelled the same in both languages, also "means" in both languages, but the simultaneous meanings are not the same. The concealed (Spanish) phonetics harbors a repressed signification, and the poetics of convergence and divergence underlies an everyday politics of the break in cultural and historical memory.

"La memoria rota," evocative image of the fragmentation of Puerto Rican historical consciousness, is thus most appropriate, especially as it refers to the migratory experience, when reimagined as an active process of breaking and re-membering. Arcadio Díaz-Quiñones has succeeded in placing those lapses and exclusions indelibly on the contemporary intellectual agenda and has signaled the attendant political implications of a needed historical revision. But for Puerto Rican memory to be "repaired," for it to assume greater coherence and continuity, its incoherences and discontinuities must be probed and interrogated as they manifest themselves in lived experience and expression. "Este revolú que nos identifica," the elusive mortar of Puerto Rican cultural identity, appears as a magnetic field of unity and diversity, relations and translations. Puerto Rican memory gets "unbroken" by Melao, and by Melaíto, his "disparate sounding" son, and by Melaíto's "spanglish speaking son" when he affirms his "dual mixture" by proclaiming, "así es la cosa papá."

Contributors

CARLOS J. ALONZO is Professor and Chair of Spanish at Emory University. He is author of *Modernity and Autochthony: The Spanish American Regional Novel* (1990) and *The Rhetoric of Cultural Discourse in Spanish America* (forthcoming). He is also senior consulting editor for the *Latin American Literary Review*.

ANTONIO BENÍTEZ-ROJO is Thomas B. Walton Jr. Memorial Professor of Romance Languages at Amherst College. His most recent book is *The Repeating Island: The Caribbean and the Postmodern Perspective* (1992). An expanded edition is forthcoming.

JOHN BEVERLEY is Professor of Hispanic Languages and Literatures and of Communications at the University of Pittsburgh. He is author of *Literature and Politics in the Central American Revolutions* (1990), with Marc Zimmerman, and *Against Literature* (1993), and is editor of *The Postmodernism Debate in Latin America* (1995), with José Oviedo and Michael Aronna. He is a founding member of the Latin American Subaltern Studies Group.

DEBRA A. CASTILLO is Professor of Romance Studies and Comparative Literature at Cornell University. She is author of *The Translated World: A Postmodern Tour of Libraries in Literature* (1984) and *Talking Back: Toward a Latin American Feminist Literary Criticism* (1992). Her most recent book is a translation of Federico Campbell's *Tijuana: Stories on the Border* (1995).

ARCADIO DÍAZ-QUIÑONES is Professor of Spanish and Latin American Studies at Princeton University. His most recent book is *La memoria rota: Ensayos sobre cultura y política* (1993). He is currently working on a book on late-nineteenth- and early-twentieth-century Caribbean intellectuals.

JUAN FLORES is Director of the Center for Puerto Rican Studies and Professor of Black and Puerto Rican Studies at Hunter College, City University of New York. With Jean Franco and George Yúdice, he edited the collection *On Edge: The Crisis of Contemporary Latin American Culture* (1992). His most recent book is *Divided Borders: Essays on Puerto Rican Identity* (1993).

MARY M. GAYLORD is Professor and Chair of Romance Languages and Literatures at Harvard University. She has written widely on all major genres of Spanish Golden Age literature and on historical prose of the same period. Her book in progress, *Tropics of Conquest*, argues for the need to reread European and American texts as parts of a shared linguistic and cultural community.

JOSÉ E. LIMÓN is Professor of English and Anthropology at the University of Texas at Austin. His most recent book is *Dancing with the Devil: Society and Cultural Poetics in Mexican-American South Texas* (1994). The present essay is part of a book in progress titled *"Our Life's Work": Jovita Gonzalez, E. E. Mireles, and the Politics of Culture in Texas.*

JOSEFINA LUDMER is Professor of Latin American Literature at Yale University. Her most recent book, *El género gauchesco: Un tratado sobre la patria* (1988), will appear in English translation from Duke University Press. *El cuerpo del delito* is forthcoming in Buenos Aires.

FRANCINE MASIELLO is Professor of Spanish and Comparative Literature at the University of California at Berkeley. Her most recent books are *Between Civilization and Barbarism: Women, Nation, and Literary Culture in Modern Argentina* (1992) and *La mujer y el espacio público: El periodismo femenino en la Argentina del siglo XIX* (1994).

JOSÉ ANTONIO MAZZOTTI is Assistant Professor of Spanish and Portuguese and of Latin American Colonial Literature at Temple University. His book *Una coralidad mestiza,* on El Inca Garcilaso de la Vega, is forthcoming. He is currently doing research on colonial and postcolonial Latin American poetry.

WALTER D. MIGNOLO is Professor of Latin American Studies and Theory in the Department of Romance Studies, the Program in Literature and Cultural Anthropology, at Duke University. His main research interests are Western expansion since 1500, colonial legacies, and postcolonial thinking. He is author, most recently, of *The Darker Side of the Renaissance: Literacy, Territoriality, and Colonization* (1995) and editor of "Loci of Enunciation and Imaginary Constructions: The Case of (Latin) America," a double issue of *Poetics Today* (1994–95).

SYLVIA MOLLOY is Albert Schweitzer Professor of Humanities at New York University. Her most recent book is *At Face Value: Autobiographical Writing in Spanish America* (1991). She is currently working on a book about decadence, national health, and the construction of sexualities in turn-of-the-century Latin America.

MARY LOUISE PRATT is Professor of Spanish and Portuguese and of Comparative Literature at Stanford University. Her most recent book is *Imperial Eyes: Travel Writing and Transculturation* (1992). She is currently coediting the essays of Jean Franco and doing research on culture and neoliberalism.

VICENTE L. RAFAEL teaches at the Department of Communication, University of California at San Diego. He is the author of *Contracting Colonialism: Translation and Christian Conversion in Tagalog Society under Early Spanish Rule* (1993), and the editor of *Discrepant Histories: Translocal Essays on Filipino Cultures* (1995) and *Figures of Criminality in Indonesia, the Philippines, and Colonial Vietnam* (1998).

JULIO RAMOS is Professor of Latin American and Caribbean Literatures at the University of California at Berkeley. He is author of *Desencuentros de la modernidad en América Latina* (1989), to appear in English translation from Duke University Press, and *Paradoias de la letra* (1996), and is editor of *Amor y anarquía: Los escritos de Luisa Capetillo* (1992). He also codirected *La promesa*, a video documentary of religion and politics in contemporary Cuba.

SUSANA ROTKER is Associate Professor of Spanish and Portuguese at Rutgers University. Her most recent books are *La invención de la crónica* (1992), *José Martí: Crónicas* (1993), and *Ensayistas de Nuestra América:*

Siglo XIX (1994). She is currently working on an edition of Fray Servando Teresa de Mier's works.

ROBERTO SCHWARZ is retired professor of Brazilian literature at UNICAMP(Campinas). His most recent book is *Um mestre na periferia do capitalismo: Machado de Assis* (1990). A collection of writings has appeared in English translation under the title *Misplaced Ideas: Essays on Brazilian Culture* (1992).

DORIS SOMMER, Professor of Latin American Literature at Harvard University, is the author of *One Master for Another: Populism as Patriarchal Rhetoric in Dominican Novels* (1984), *Foundational Fictions: The National Romances of Latin America* (1991), and coeditor of *Nationalisms and Sexualities* (1991). Thanks to grants from the Guggenheim Foundation and from the ACLS, she is writing *Proceed with Caution: A Rhetoric of Particularism.*

DIANA TAYLOR is Professor of Spanish and Chair of Comparative Literature at Dartmouth College. She is author, most recently, of *Disappearing: Acts: Spectacles of Gender and Nationalism in Argentina's "Dirty War"* (forthcoming) and is coeditor of *Negotiating Performance in Latin/o America: Gender, Sexuality, and Theatricality* (1994) and *Radicalizing Motherhood: Activists from Left to Right* (forthcoming).

NANCY VOGELEY is Professor of Spanish at the University of San Francisco. She is writing a book on José Joaquín Fernández de Lizardi and the birth of the novel in Spanish America.

Index

Library of Congress Cataloging-in-Publication Data
The places of history : regionalism revisited in Latin America /
edited by Doris Sommer.
Includes bibliographical references and index.
ISBN 0-8223-2310-9 (alk. paper).
ISBN 0-8223-2344-3 (pbk. : alk. paper)
1. Latin American literature—History and criticism.   2. Literature and
history—Latin America.   3. Regionalism in literature.   I. Sommer, Doris.
PQ7081.A1P53   1999   860.9'98—dc21   98-40998 CIP